Globalisation and Pedagogy

The reconfiguration of pedagogical practices around the globe has taken on a momentum that an earlier generation might well have considered startling and disorientating. Many still working in the education and training arenas do experience a high degree of disorientation and dislocation. With different pedagogic practices come different ways of examining them and fresh understandings of their implications and assumptions. It is the examination of these changes and developments that is the subject of this book.

The authors examine a number of questions posed by the rapid march of globalisation, including:

- What is the role of the teacher, and how do we teach in the context of globalisation?
- What curriculum is appropriate when people and ideas become more mobile?
- How do the technologies of the Internet and mobile phone impact upon what is learnt and by whom?

The second edition of this important book has been fully updated and extended to take account of developments in technology, pedagogy and practice, in particular the growth of workplace, distance and e-learning. Drawing upon a wide range of literature, it explores the changing configurations of pedagogy in response to and as part of globalising processes and raises questions about identity and difference, homogeneity and heterogeneity, in the practices of education and training.

Richard Edwards is Professor of Education at the Institute of Education, University of Stirling, UK.

Robin Usher is Professor of Education at the Royal Melbourne Institute of Technology University, Australia.

Globalisation and Pedagogy

Space, place and identity

Second edition

Richard Edwards and Robin Usher

LONDON AND NEW YORK

First edition published 2000 by Routledge

This edition published 2008 by Routledge
2 Park Square, Milton Park, Abingdon, Oxon OX14 4RN

Simultaneously published in the USA and Canada
by Routledge
270 Madison Ave, New York, NY 10016

Routledge is an imprint of the Taylor & Francis Group, an informa business

Typeset in Goudy by
GreenGate Publishing Services, Tonbridge, Kent

Printed and bound in Great Britain by
TJ International Ltd, Padstow, Cornwall

British Library Cataloguing in Publication Data
A catalogue record for this book is available from the British Library

Library of Congress Cataloging in Publication Data
Edwards, Richard, 1956 July 2-.
  Globalisation and pedagogy : space, place, and identity / Richard
Edwards and Robin Usher. -- 2nd ed.
        p. cm.
  Includes bibliographical references and index.
  ISBN 978-0-415-42896-5 (pbk. : alk. paper) -- ISBN 978-0-415-42895-8
(hardback : alk. paper) -- ISBN 978-0-203-94500-1 (e book) 1.
International education. 2. Internationalism. 3. Education and
globalization. I. Usher, Robin, 1944- II. Title.
  LC1090.E33 2007
  370.116--dc22
                                        2007020407

ISBN-10: 0-415-42895-5 (hbk)
ISBN-10: 0-415-42896-3 (pbk)
ISBN-10: 0-415-94500-X (ebk)

ISBN-13: 978-0-415-42895-8 (hbk)
ISBN-13: 978-0-415-42896-5 (pbk)
ISBN-13: 978-0-415-94500-1 (ebk)

Contents

Acknowledgement

Part of Chapter 8 has arisen from work for the Economic and Social Research Council Teaching and Learning Research Programme Thematic Seminar Series, *Contexts, Communities and Networks: Mobilising Learners' Resources and Relationships in Different Domains* (RES-139-25-0174). Richard Edwards would like to thank all those who contributed to the work of the seminar series.

Introduction
Glimpsing

Thrown into a vast open sea with no navigation charts and all the marker buoys sunk and barely visible, we have only two choices left: we may rejoice in the breath-taking vistas of new discoveries – or we may tremble out of fear of drowning. One option not really realistic is to claim sanctuary in a safe harbour; one could bet that what seems to be a tranquil haven today will soon be modernised, and a theme park, amusement promenade or crowded marina will replace the sedate boat sheds.

(Bauman 1998: 85)

Contemporary societies require constant mappings and re-mappings because of the intensity of change and speed of current social transformations.

(Kellner 1995: 26)

In so far as globalisation can be represented at all, it is through the contradictory pluralities of such enforced in-betweenness and the tactics of serious play to which it gives rise. Glimpsed, but not grasped.

(Perry 1998: 166–7)

Opening a (renewed) space?

To write about globalisation and pedagogy did not seem either the most obvious or the most useful thing to do, when much of this text was first published in 2000. At the time, while there was a good degree of discussion of globalisation in the broader social sciences, there was little in the discussions of education. Where globalisation was discussed, it was largely in relation to educational policy. Little attention had been paid to questions of pedagogy in relation to globalisation. Since 2000, there has been an explosion of writing and research on the multiple aspects of globalisation. Books, journals, articles and programmes have been produced in abundance. These largely focus on the economic, political and cultural significance of globalisation. While there has been a similar growth in writing about globalisation and education, the tendency has still been towards a focus on policy and the largely perceived negative impacts of globalising processes, which are often positioned as a code for neo-liberal capitalism. What cannot be denied is that globalisation is increasingly thematised by the writing about it, in the sense that it has become a more solid concept through the increasing writing and discussion of it. The world has been increasingly *realised* as globalised whether we like it or not.

Thus, in coming to write a second edition of this text, we have found ourselves both swimming in a far bigger literature than previously existed, but also strangely finding ourselves away from the main currents of debate, given that our core interest is in the spatiality of globalising processes and their pedagogical significance. For the interest in globalisation has mirrored, fed upon and fed the interest in matters of space and it is here that we have and continue to find much of interest for educators. Of course this might be read as avoidance of what is *really* important in the discussion of globalisation and education. Our contention is that there are other areas of importance which educators are overlooking or not giving sufficient attention to, and it is these which remain the focus of this text.

Edition two is therefore similar in terms of the overall thrust of our discussion. However, where relevant, we have attempted to update and engage with more current discussion of topics. We have also removed two of the original chapters and included two new ones. This takes account of the changing significance of some issues over others. In particular, we have introduced new work on workplace learning and pedagogy, given that workspaces are increasingly identified as important sites of learning and learning is articulated as crucial to the competitive edge upon which organisations need to capitalise within the global economy.

The reconfiguration of pedagogical practices around the globe has taken on a momentum that an earlier generation might well have considered startling and disorienting. Indeed, many still working in the education and training arenas do experience a high degree of disorientation and dislocation. With different pedagogic practices come different ways of examining them and fresh understandings as to their assumptions and implications. This only adds to feelings of dislocation as the authority and authoritativeness of particular perspectives comes to be questioned. Both temporal and spatial frontiers are troubled, and this itself is existentially troubling. It is the ongoing examination of those troublings that has led us to write this text and to bring together discussions of globalisation and pedagogy, a move that itself is troubling and that will no doubt trouble many. But it is also in such spaces that possibilities lie. As Derrida (1996: 84) puts it:

> This chaos and instability, which is fundamental, founding and irreducible, is at once, naturally the worst against which we struggle with laws, rules, conventions, politics and provisional hegemony, but at the same time it is a

chance, a chance to change, to destabilise. If there were continual stability, there would be no need for politics, and it is to the extent that stability is not natural, essential or substantial, that politics exists and ethics is possible. Chaos is at once a risk and a chance.

It is in this spirit that we have entered into the discussions that follow.

There are many routes/roots (in)to this text. First, there is our ongoing writing on and about postmodernity and its implications for the study and practices of education and training. For over a decade, both separately and in collaboration, we have pursued our interests in the postmodern. Our early book, *Postmodernism and Education* (Usher and Edwards 1994), examined the work of some of the leading writers associated with the development of postmodern perspectives and explored the implications of their writings for educational practices. One area of exclusion in that work, and a criticism that has been made more generally about our writing, is that it failed to engage sufficiently with questions of pedagogy. While until recently it has not been our intention to focus on pedagogy, we have nonetheless wanted to address this as an issue. Thus, pedagogy is the specific focus for this text. However, a second implication of our examinations of postmodernity is that we have had to engage also with other literatures and with attempts to conceptualise the contemporary period, exploring the relationships and enfoldings found there. Any discussion of postmodernity is inevitably enfolded with debates about post-Fordism, post-industrial society, the information society, the knowledge economy, the risk society, late modernity, the learning society and, of course, globalisation.

Globalisation has come to the fore as a result of some of the other routes/roots (in)to this text, the second of which is our developing interest in the growth of spatial metaphors in the discussion of pedagogy and wider cultural practices. In our reading of texts, it was hard not to become aware of the widespread use of such metaphors. Alongside and as part of this was our growing awareness of the increased importance being given to questions of space in the social sciences and the theorising of space in social theory. Within these wider debates, there is the discussion more specifically of globalisation, and one of us has previously begun to explore the significance of space–time compression for pedagogy in relation to open and distance learning (Edwards 1995). The various strands therefore began to be woven together whereby it seemed to be productive to examine globalisation and pedagogy as interrelated, exploring the spatial metaphors and learning spaces in relation to wider debates about the spatial within the social sciences, and the implications for pedagogical practices and their study.

Through these enfoldings, we have begun to open a space which itself has been used to create the enfoldings. Our first attempt to explore these ideas was in a conference paper in the UK in 1997 (Edwards and Usher 1997a). A journal article followed (Edwards and Usher 1997b), and this was followed in 1998 by two further journal articles (Edwards 1998; Edwards and Usher 1998a) and conference papers delivered in the USA, the UK and Belgium (Edwards and Usher 1998b–d). We have also presented seminars on our ideas in Europe, North

America and in Australia. This was the forerunner to the first edition of this text in 2000. The space opened up to examine these ideas has grown therefore and has encompassed a range of forms, participants and responses. All of these have fed into this text.

Outlining the presentations that we have made alerts us to another route/root (in)to this text. This is our own experience of globalisation. As academics, we are privileged participants in, and consumers of, globalisation and we do not pretend otherwise. We have access to consumer products from around the globe in our local shopping areas. The media bring us news, views and entertainment of and from around the world. We travel for work and leisure. We are part of an international academic community – the 'global academic' – to which we will refer later. We have lived and worked in various parts of the world. We regularly use e-mail and the Internet. Indeed, this text has been written largely while one of us has been in the UK and the other in Australia, although we have met at various points in both the UK and Australia to discuss progress. Professionally, then, our auto/biographies are enfolded within that about which we write. In a sense, we have lived aspects of that which is the theme of this text.

Having opened this particular space, we fill it – at least to the limit prescribed by the publisher – and, in filling it, we open it. Having indicated some of the background for this text, we enter into the rationale for that which we write.

A global virus?

As we have indicated, there is considerable debate as to the nature, extent and significance of globalisation. There is also much discussion of its implications for education (e.g. Green 1997; Burbules and Torres 2000; Apple *et al.* 2005; Lauder *et al.* 2006). This has been most noticeable in a number of areas, in particular those to do with the global spread of policy approaches and the role of international organisations such as the Organisation for Economic Co-operation and Development (OECD) in global policy transfer (Taylor *et al.* 1997; Ball 1998; Levin 1998; Dale 1999; Marginson 1999).

It could be argued that the contemporary *is* the moment of policy in the sense that we are witnessing a significant increase generally in questions of policy construction, implementation and impact, and the role of research and evidence in these processes. Governing and policy have become almost a form of hyperactivity. Education is not immune from this development. The discussion of globalisation and educational policy has two interrelated aspects. First, there is the examination of the content of policies as they migrate around the globe. Second, there is the exploration of the processes of migration, of how similar policies emerge in different national and regional contexts (Nicoll 2006). In many ways, this discussion is still bounded by the assumptions and conventions of comparative education insofar as there is a focus on the unifying effects and homogeneity of policy development around the globe, rather than the latter being examined within the wider framework of the heterogeneity and associations of globalisation. This is what we set forth in this text, highlighting that trends towards similar policies in some areas in some countries are matched by, and even contain, difference and diversity within them. In following certain actors as they migrate, therefore, we also have to be alive to their translations and transformations. For instance, the notion of national curricula might have a global reach, but the substance will be very different because of the particular situatedness of such curricula within specific national contexts.

Policy migration can be seen in relation to all sectors of education and training, impacting upon institutional structures, curricula and pedagogic practices. Both a condition and consequence of these, the cultures of education and training around the globe are being transformed in various ways and with various effects. Levin (1998), for example, in discussing schooling, identifies a certain commonality of themes in the frameworks through which education policy is constructed and which shape its substance. These are:

- The need for change is largely cast in economic terms.
- There is increasing criticism of schools and their failure to deliver what is required.
- Changes in schooling are being required without a significant increase in resourcing from governments.
- Educational reform is promoted through changes in forms of governance.
- Schools are being required to work in more commercial and market-like ways.
- There is an emphasis on standards, accountability and testing.

Carter and O'Neill (in Ball 1998: 122) identify five similar central elements in the reform of education – once again assimilated to schooling – around the globe, as follows:

- improving national economics by tightening the connection between schooling, employment, productivity and trade;
- enhancing student outcomes in employment-related skills and competencies;
- attaining more direct control over curriculum content and assessment;
- reducing the costs of education to government;
- increasing community input to education by more direct involvement in school decision making and pressure of market choice.

Ball (1998) himself then goes on to identify the influences which are increasing and which have resulted in certain global commonalities. These are:

- neo-liberal approaches;
- new institutional economics;
- performativity;
- public choice theory;
- new managerialism.

The identification of such trends and influences is important. Yet caution is also necessary on a number of counts. First, there is the point to which we have already alluded, i.e. that the focus for these discussions is largely schooling and not the full range of education and training. Second, the spread of these trends is most readily identified in the English-speaking centres of economic power. Thus, their identification specifically as *trends* is itself problematic because it assumes starting points and trajectories that may be those of some countries' policies on schooling, but could not be generalised to include those, for instance, where initial schooling is not available to all or those wherein direct control of the curriculum is not a recent development. Third, the very notion of *trends* needs to be questioned, given its role in a particular contemporary discourse of governmentality. In a sense, the very narrative of globalising trends we have been outlining is itself already located within a particular framework of assumptions which we would argue need to be located or perhaps relocated within a more critically informed notion of globalisation, which is sensitive to the complexity of the actors and practices in play. The way in which globalisation is formulated in policy itself needs to be located as a particular discourse that constructs future directions in a particular and often problematic way (Edwards *et al.* 2004).

This is not to deny the importance of examining policy migrations, but there is a question of what is identified, by whom and where, as the migrations will look different from the standpoint of different locations. And there is also the question of the technologies and techniques through which those migrations take place. Nor will the migrations be singular or unidirectional. Thus, in addition to those identified above for schooling, it is possible to suggest also global migrations in the areas of vocational education and higher education. In the former, there has been, for instance, the growing influence of competence-based approaches and work-based learning. In the latter, there are shifts towards extended participation and the deployment of various forms of flexible-, distributed-, blended-, open- and distance-learning approaches. For these post-school sectors, many of the influences and trends identified for schooling in certain countries would be similar. In addition, we could highlight the increased demands for flexibility in support of lifelong learning as a significant migrating policy and one which is now affecting all sectors of education. Yet, despite these significant commonalities, it would still be unsafe to conclude that all these migrations are universal or uniform or that local variations are no longer significant. Certainly, as far as the latter is concerned, it is invariably the case that 'global facts take local forms' (Appadurai 1996: 18).

Ball (1998: 126) suggests:

> national policy making is inevitably a process of bricolage: a matter of borrowing and copying bits and pieces of ideas from elsewhere, drawing upon and amending locally tried and tested approaches, cannibalising theories, research, trends and fashions and not infrequently flailing around for anything at all that looks as though it might work.

Thus, generic policies are polyvalent, 'they are translated into particular interactive and sustainable practices in complex ways' (Ball 1998: 127). In addition, and as with policy within nation states, there can be various strands in tension and conflict with each other. For instance, prior to the economic recession of the late 1990s, it was suggested that Malaysia's state economic interest lay 'in supporting the trends towards international private education, but its interests in nation building suggests that it should attempt to expand its public education sector' (Taylor *et al.* 1997: 67). Such configurations can themselves change with the emergence of different economic, social and cultural circumstances. The main point, however, is that the location of policy migrations is as important as the migrations themselves.

This brings us to the question of the techniques and practices of migration. Dale (1999) provides a helpful typology of the mechanisms through which the globalisation of policy is effected – harmonisation, dissemination, standardisation, installing interdependence and imposition. He contrasts these with more conventional notions of policy borrowing and policy learning that work from a more national policy focus. Levin (1998) suggests that there is little systematic learning in the processes of national policy borrowing and that the latter may be largely symbolic. He suggests the alternative metaphor of the 'policy epidemic' to assist in understanding such practices:

> New agents of disease tend to spread rapidly as they find the hosts that are least resistant. So it is with policy change in education – new ideas move around quite quickly, but their adoption may depend on the need any given government sees itself having. Although many people may be infected with a given disease, the severity can vary greatly.
>
> (Levin 1998: 139)

Here, it is possible to suggest a relationship between the notion of policy epidemic and Foucault's (1979) notions of biopower and biopolitics. The former can be seen as an extension of the latter, as it seeks to reform and renew education and training to extend the capacities of government to produce healthy and productive populations. At the same time, the notion of policy epidemic resonates with the viruses that are a feature of computer-mediated communication – itself an aspect of the information technologies associated with globalisation.

The spread of these 'diseases' may be through a variety of direct and indirect means. The indirect means may be through the reports, books and online postings produced and circulated by individuals and organisations and through various types of electronic and other media. There is a significant link here with the notion of new modes of knowledge production that we shall explore further at a later point and the attempts to understand the distributed production of knowledge through actor-network theory (Latour 2005). The direct means can be through the circulation of ideas based on the movement of individuals among and between certain networks. These have been facilitated and significantly expanded by the global spread of information and communication technologies.

Politicians, policy advisors and members of 'think tanks' migrate around the globe both actually and virtually spreading certain messages. The same is true for many academics. There is also the influence of members of international agencies such as the OECD, Unesco and the World Bank, which point 'towards the emergence of a global policy community, constituted by an overlapping membership of globalising bureaucrats...senior public servants, policy-makers and advisers' (Lingard and Rizvi 1998: 262).

All this has interesting implications for us as academic writers and for this text specifically. We indicated in the opening section that, as academics, we travel to various parts of the globe and we are in touch with academics and others globally through computer-mediated communication. Indeed, this text is being constructed through this means given our locations in Australia and the UK. As such, we are involved in the spreading of certain ideas. We might be said therefore to be carriers of various 'diseases' – and, indeed, we are convinced some see us in this way! Similarly, what of the status of this text? It both examines and puts forward certain ideas and it will be distributed to various parts of the globe with various degrees of effectiveness. In a sense then, this text might be said to be 'infectious', a carrier of certain viruses, part of an epidemic, an artefact and actant, in that it itself becomes an actor in the realisation of globalisation as a phenomenon. Or maybe, and perhaps more positively, part of an antidote with all the concern for side-effects that such an idea can raise!

Spatial metaphors

In addition to the discussion of globalisation and policy, there is also the discussion of, for instance,

- open and distance learning as a response and contributor to space–time compression and globalising influences (Edwards 1995; Evans 1995; Rowan *et al.* 1997);
- educational responses to global economic change (Ashton and Green 1996);
- the need for 'multiliteracies' to address linguistic and cultural differences (New London Group 1995; Kellner 1998);
- global education and the curriculum (Gough 1998).

Although, to some extent, these discuss the significance of globalisation for educational practitioners, and the opportunities and challenges now opened up for learners, the discussion generally is limited.

Our purpose in this text, therefore, is to make a contribution to these ongoing and developing discussions by exploring the implications of globalising processes in reconceptualising, or thinking differently about, pedagogical practices. In this book, we will attempt in the main to survey the outlines of a theoretical terrain rather than present a detailed picture of pedagogical practices. However, we would suggest also that the theoretical terrain provides a starting point for more detailed analysis of particular pedagogical practices, some of which will be outlined and explored within the text. Furthermore, our concern is not so much with the micro-practices of pedagogy in the classroom. For one thing, we take the view that globalisation has highlighted that learning and pedagogy are not confined to the classroom but take place in a whole variety of life settings. Indeed globalising processes and associated trends towards discourses of lifelong learning raise questions over what precisely we designate as specifically a learning context. Pedagogy, therefore, now has to be seen in a context wider than the classroom both temporally and spatially – in relation to curriculum, the identity of learners and socio-economic and cultural contexts.

Issues of position, borders and boundaries already play an important part in the framing of political and pedagogical questions, as witnessed by the presence and significance of 'location' in many recent discussions. Spatial metaphors, such as border crossing (Giroux 1992; Tuomi-Grohn and Engestrom 2003), border pedagogy (Study Group on Education and Training 1997), speaking from the margins (Spivak 1993), spanning the abyss (Elam 1994), occupying in-between spaces (Bhabha 1994), actor-networks (Nespor 1994) and legitimate peripheral participation (Lave and Wenger 1991), have all emerged to characterise educational and other cultural practices. As we have indicated, there is an increasing exploration of space in social theory, and geography itself has begun to be redefined as a cultural and political practice (Pile and Keith 1997; Massey 2005). These trends are noticeable particularly in critical, feminist and post-colonial pedagogy influenced by post-structuralist and postmodern theory, but are also to be found in socio-cultural theories of learning. Increasingly, problematised notions of positionality and voice in relation to power and authority have proved important areas of debate (C. Luke 1996).

We believe that globalising processes and their effects and globalisation itself as an effect are implicit in most of these debates and that the emergence of spatial metaphors signifies in part a response and contribution to the reordering of space–time with which it is associated. The compressions and associations of space and time surfaces the locatedness of each and all, thus contemporary globalising processes serve to highlight the significance of location and practices of locating. As Wiseman (1998: 17) points out, the question that is posed increasingly is how to describe 'a world in which relationships are becoming less two dimensional and hierarchical and more like networks, rhizomes and Internet links'. Or as Latour (2005: 245) suggests, 'the world is not a solid continent of facts sprinkled by a few lakes of uncertainty, but a vast ocean of uncertainties speckled by a few islands of calibrated and stabilised forms'. Given all this therefore, it is perhaps not surprising that globalising processes are having profound effects on conceptions of what constitutes learning and with that on the nature of education and pedagogy. The aim of this text, therefore, is to explore some of these effects and, in particular, the potential offered by the emergence of *location* as a central interpretative metaphor in reconfiguring a notion of pedagogy that resonates more clearly with current times.

Whereas it could not be claimed that these spatial metaphors are new, often they have been developed in educational thinking and practices in order to articulate forms of critical-emancipatory pedagogies. Spatial metaphors have been deployed to uncover education's domesticating thrust and to provide a basis for 'empowering' pedagogical alternatives. Here, critical-emancipatory pedagogies can be more aptly understood as involving forms of *relocation*, the changing from one bounded location or space (domestication) to another (empowerment). However, we want to argue that the increased emphasis given to location is more aptly situated in current globalising trends where forms of location – of positioning and of being positioned – also and inevitably entail forms of dislocation – of dis-identifying and being positioned as other. We will refer to this as *(dis)location*, a conception that we believe provides a useful, non-essentialising metaphorical resource through which to analyse, understand and develop changes in pedagogy in conditions of globalisation. The space of (dis)location is not closed, bounded or secure, but rather constitutes what Brah (1996: 242) terms 'diaspora space' – a space that 'marks the inter-sectionality of contemporary conditions of transmigrancy of people, capital, commodities and culture'. For us then, globalisation is characterised by diaspora space and (dis)locating rather than simply relocating practices – with consequent implications for opening up pedagogy and our understanding of it. Here, we can say that for us globalisation (dis)locates questions of pedagogy, which in turn provides the possibility for a framing of pedagogies of (dis)location. All of which may seem obscure at this point in the text – an unknown virus perhaps, but, hopefully, and to mix metaphors, a (tasty) hors-d'oeuvre for what is to come.

The text as (globalising) space and pedagogy

The attempts to characterise contemporary change are many and varied. Notions of a post-industrial society, a knowledge economy, an information society, postmodernity, a learning society, globalisation, among others, have all been posited as ways of understanding contemporary processes by certain people in various parts of the world. Some of these are to be found in popular and media discussions as well as academic debates. Each of these attempts to characterise change opens a space within which there is debate over not only the nature of the characterisation but also its empirical validity. Nor are these characterisations hermetically sealed from one another since their relationship to each other is itself an area of debate. What is surprising about many of these characterisations is how little attention they give to education. Even Castells (1999) in his monumental three-volume work on the information age makes only a few passing remarks about education. Yet education and lifelong learning have become key themes of many organisations and governments around the globe. Indeed, they may be thought of as central to contemporary governmentality.

However, it is the idea that these concepts open up a space, and that these spaces are networked effects, that indicates reflexively the increased importance given to questions of space, location and the flows and relations through which they are constituted in debates in many parts of the social sciences and humanities at the present; and, with that, the centrality of the notion of globalising processes and associated practices that are explored within this text. Indeed, there is a reflexive dimension to this very text insofar as it itself involves opening a space – literally in the files on our computers in which we are constructing it, but also metaphorically in the openings that the argument put forward here attempts in relation to questions of pedagogy. Thus, we work with the notions that 'signs (and words), rather than being attempts to represent something (a referral to something that is external to them), or even residual attempts to refer to an absence, are first and foremost *actions*' (Jones *et al.* 2004: 730–1, emphasis in original). At the same time, we are aware that our openings also involve closures – consequent upon our auto/biographies and positioning in the educational domain. Hence, although we have not ignored schooling, it remains the case that our text focuses more closely on post-school education, higher education and lifelong learning.

At its most general, it is often said that the world is experiencing intensified globalisation, particularly in the economic arena, resulting in what an earlier generation of thinkers referred to as the 'global village' in which there is the collapsing of all frontiers. This is apparent increasingly in much popular and media debate. In particular, there is a highlighting of the experience of space–time compression enabled by the deployment of new media and information and communications technologies. Globalisation brings to the fore questions of space, place and identity and indeed, some would argue, is a condition for their emergence as problematics to be addressed.

However, with the characterisation of the contemporary in terms of globalisation, a space is being opened within which the nature and extent of globalisation itself can be debated. Here, we are interested in globalisation as a discursive practice – as a way of thinking, speaking and acting that interacts with changes in socio-economic and cultural structures, configurations and relationships. This serves to highlight the potential of globalisation to characterise the space of spatial metaphors, in opening a space through which to challenge and disrupt certain established assumptions and binaries, most powerfully those of the international and national, the universal and particular, the cosmopolitan and parochial, and the global and local. For instance, no clearer example of these disruptions can be found than in the attempts to inscribe a notion of 'global warming' into the popular imagination.

In this context, we need to emphasise that our use of the term 'globalisation' is generally shorthand for 'globalising processes'. Privileging the verb rather than the noun form is an important tactical move since we do not wish to convey the impression that we understand globalisation in reified and purely naturalistic ways. Globalisation is effected and realised through practices, exercises of power and has powerful effects. Our position rather is that globalisation refers to processes and practices that result in globalised outcomes. In other words, globalisation is realised through globalising processes and practices. This also enables us to avoid the determinist trap. While recognising that globalisation is itself both material and discursive with all that implies in terms of constitutive effects, we can still locate ourselves in a discourse which does not leave us open to accusations of eliminating agency or inducing fatalistic pessimism. Things could always be other than they are and what they are is always diverse. Thus our reference to Derrida earlier.

We can touch upon only some of the debates concerning globalisation in a book such as this, although in doing this we wish to put forward an understanding of globalisation that will allow us to discuss framing a spatialisation of pedagogy and a pedagogy of spatialisation – in other words, what we will term pedagogies of (dis)location. We will suggest that the latter terms both respond and contribute to space–time compression, to the rhizomatic, to hybridity and to the constitution of diaspora space. Here, although 'globalisation and diasporisation are separate phenomena with no necessary causal connection, [they] "go together" extraordinarily well' (Cohen 1997: 175). In the process, we will touch upon the relationships between globalisation and other framing notions, such as postmodernity, to indicate the ways in which the former both contributes to, and is a result of, the latter. Indeed, the hybridity characteristic of contemporary globalisation can be said to create conditions of possibility for the flourishing of diverse frameworks of understanding and for what we will later argue to be the need for a locating, mapping and translating of such frameworks.

Central to processes of globalisation are new forms of economic organisation and the spread worldwide of cultural messages through new media and information and communications technologies. Globalisation is responsible for, and responsive to, space–time compression where distances, both virtual and actual, can be covered far quicker than in previous times and where people, goods and images encounter each other on an almost instantaneous basis. Space–time compression thus brings to the fore the significance of place and location through the associations and interconnections that are enacted and the transformations and translations that they produce. Yet, with this de-territorialising thrust and the growth in awareness of the globe as one place and a certain cosmopolitan opening, there is at the same time, and paradoxically, an assertion of the local, the parochial and the specific arising from the heightened consciousness induced by globalisation of the relativity and significance of place. The discourse of globalisation 'captures the increasingly widespread consciousness or "reflexive" awareness of the interdependence of local ecologies, economies and societies' (Wiseman 1998: 14). With the surfacing of the locatedness of each and all, the significance of location in interpreting the contemporary condition is accompanied by a sense that location is complex and ambiguous, with a diasporan quality, 'a process of multi-locationality across geographical, cultural and psychic barriers' (Brah 1996: 194). Here the local is not a bounded container but precisely an effect of the associations and networks through which it is constituted. It is thus the attempt to think across frontiers that is part of the endeavour of this text, to create a different type of space through which to discuss pedagogy, even as we question any simple notion of their collapsing.

Globalisation then is no single or simple phenomenon – another reason perhaps why globalising processes is a better term. To speak in this way means that notions of flow, relationality, association, (en)counter, movement and networks tend to be given heightened priority, something which reflexively we have adopted in the writing of this text. Rather than simply presenting a bounded and progressive argument, tidily chunked into chapters and sections in the manner of a text book, we adopt a process of fluidity and migration in the writing of the text, where issues may be returned to a number of times to be reframed and re-enfolded to produce different perspectives and interpretations. Indeed, in the construction of the narrative, the ordering of the chapters has changed a number of times, as the ideas have developed and enfolded one another in successive attempts to locate and relocate the issues under discussion.

Our intention therefore is to open a space through which hopefully glimpses of globalising processes at work can be discerned. A modest aim, perhaps, which some may take as too modest. They will ask, for example, where is your emancipatory aim? We believe that this text has an emancipatory thrust, but it is neither explicit nor obvious. For us, education has been too often concerned with emancipatory messages and the result has too often been totalising, disappointing and sometimes oppressive. This is something we deliberately wish to avoid. Of course, we are not so naive as to believe that texts can be written in a neutral and apolitical way. Nor do we take the view that what is about to unfold is merely a description of the 'facts' of globalisation. We recognise that texts have effects and are read with meanings that do not coincide with the authors' intentions. Thus, for example, we accept that this text might be read as an uncritical celebration of globalisation or as advocating a total embracing of information and communication technologies. We can but reiterate that this is neither our intention nor our position, and that our hope is that the openness of our text will stimulate and contribute to an openness of debate – and it is here that the emancipatory thrust of the text is located. However, the translations to which this text will be subject are beyond us as actors to control.

In opening a space, a text also inevitably entails closure, however provisional, for 'to engage in the act of writing one story in one way, is always to opt (consciously or not) not to write something else' (Stronach and MacLure 1997: 53). To reach this point then has entailed closing the files on our computers and the arguments herein, although as a published text new openings are now possible. This text, like globalisation itself therefore, does not attempt to be singular or simple, nor are its arguments intended to be universal in their scope. In a messy and complex world, why as Law (2004) rightly asks should understandings be simple? The text too is as subject to the processes it outlines as any other text and will itself no doubt be located, relocated and dislocated.

Which brings us to the final point of this initial glimpse. This text is deliberately reflexive in the sense that it attempts to provide an account of a 'reality' (globalisation) which also explains how we as authors of the text came to hold such an account. We have done this by locating our account in the globalising processes within which we are enfolded at the personal, professional and cultural levels and by recognising that we are by this very writing both contributing to, and shaped by, a powerful contemporary discourse which presents both limitations and uncertainties as well as possibilities and potentialities. We have certainly not positioned ourselves as detached and neutral observers nor presented ourselves as involved in a process of unveiling the deep and hidden truth about globalisation and pedagogy. We recognise that we are both co-products and co-producers of this moment and that the best we can do is offer glimpses.

Thus, as well as being subject to its own arguments about globalisation, this text is also subject to its own articulations of pedagogy. The text itself, therefore, can be positioned as offering a pedagogy of (dis)location about which it speaks. The arguments herein can be seen as providing a framework through and within which to locate, map and translate something with which readers can identify, counter-identify or dis-identify. As well as being a text about pedagogy, it is globalised and globalising, itself a pedagogical text.

Glimpse one

Globalisation – lost in space–time

> (T)he globalisation/spatialisation of the story of modernity has provided a commentary upon, and thereby challenged, *both* a system of rule and a system of knowledge and representation.
>
> (Massey 1999: 31, emphasis in original)

Rethinking the globe

Until relatively recently, 'the world' has been theorised overwhelmingly either in terms of a realist view where the focus is on relations between sovereign entities or in terms of world system theory. The former focuses on the relations between nation states, the latter on the capitalist economic system. Each has been criticised on the grounds that through their particular focus on large and significant trends they marginalise and exclude, in particular, the cultural dimensions and the impact of space–time compression through the spread of information and communication technologies (ICTs). In response to these perceived limitations, different theorisations of globalising processes have emerged. We shall discuss these in more detail later.

These have stimulated debate about the nature, extent and novelty of the globalisation phenomenon, particularly in relation to the economy (Hirst and Thompson 1996a) but also in relation to politics and culture (Waters 1995). Broadly, two very diverse camps can be identified (Held and McGrew 2003). On the one hand, there are the globalists, who view globalising processes as a significant trend in the contemporary world. On the other hand, there are the sceptics, who, on a historical or comparative basis, argue that things have not changed as significantly as some suggest. The globalists include those who promote globalisation as well as anti-globalisation protesters.

In many ways, globalisation has come to the fore in recent years as a response to the limitations of more established theorisations, from the trends and challenges arising from socio-economic and cultural change and from the political and epistemological challenges of post-structuralism, postmodernism, feminism and post-colonialism with their disruption of dominant meanings of metaphors of space and place. One increasingly influential way of theorising globalisation, often referred to as 'world culture' theory, highlights 'the compression of the world and the intensification of consciousness of the world as a whole' (Robertson 1992: 8), or, as Waters (1995: 3) suggests, globalisation is 'a social process in which the constraints of geography on social and cultural arrangements recede and in which people become increasingly aware that they are receding'. Robertson argues that global consciousness has heightened as world systems become more fluid, the prospects for humanity more hazardous on a global scale and with the increasing consolidation of global communications and global media. Here then the signification is of a shrinking world where people, services, information and goods are available to each other across the globe through a variety of means and in increasingly immediate ways. Airline tickets bought in England are processed in India. CNN and McDonald's are available on a global scale, albeit with local variations. People migrate globally for work and increasingly as refugees, people travel globally for business and leisure. The Internet, fax and mobile telephone put people instantly in touch with each other, although they may be in different hemispheres and different time zones. Investment decisions taken in one country affect workers and investors in other countries. What in the past would have taken months to move around the globe now takes hours or even seconds. In 1924, a telegram took 80 seconds to circle the world (Thompson 2003). Now, with the digitalisation of information, it is almost instantaneous.

Giving rise to, and stemming from, these globalising processes, space and time increasingly are compressed. The argument here then is that the compression of the world and the intensification of the consciousness of the world as one produce an interdependence that in turn compresses the world even more, with heightened intensification and so on. In this theorisation therefore globalisation is a process that both *connects* and stimulates awareness of connection and interdependence. Here also 'the local becomes embedded within more expansive sets of interregional relations and networks of power' (Held and McGrew 2003: 3). The local is constituted as an effect of the associations and networks of which it is a part.

Much popular discussion of globalisation often takes it to be an entirely new phenomenon arising from the conditions of the immediate present. However, globalisation has a history and geography of its own. In this context, the contemporary interest in globalisation can be understood as the result of an intensification of certain processes and the awareness of the globe as a single environment. Robertson (1992), for example, provides one outline of the historical phases of the long, uneven and complicated process of globalisation. First, he identifies the 'germinal phase', which lasted in Europe from the early fifteenth to the late eighteenth century. While this is associated with the growth of national communities, it also embraces the spread of ideas about humanity and perhaps more importantly the Gregorian calendar, a step towards a global conception of time. The 'incipient phase' followed until the 1870s, once again mainly grounded in Europe. This period saw the consolidation of the nation state and the development of international relations. The 'take-off phase' lasted until the mid 1920s, where there were growing global assumptions about what a nation state should be and how it should act. In this period, there was the implementation of 'world time', a sharp increase in the amount and speed of global communication and a growth in global competitions, such as the Olympic Games. Between the mid 1920s and the late 1960s, there was the 'struggle for hegemony phase', particularly between the Second World War and the Cold War adversaries seeking to determine the direction of the globalising processes in line with their own ideologies and interests. The Holocaust and the atom bomb provided defining perspectives on the prospects for humanity within this period.

The current phase, since the late 1960s, is what Robertson terms the 'uncertainty phase', in which global consciousness has heightened with international systems more fluid, at the same time, the prospects for humanity more fraught in the light of environmental and other risks, and with the growth in global communications and the consolidation of the global media. Alongside trends towards global integration and in response to them, white 'Western' male assumptions that underlie dominant conceptions of humanity and society have been problematised by considerations of gender and sexual, ethnic and racial difference, the increased multiculturalism of societies and the notions of the hybridity of cultures.

Robertson claims that these phases are only an outline in need of more rigorous analysis. In particular, the Eurocentric framing of globalisation in conjunction with the development of the nation state and colonisation suggests a particular perspective on the history and geography of the processes he identifies. For globalisation 'can be seen as being a condition resulting from a long history of international exploration, invasion and colonisation, fuelled by economic, military, religious and political interests, and enabled through enormous developments in transport and communications technologies' (Evans 1997: 12). Shields (1997: 194, emphasis in original) argues that notions of spatial zones generally are all

> socio-political constructions ideologically coded into cartographic conventions and reified in socio-cognitive mappings of the world...these serve to exemplify the extent to which we live within the territorialising and boundary-drawing impulse of the *imaginary geography* of the nation-state...*Representation of space* such as national air space and 200-mile limit inform and delimit our *practical* interventions in these spaces.

The particular representations inscribed in different theorisations of globalisation, and indeed in globalisation as a conceptualisation of space–time, therefore always need to be borne in mind. Mapping and remapping are powerful practices, and this is as true for notions of globalisation as for other signifying practices. 'Space' and 'place' are articulated and performed within the spatialising practices of 'imaginary geographies' and political moves (Pile and Keith 1997). Here, globalisation can be seen as forms of re-imagining geography in the cause of re-inscribing different meanings into and within the world.

However, there are distinct limits to the re-imaginings that are taking place. As Massey (1994: 166, emphasis in original) highlights, globalisation has ironically 'been analysed from a very *un*-global perspective'. As a process, both particular periodisations and spatialisations are exercises of power through a naming/framing process and could no doubt be rewritten from other locations. Indeed, we may speculate how discourses of globalisation could be constituted in global ways that would not involve the forms of centring and peripheralising, in which the site of the other, for example religious fundamentalism of whatever form, is invariably one of terror. For, as Tomlinson (2003: 271, emphasis in original) argues, globalising processes do not result in a simple destruction of identities but 'attest to an *amplification* of the significance of identity positions'. The possibilities for the other to be recognised in their position as powerful in both constituting and being a point of deconstruction of the centre therefore (Natter and Jones 1997) need further development and would certainly involve more than a book written by two Anglo, white, male, academic authors.

However, despite and maybe because of these problems (see, for example, Hesse 1999), the framework of world polity theory that Robertson presents is useful in bringing to the fore that, although globalisation as a concept may be a relatively recent reflexive set of understandings, globalising tendencies and processes do have a history and geography, of which the current heightened awareness about the 'globe' is only the most recent manifestation. What is significant here is that it is only with the increased weight given to the concept of globalisation that we are able to view current trends as having a history, as 'much of the conventional sociology which has developed since the first quarter of the twentieth century has been held in thrall by the virtually global institutionalisation of the idea of the culturally cohesive and sequestered national society...' (Robertson 1992: 50). This is a point also argued in those attempts to move sociology from a science of the social to the 'tracing of associations' (Latour 2005). In other words, to conceptualise the contemporary condition, it is necessary to go beyond the categories of classical sociology and economics, which already assume the nation state and economy as privileged and society as the foremost explanatory concept. In the process state, economy and society become reified and unquestioned as ways of framing understanding. Conceptually, globalisation can provide an alternative space within which to frame the contemporary practices of nation states and social orders, since the boundaries around the two can no longer be assumed coterminous, nor can they be held to be as solid or impermeable as classical sociological and economic understandings suggest. We can argue then that globalisation both problematises, and is itself a response to, the limitations of traditional notions of the 'national' and 'international' as distinct and opposite polarities. It is such questionings of boundaries that are central to the debates being engendered in and around the meaning and significance of globalisation.

Globalisation – it's all the same to me

Robertson's view on the need to rethink interpretative frameworks as itself an aspect of globalisation is paralleled by other writers. For instance, in his analysis of trends in the global economy, Reich (1993) argues that much economic thinking is based on the 'vestigial thought' of national economic interest. With the increased decoupling of capitalism from particular nation states, he suggests this no longer reflects the reality of contemporary economic life. He argues that new ideas and fresh conceptualisations are necessary to help explain the contemporary condition. If this is the case, it becomes important to reflect on how trends in globalisation may disrupt established images and categories of, for instance, First, Second and Third Worlds, or notions of the core and periphery in the global economy (Soja 1989). Similarly, and as we intend to do, there is the need to investigate the vestigial thought of education, those assumptions which may be losing their significance and potency in contemporary conditions.

Reich argues that economic interests are nowadays articulated not so much in terms of supporting particular national companies, but through making geographical areas attractive for inward investment by more mobile transnational capital, serviced by a variously skilled workforce. Whether this itself constitutes a *reformed* national economic interest rather than its replacement by other concerns is open to debate. As with national economies, so with regions and even cities 'in a world in which inter-urban competitiveness operates on a global scale, cities are propelled into a race to attract increasingly mobile investors (multinational corporations), consumers (tourists), and spectacles (sports and media events)' (Robins 1993: 306). Given that national policies aim to support economic competitiveness, despite and perhaps because of the increased global mobility of finance capital and the variety of models of capital accumulation around the globe, the evidence is contradictory and certainly not clear-cut.

Ashton and Green (1996: 71) maintain that:

> though trade has increased its importance in the post-war economic life of most countries, the largest economies are still served by national-based firms...the truly transnational corporation which has no national bases and no concern for national specificities remains in a small minority.

They, like Hirst and Thompson (1996a and b), argue that this raises questions about the *extent* of globalisation. Here the argument is that 'globalisation operates as a "necessary myth" through which politicians and governments discipline their citizens to meet the requirements of the global marketplace' (Held and McGrew 2003: 5). What is suggested is that net economic flows are less now than during the period 1890–1914 and that internationalisation is complementing national economies rather than being supplanted by globalising processes. However, within this sceptical position, globalisation is taken to be an undifferentiated process of integration of the world economy. We are not in sympathy with this argument and we do not offer it further here. We feel more sympathy with Massey (1994: 159), who argues that while most companies have a national origin and with that a clear direction of flows in foreign investment 'the geography of these flows has been changing and becoming more complex'. However, the alignment of certain corporate interests with those of specific nation states has indeed become questionable, not least because of the growth of regional economic blocs in various parts of the globe. The growth of transnational corporations without commitment to any national economy may be more limited than Reich suggests, but the influence of more general globalising tendencies cannot be denied as, for instance, in 'the increasing importance of targeting consumers on the basis of demography and habits rather than on the basis of geographical proximity' (Morley and Robins 1995: 110). The productivist focus of much of the critique of the scope of economic globalisation therefore may miss the point.

Economic globalisation is usually held to be central to globalising processes in general with the economic articulated as the motor of globalisation. Indeed in world system theory the argument is that globalisation consists of the process whereby capitalism spreads across the globe. In this world economy nation states inevitably have to compete with one another. There is a decline in the power of any one nation state to regulate and limit capitalism and no single political centre to take its place and assume these functions. Capitalism therefore assumes a virtual freedom of manoeuvre. This raises questions not only about the competence of the nation state to govern and the status of national companies and economic interests but also about what and who constitutes civil society. As suggested by Robertson, the coexistence of nation state and civil society is broken by globalisation. This provides the basis for an increase in the power of the neoliberal market as the contemporary form taken by capitalism. However, contrary to world system theory this also opens up different possibilities for globalised forms of sociality and practices, for what some term 'globalisation from below' (Falk 1993; Korsgaard 1997; Kellner 2000; Singh *et al.* 2005). Here, the link between nation state and citizenship may be loosened with people playing an active role addressing issues of shared concern in and through global networks that can be understood as a form of cosmopolitanism. National governments become only a partial focus for certain forms of popular intervention, as demonstrated by such environmental groups as Greenpeace, humanitarian groups such as Amnesty and the anti-globalisation movement itself. Globalisation therefore provides possibilities as well as threats in the spread of capitalist relations. On the one hand, for instance, there is the feminisation of labour where

> global assembly lines are 'manned' by women workers in free trade zones; subcontracted industrial homeworking is performed at kitchen tables by women who 'have time on their hands'; home-based teleworking is carried out by women who can't afford day-care costs and are grateful to have paid work.
>
> (Manicom and Walters 1997: 72)

However, practices also develop which bring together groups affected by economic restructuring in new ways, such as trade unions funding labour and community projects outside their own national base (Marshall 1997). Similarly, information and communication technologies (ICTs) can be utilised by differing groupings.

> Affinity groups of 'senior' or retired citizens, feminist scholars, individuals who share knowledge on health afflictions, hobbyists, professionals, political organisations and many others are...using the Internet to educate, proselytise and organise, cutting across national boundaries with apparent ease.
>
> (Goodenow 1996: 200)

While notions of globalisation both from below and from above help to reframe some of the different possibilities within globalisation, they also present a certain spatial relationship that seems to be set within certain binaries of 'above–below', 'power–resistance' and 'oppression–emancipation', which themselves constrain debate and understanding through the very processes of categorisation in play (Bowker and Star 1999). In other words, this is a notion of globalisation already subsumed within a particular politics, rather than, as Pile (1997) suggests, a reframing of the political and indeed a resistance to it.

The intensifying processes of globalisation are undoubtedly triggering a reconfiguration of governance and the political generally. The state itself may be said to be as much subject to the paradoxical pulls of globalisation as any other institution. Waters (1995) suggests that there is evidence of the aggregation and decentralisation of state powers and the growth of international organisations. Whilst these are relatively powerless at present, their numbers continue to grow and they now constitute a significant part of what has been the termed the world 'polity'. In his outline of contemporary globalisation as a side effect of economic deregulation, Scott (1997: 10) argues that:

> it is deregulation which undermines the ability of nation states to protect themselves and the community they represent from the social destructiveness of markets, but it is also the nation state that is the key actor in bringing deregulation about both internally (e.g. through privatisation and lowering social costs within its borders) and externally (e.g. by participating in and agreeing to proposals emerging from international fora – GATT negotiations etc.).

Cunningham and Jacka (1996: 14) argue that globalisation has 'gradually led to the erosion of the appearance of congruity between economy, polity and culture within the nation-state'. However, a continued role for the nation state is taken by some (Hirst and Thompson 1996a; Green 1997) to be evidence against the thesis of globalisation and the point here must surely be the need to contest simplistic and overgeneralised views of the latter.

In his detailed argument for the role of the nation state in supporting different forms of nationalism through education – civic, ethnic and economic – Green (1997), in particular, is cautious in his assessment of globalisation. However, this is in part because he views the argument to be one over whether there is an increased or a decreased role for the nation state and nationalism. By contrast, we believe it is also possible to explore the *changing* role of the state as *part* of globalisation, where the state signifies a conceptual framework that deconstructs the fixities and fixations of the binary of 'national–international'. Here, a distinction needs to be drawn precisely between internationalisation and globalisation (Edwards 1995; Taylor *et al.* 1997). It is part of the paradoxes of globalisation rather than a refutation of it that the role of the nation state and specific nation states might actually be enhanced in certain ways with globalisation.

Globalisation, therefore, can tell us different stories of the nation state, surfacing its relationality and contested internal and external boundaries. Other than world system theorists, there would be few people interested in globalisation who would, as Green (1997: 157) seems to suggest, think that 'the nation state was disappearing', even if its taken-for-granted status comes to be questioned and attempts at self-reproduction become ever more transparent. The spatial–temporal location of the nation state is itself brought to the fore by globalisation. Nationalism can therefore be located best in an interpretive framework that foregrounds globalisation.

Globalisation is often taken to have a single trajectory or logic resulting in an increased uniformity or homogeneity across the globe. The argument of world system theory that everything is now commodified would be a good example here. However, despite the powerful effects of transnational capital and international media conglomerates, this is unsustainable and is not the stance adopted here. To assume that globalisation is about, or results in, homogenisation is to simplify the processes at work and, in a sense, to distance oneself from the very complex effects on space, place and identity that globalising processes bring to the fore. As Giddens (1990) among others suggests, while globalisation has resulted in the spread of 'Western' institutions across the globe, that very trend produces a pressure for local autonomy and identity. In other words, globalisation is about examining places as simultaneously traversed by the global and local in ways that have been intensified by the contemporary compression of space and time. Thus, alongside the global availability of satellite television, McDonald's, Nike and Harry Potter films, there is an affirmation of, for instance, local, regional and ethnic identities. Indeed, some transnational companies have explicitly adopted strategies of 'glocalisation', extending their influence around the globe, while situating themselves and their products and services within local conditions. Localisation can therefore be part of the strategy of companies in seeking a competitive edge. These may be a response to global influences, but they are nonetheless a part of globalisation rather than a rejection of it.

What this suggests is that the local is as much a condition for globalisation as the global; space and place are traversed by the global–local nexus of globalised space–time compression – 'time–space distanciation, disembedding, and reflexivity mean that complex relationships develop between local activities and interaction across distances' (Waters 1995: 50). The integration of the globe *reconfigures* rather than supplants diversity. Globalisation 'does not necessarily imply homogenisation or integration. Globalisation merely implies greater connectedness and de-territorialisation' (Waters 1995: 136). A global world may be interdependent but not necessarily harmonious. It may be a 'single place' as Robertson and other proponents of world polity theory argue, but that can also mean diversity and fragmentation. To understand the current situation in this way is to problematise a particular Eurocentric culture that can no longer be considered an 'authentic, self-evident and true universal culture in which all the world's people ought to believe' (Lemert 1997: 22) – a position which of course itself would not command universal assent.

The assertion of heterogeneity by the locale or by the region may take many forms. For instance, it may involve the protection/assertion of a specific identity as a reaction against the perceived homogeneity introduced by the global. As Turner (1994: 78) argues in relation to contemporary religious fundamentalism, it 'is a two-pronged movement to secure control within the global system and also to maintain regulation of the lifeworld...Fundamentalism is therefore the cultural defence of modernity against postmodernity'. Within the global–local nexus, fundamentalism attempts, through the deployment of notions of religious community bounded together by spiritual belief and sentiment, to contain if not negate the assertion and spread of difference and secular consumerism. Fundamentalists are opposed to a globalised culture based on secularism, consumerism and modernisation, but they themselves have a vision and modus operandi which only makes sense, and indeed is only possible, within a globalised world.

Thus paradoxically such movements also take their own world-views to be universal and seek to promote themselves more effectively through the use of new technologies. For instance, 'Islam is now able to self-thematise Islamic religion as a self-reflective global system of cultural identity over and against the diversity and pluralism involved in the new consumer culture' (Turner 1994: 90). Nor is this the case only for parts of Islam. Here, then, fundamentalism is as much subject to globalisation as a response to it. Any movement of this kind is likely to be globally mediated and as much subject as other practices to the cultural processes it opposes. In this sense, fundamentalism cannot be seen simply as a return to traditions, even if it is reflexively asserted as such. Tradition is itself reworked, even in some cases into self-parodying forms found in heritage centres and theme parks (Rojek 1993; Heelas *et al.* 1996).

What we can say then is that globalisation brings to the fore the paradoxical and the complex. For instance, rather than a rejection of the integration of the globe by for example certain forms of fundamentalism, the competition between regions for investment and jobs may involve a greater participation in the integrating processes. Here, the very processes of globalisation encourage regionalism. By contrast, the risks to humanity as a species through nuclear or environmental catastrophe encourage a more generalised consciousness of the globe as 'one world', expressed at least in part through international conferences and agreements. As Beck (1992: 44) argues, 'the multiplication of risks causes the world society to contract into a community of danger'. Here, environmental risk itself is globalised, both unbounded and universal, yet also unequally distributed. Thus as we have argued, the integration of the globe reconfigures rather than supplants diversity, in the process introducing forms of economic, social and cultural creolisation, even when these are often framed in discourses of authenticity. Here, notions of authentic and inauthentic themselves deconstruct under the globalised mediation. Drawing a distinction is now necessary between internationalisation and globalisation, the former concerned with the spread of Western (or as some would argue American) institutions, culture and practices, the latter with the paradoxes of hybridity and diaspora space, the global–local nexus. Here, in some ways, 'what is being globalised is the tendency to stress "locality" and "difference", yet "locality" and "difference" presuppose the very development of worldwide dynamics, institutional communication and legitimation' (Poppi 1997: 285). We are reminded of the argument articulated in world culture theory that we all now have to assume a position and define an identity relative to the emerging global whole – a process referred to as 'relativisation' where comparisons with others continually have to be made. This assumes that there is a common reference point of 'humankind' as a significant aspect of the development of a world culture even though all universals have to be made concrete in order to be effective. Hence any apparent universal such as humankind will be subject to local interpretation and variation in the way it is concretised.

While clear differences about the nature and significance of globalisation do exist, in much of the literature there is a shared sense of the centrality of the contribution that media, communication and transport have made to that process (McChesney 2003; Thompson 2003). In many ways, it is the development of these technologies in the widest sense that has underpinned globalisation, as information about and from around the globe is gained directly through travel and indirectly, yet increasingly instantly, through electronic media. Perhaps, most importantly, these developments have enabled financial flows around the globe to be speeded up on an almost continuous basis. The globe also enters our homes through the media with which we engage and the products and pollutants we consume and emit. Most arguments regarding globalisation therefore focus on the significance of the development of technology and particularly the speeding up of communication and transportation that this development has made possible. Here, 'globalisation has reordered both time and space and "shrunk the globe"' (Held 1993: 5). Globalising processes have brought different cultures into contact and collision with each other through information technology, travel, migration and the media. Airplanes, satellites, computer networks and mobile phones have all contributed to the process of shrinking and relativisation. Speeding up increases the range of what Rowan *et al.* (1997) term '(en)counters', but it also raises questions about structuring metaphors of boundaries and boundedness which, as we saw, have been associated with knowledge structured by notions of the nation state and society. For Morley and Robins (1995: 75), new technologies

are implicated in a complex interplay of deterritorialisation and reterritorial-
isation...Things are no longer defined and distinguished in the ways that
they once were, by their boundaries, borders or frontiers...We can say that
the very idea of boundary – the frontier boundary of the nation-state, for
example, or the physical boundaries of urban structures – has been rendered
problematical.

Dependent upon which part of the globe one lives within and one's position
therein, lifestyles, life courses and decision making are increasingly mediated and
re-inscribed through globally integrated and integrating processes. However, care
needs to be taken in the framing of the centrality of ICTs to contemporary globalisation, as the result is often a crude form of technological determinism.
Technological development is necessary but not sufficient to these processes,
since their development, articulation and deployment is subject to a range of factors and possibilities. As Scott (1997: 15, emphasis in original) cautions, 'while
financial flows and the information super highway may be global in *range*, their
scope of influence will become the object of regulation and restriction'.

Globalisation, modernity and postmodernity

Differences lie not only in the significance given to globalisation but also in its
relationship to debates about modernity and postmodernity. The meaning, significance and existence of modernity and/or postmodernity are heavily contested
and, therefore, the positions outlined here are by no means definitive. Robertson
(1992) and Giddens (1990), for example, take differing positions on the relationships between globalisation, modernity and postmodernity, and we will use
their views as a springboard. Giddens (1990) argues that modernity brings forth
modes of life that sweep away the traditional social order. While it cannot do
away with historical continuity completely, modernity is constantly disruptive,
with social relations disembedded from their immediate contexts and restructured across space–time. In contrast to traditional social orders therefore,
modernity is characterised by both a previously unknown pace and a scope of
change, with a set of institutional arrangements, most notably the nation state
and capitalism which are integral to this process, and what Giddens terms institutional reflexivity. This last 'consists in the fact that social practices are
constantly examined and reformed in the light of incoming information about
those very practices, thus constitutively altering their character' (Giddens 1990:
38). This reflexivity is marked by an increasing emphasis on the accumulation of
information, on what is done as a condition for making decisions about what is to
be done.

It is these processes of modernity which for Giddens result in globalisation
because, as universalising tendencies, they seek to displace all traditional forms of
social order. In the current period of what he terms late modernity, it is 'the intensification of worldwide social relations which link distant localities in such a way
that local happenings are shaped by events occurring many miles away and vice

versa' (Giddens 1990: 64). As human consciousness of risk grows, reflexivity actually begins to undermine the basis upon which modernity has developed. Globalisation thus results from the drive of the 'juggernaut' of modernity, where 'globalisation is really the globalisation of modernity, and modernity is the harbinger of identity' (Tomlinson 2003: 271). However, in the process, this produces an increased awareness of its own conditions of possibility and therefore reflexively produces more uncertainty as to the course of modernity itself. The reflexivity that is central to the disjunctive development of modernity gives knowledge an uncertainty and provisionality that is socially and personally troubling. For Beck (1992), unlike Giddens, increased risk results in a form of reflexive modernisation rather than in the simple modernisation of industrialisation.

Giddens (1990) provides a view of globalisation framed in an overarching narrative of modernity which, although it tells a story of change, instability and heterogeneity, is ultimately a unifying and reified narrative in which globalisation is 'simply an enlargement of modernity...modernity on a global scale' (Robertson 1992: 162). Although modernity may have been the spur for globalisation, for Robertson the effects of that process is to begin to throw that narrative itself into doubt. Rather than being seen as a condition within modernity, therefore, reflexivity can be turned on the very notion of modernity itself, as the impact of globalisation and the heterogeneity that results throws doubt on the possibility of an overarching and unifying narrative. The global spread of modernity therefore undermines its very conditions of existence as diverse others are brought into relation with each other through a variety of means. Here, globalisation can be seen as providing the grounds for and necessitating a conceptualisation of heterogeneity, where diverse others and other cultures are not subsumed within a narrative of modernity but where there is rather a 'relativisation of "narratives"' (Robertson 1992: 141) that we mentioned earlier.

With Robertson's argument globalisation, therefore, does not result in a global narrative, but points to the very impossibility of such a narrative because the globe is constructed as a diaspora space. In other words, while space–time compression, in bringing the globe under increasingly integrated processes, has tendencies towards uniformity, it also provides the basis for a questioning of the guiding assumptions which have underpinned those very processes of globalisation, providing a basis for the recognition of, and support for, cultural difference. Therefore rather than globalisation resulting in the universalising and homogenising of modernity, the modern is thrown into doubt and question, for as things move and spread so they are translated and take different forms. This still allows the possibility of a continuation of the privileging of 'Western' views of the world – the discourse of modernity and the project of enlightenment, progress and emancipation through the application of science and processes of economic development – the overarching legitimating models of thought and action privileged by world culture theory. However, for us, Robertson's view on the very impossibility of such a narrative is persuasive. It is a view associated with the discourse of postmodernity and the assertion of difference and doubt as to the inevitable emancipatory consequences of modern forms of development.

Through the processes it sets in play, the universalising and internationalising logic of modernity thereby undermines the conditions for its own hegemony. The more effective modernity has become then the greater the compression of space–time and integration of the globe and the less universal modernity appears, a surfacing of difference which both frames and is framed by postmodernity. Thus globalisation 'is provoking new senses of disorientation and orientation, giving rise to new experiences of both placeless and placed identity' (Robins 2003: 242). In some ways, therefore, the strength of the challenges to the politics and epistemology of the West by feminist, post-colonial and post-structuralist writers in their bringing to the fore of difference can be said to respond to, help to produce, as well as be part of, globalising processes.

Taking a breath – space–time compression

Central to these globalising processes is the reordering of space and time and in particular its compression. Giddens (1990) argues that with the wide availability of the mechanical clock at the end of the eighteenth century a separation of time and space took place that eventually resulted in a global spread of a specific ordering of 'time' as a universal phenomenon. For Giddens, this separation was crucial to the development of modernity as it resulted in a particular set of possibilities associated with the advance of capitalism and colonialism where history (time) was asserted over and played out on the inert body of geography (space) (Massey 1993; Blunt and Rose 1994). In this separation of space and time, one that is still powerful, 'geography is an inert, fixed, isotropic back drop to the real stuff of politics and history' (Pile 1997: 4).

This separation is crucial in modernity's understanding of its own development, with the assertion of the temporal and historical over the spatial and geographical; as with the global–local nexus in understanding the development of globalisation, so space and time need to be understood in terms of the different ordering of space–time. Foucault's (1979) analysis of the development of modern institutions demonstrates how fundamental timetables were to the organisation of time and space in enabling the governance of the population of the developing nation state. The ordering of time is therefore also and always an organisation of space and vice versa. It is thus unsurprising that the contemporary period has seen the emergence of new forms of geography and the development of a sociology and politics of space and location that both undermines and counteracts the dominance of the temporal and historical and their production of linear and singular interpretations (Mohanty 1992; Urry 1995; Pile 1997). Thus 'the discourse of geography has become much wider than the discipline' (Gregory 1994: 81), something itself illustrated by this text. In the process, the very notion of space–time has been reconfigured with attempts to reposition understanding and practice in different spaces – margins (Spivak 1993), interstitial third space (Bhabha 1994) and diaspora space (Brah 1996).

The ordering of space–time therefore has a history, and it may be possible to categorise this into phases as with Robertson's conception of the globalising process discussed earlier. However, as Soja (1989) suggests in relation to the restructuring of space–time, globalising processes do not simply displace previous conditions but rather *overlay* and *interweave* them. This undermines established patterns of uneven development and produces new centres of urbanisation, but does not completely replace what existed previously. Notions of a post-industrial world are therefore partial and misplaced, the continuation of a purely Western rather than a globalised perspective. Here, 'globalisation' and indeed 'postmodernity' do not signify completely new spaces, but rather the attempt to conceptualise and articulate the complex, chaotic, layered and hybrid character of contemporary diaspora space, 'the intersectionality of diaspora, border, and dis/location as a point of confluence of economic, political, cultural and psychic processes' (Brah 1996: 208).

While there may be debate about the conceptualising of space and time as part of globalising processes, what has become accepted generally is the experience engendered by space–time compression under the influence of developments in transport and communications and more generally through the increased significance of speed. We shall say more about the latter later. Compression is basically the notion that the world feels smaller, and in an important sense *is* smaller, as more people, goods, information and services are now able to travel around it and communicate across great distances much more quickly and easily than was previously the case. However, the process of compression is itself one of uneven development, as there have been periods and places of greater compression than others. As an aspect of globalisation, space–time compression can be seen to have been significantly enhanced with the advent of modernity and the revolutionary forces which were let loose within it.

Probably the most systematic attempt to chart this process of compression from the Enlightenment to the present is to be found in the work of Harvey (1989), which situates globalisation and space–time compression within the current restructurings of capitalism. Here, it is the search for increased profits and social discipline on a global scale under conditions of enhanced competition for goods and services which it is argued leads to contemporary change. Drawing on a neo-Marxist framework, Harvey argues that the crises in capital accumulation at various stages in the history of capitalism have resulted in the disruption of established patterns of spatial arrangements and their continual reordering around new centres and forms of production. Thus, the crisis of over-accumulation and revolutionary upsurge in Europe in the 1840s was resolved in part by the expansion of investment and foreign trade through imperialist appropriation. This compression of space–time was made possible by the

> expansion of the railway network, accompanied by the advent of the telegraph, the growth of steam shipping, and the building of the Suez Canal, the beginnings of radio communication and bicycle and automobile travel at the end of the century...
>
> (Harvey 1989: 264)

As a result of these developments, global processes and change were speeded up. This was enhanced by the tight ordering of space–time on Fordist production lines, the first of which was built in 1913. For Harvey, the period of the late 1980s is marked by a further intensification of space–time compression, as capitalism is reconfigured with Fordist forms of capital accumulation, giving way to flexible accumulation and post-Fordism. Here, the development of new organisational forms engendered through the development of new technology and faster means of communication have resulted in an acceleration in production, also matched by an acceleration in exchange and consumption.

Fordism was deeply paradoxical for capitalism. Industrialisation provided the basis for the expansion of capital accumulation. However, the urbanisation processes associated with industrialisation – the bringing together of large numbers of people to work in factories – also provided the ground for a sense of solidarity and forms of union organisation to oppose capital. In other words, the very processes which created the conditions for the development of capitalism, through the creation of an urban working class, also provided the possibility of a challenge to capitalist organisation. Therefore, there is a sense in which, as Harvey (1993: 88) suggests, 'spatial dispersal and geographical isolation' have played an important part in capital's attempts to sustain labour market discipline and control, and to displace the challenge potentially posed by an urban working class. Now, this dispersal has been enhanced further by the globalisation underpinned by new forms of transport and communication, such as satellites, air travel and information technology. These compress space–time, allowing new forms of spatial dispersal to develop across the globe and thus for capital to locate and re-locate where returns are highest. Thus as we have seen, this gives place a greater significance for capital as it seeks out the most favourable conditions for its accumulation, a process enhanced by regional competition for inward investment and employment – 'the less important the spatial barriers, the greater the sensitivity of capital to the variations of place within space, and the greater the incentive for places to be differentiated in ways attractive to capital' (Harvey 1989: 295–6). This echoes the earlier argument that globalisation is not in opposition to localisation, but rather that the latter can be understood as part of the former and the former as expressing itself through the latter. New patterns of economic inequality are inscribed and re-inscribed in this process, as the current changing economies of China and India illustrate.

This geographical dispersal is also taking place within the nation, region and locale. Developments in the organisation of work have implications for the reorganisation of geographical distances between paid and unpaid work, leisure and other social practices. The need for populations to be concentrated into urban conglomerations is undermined by increasing physical distances, with technology enabling people, goods and services to be brought together by means other than physical proximity. At its most extreme, this provides the possibility for certain groups of people not to have to visit a workplace at all. They may live some distance from their employers or even in different countries, but technology and forms of communication enable them to have their activities based within their own homes. The very notion of the employer and workplace being geographically unified is lost. Post-Fordism can be seen as the means of organising that spatial dispersal as the acceleration of time engendered by developments in technology and communications increases the possibility of capital accumulation. However, dispersal from the traditional heartlands of capitalism and industrialisation should not blind us to the concentrations, industrialisation and urbanisation that is taking place in different parts of the globe. As Massey (1991) rightly cautions, globalising trends have not been experienced evenly and look different from different vantage points. Further, the replacement of Fordism by post-Fordism is not complete. Fordism, post-Fordism and neo-Fordism may all exist in the same country and even in the same organisation, with other means of organising production also possible.

The space–time compression of globalisation and responses to it are therefore neither uniform nor homogenising. Rather they present a number of contradictory positions in which the importance of distance and place appear to be reduced, even as their importance is reasserted as a reaction to the unifying effects of global integration. Thus, 'the globalisation of social relations is yet another source of (the reproduction of) geographical uneven development, and thus of the uniqueness of place' (Massey 1991: 29). The strength of these processes is dependent upon the intensity of the space–time compression and one's place in the global–local nexus. Thus, as Massey (1994: 148–9) argues in suggesting the need for a power geometry of space–time compression, the globalising processes need 'differentiating socially...different social groups, and different individuals, are placed in very distinct ways in relation to these flows and interconnections'.

Here, it is important also to remember that capitalism itself is not a uniform set of practices. National, international and regional organisations adopt different stances in the pursuit of capital accumulation and indeed skill formation. For instance, Lash and Urry (1994) suggest certain governments, most notably in the UK, North America and Australia, have both responded to and directed policy at increasing flexibility more enthusiastically and in different ways from others, for instance in Germany, France and Japan. Each set of policies rests on different conceptions of the relationships among the state, business and the workforce. However, the aim of sustaining competitiveness in global markets is shared across nations and, increasingly, across previous ideological divides.

As capital becomes more internationalised and the globe more integrated into market mechanisms, flexibility in its many manifestations can be seen as an attempt to resolve the problems of capital accumulation. Here, space–time compression is not only significant in relation to the restructuring of the places of production and production processes, but also in relation to its impact upon exchange and consumption. The acceleration of production can only be sustained if there is greater and faster consumption. Greater importance is thereby bestowed on the consumer, on branding, advertising and marketing. It is significant that debates about the 'consumer society' have developed alongside the shift in capital accumulation associated with globalisation. The primacy given to production, the workplace and the politics of the producer have been displaced and overlaid increasingly by consumption, the shopping mall and the politics of the market. Whereas Fordism provided the basis for constituting and satisfying the desires of a mass market, post-Fordism is held to serve the swiftly changing desires of market niches, to which instantaneity and disposability have become central. Here, the socio-cultural distinctions based on status and lifestyle overlay and, for some, displace the centrality of socio-economic class divisions, with 'a shift in patterns of differentiation from the social to the cultural sphere, from life-chances to lifestyles, from production to consumption' (Crook *et al.* 1992: 133). Consumption has a symbolic as well as material value, and image and lifestyles an increased volatility. The consumer market is one in which difference is the mark of distinction rather than uniformity. Any desire to 'keep up with the Joneses' means not having the same as them, but being able to distinguish oneself positively from them (Usher *et al.* 1997). This gives rise to a proliferation of possibilities for differing lifestyles, images and identities, despite and perhaps maybe because of the increased integration of the global economy.

Making sense of/through globalisation – representation and signifying practices

For Harvey (1989), the processes of space–time compression find a specific cultural expression in the transformation of capitalism at the turn of the twentieth century, resulting in the onset culturally of modernism as a reaction against realism. The latter was held to no longer express the sensibility of experiencing, or to represent the world as it was being experienced. The resolution of the crisis of capitalism therefore resulted in a crisis of representation, or of how to represent 'the world' under the new conditions of compression. In a sense, realism represented vestigial thought in the cultural domain with limited capacity to make sense of the changing conditions of the times:

> New senses of relativism and perspectivism could be invented and applied to the production of space and the ordering of time…despising history, [modernism] sought entirely new cultural forms that broke with the past and solely spoke the language of the new.
>
> (Harvey 1989: 270–1)

In this, cultural modernism aligned itself with radical causes and the internationalist and cosmopolitan aspirations made possible by space–time compression. Localised place was rejected as the space of tradition, parochialism and reaction. However, even as this cultural internationalism developed, the 'shrinkage of space that brings diverse communities across the globe in competition with each other implies localised competitive strategies and a heightened sense of awareness of what makes a place special and gives it a competitive advantage' (Harvey 1989: 271). Thus, the local had to be 're-located' and 're-presented' within the global in order to establish itself as a specific place, i.e. one of competitive advantage.

Harvey suggests that more recently the compression of space–time is almost at the point of collapse because 'we' can watch global events on television and the Internet as they happen, visit the local supermarket where the world's goods are available to 'us', and explore the history/geography of the globe brought to us in accessible theme parks (Rojek 1993). Here, 'the natural landscapes, village settings, organic communities, city grids, and colonial outposts of earlier times give way to unrepresentable, bewildering spaces that render experience and the life world unmappable' (Leitch 1996: 119). Further, the volatility of capital in the globalised economy is disrupting and disorientating. There is an argument therefore that, in this current phase of globalisation in which people are bombarded with stimuli and information, the cultural force, representations and representational practices of both modernism and realism are no longer so relevant. Thus, as modernism challenged realism in the attempt to make sense of the changes taking place in late nineteenth- and early twentieth-century capitalism, so new ways of making sense of the current situation are necessary. This is something which is reflexively illustrated in the growing number of characterisations of the contemporary to which we made reference earlier. Included in this of course is the very notion of globalisation itself, for, as Chambers (1994: 3) suggests, 'in the accelerating processes of globalisation we are also increasingly confronted with an extensive cultural and historical diversity that proves impermeable to the explanations we habitually employ'. This new postmodern form of sense-making is in many ways a way of not being able to make sense – reflexively making sense of the bewildering suggests a bewildering practice of representation if it is to be internally consistent (Law 2004). However, this assumes a modernist view of maps as representations, whereas we wish to support the notion of *mapping* as an ongoing signifying practice. In this view, mapping is a way of making sense rather than a representation of a single, final sense made. It is a form of imagining, where 'imagination is the attempt to provide coherence between ideas and action, to provide a basis for the content of social relationships and the creation of categories with which to understand the world around us' (Rizvi 2000: 222–3). We only have to look at the proliferation of maps to see how this is illustrated in the practices of cartography itself. We will return to this argument later.

Harvey's view is that, while modernism is a crisis of representation, postmodernism points to a crisis of signification. Thus, while 'modernism conceives of representations as being problematic...postmodernism problematises reality' (Lash 1990: 13). It is this differential nature of the problematic that has led to cultural postmodernism being conceived as a manifestation of what more controversially is considered to be a wider condition of postmodernity. This also points to one of the issues in debates about discourses of globalisation – that is whether they are themselves practices of representation and/or signification, as it is the constitutive power of globalisation rather than its empirical reality which is in question, if we take the latter rather than the former stance. This is not to deny the material reality of the world but it is to view any 'reality' as always already mediated, enacted by, rather than separate from, its representations (Law and Urry 2003; Usher and Edwards 2007). This is a move 'from the analysis of social reality as such to the analysis of signs, languages, discourse, and talk – the media through which social reality comes into being and disperses itself across and through a body politic' (Lemert 1997: 74). Practices of signification are themselves material and performative. The reading of signifying practices simply as practices of representation and vice versa lies at the heart of many of the mistranslations that take place in the debates over postmodernity and globalisation.

As with the debate over globalisation, there is a contestation as to whether the changes in sensibility engendered by the current phase of space–time compression are discontinuous with modernity or not. Indeed, Harvey (1989) makes a thoroughly modernist argument for postmodernism, reproducing Marxist perspectives of the superstructural nature of representational and signifying practices in relation to the material base of the economy, a particular spatial and relational set of understandings questioned by many writers on postmodernity. As Lemert (1997: 20) argues, 'it is not just that technology allows people closer communication with each other...but that globalising processes are of such a nature as to have fundamentally changed the way the world is experienced'. Nor can the economy alone determine people's sense of space and place (Massey 1994).

This is a view of globalisation also put forward by Waters (1995). He argues that claims for globalisation rest on a relationship between social organisation and territoriality and that this link is established through the forms of exchange which predominate in any one period. Central to contemporary globalisation is the dominance of symbolic exchange over material and political exchange and the extent to which the last two themselves become subject to culturalisation. For Waters (1995: 125–6), a globalised culture

> is chaotic rather than orderly – it is integrated and connected so that the meanings of its components are 'relativised' to one another but it is not unified or centralised...[it] admits a flow of ideas, information, commitment, values and taste mediated through mobile individuals, symbolic tokens and electronic simulations.

While this is suggestive, a certain caution is also necessary for, as Cunningham *et al.* (1997: 12) point out, there is a 'need to desegregate the different elements of what is referred to as global media into: global media events; service delivery platforms; media corporations; and distribution of content'.

Waters draws upon the work of Appadurai (1990) to provide a framework for the assessment of the extent to which a global cultural economy is in the making. Appadurai identified various arenas as 'scapes' within which cultural objects flow. There are 'ethnoscapes, the distribution of mobile individuals (tourists, migrants, refugees, etc.); technoscapes, the distribution of technology; finanscapes, the distribution of capital; mediascapes, the distribution of information; and ideoscapes, the distribution of political ideas and values' (Waters 1995: 126). To these, Waters adds sacriscapes and leisurescapes, respectively the distribution of religious ideas and of tourism. In all of these arenas, Waters finds the evidence for cultural globalisation well advanced, and, with that, the increased role of the symbolic in the material and political. Massey (1994: 161) writes also that

> each geographical 'place' in the world is being realigned in relation to the new global realities, their roles within the wider whole are being reassigned, their boundaries dissolve as they are increasingly crossed by everything from investment flows, to cultural influences, to satellite TV networks.

Thus, one can travel the rural areas of parts of Africa and find satellite dishes attached to mud houses, challenging the binary of the primitive and the advanced.

The material and political therefore are to be understood increasingly as mediated by the symbolic and cultural. Reflexively, this gives rise to the locating of much discussion of globalisation within the arenas of study where it takes place, resulting in the study of globalisation in other fields increasingly having to approach its objects through forms of cultural and symbolic analysis. In this sense, therefore, globalisation itself has to be understood as a signifying rather than a representational practice – perhaps even a reflexive signification of the postmodern.

At which point, and while recognising the danger of premature closure, we move on in order to avoid this glimpse itself becoming an oppressive gaze.

Glimpse two

Putting space back on the map – space, place and auto/biography

> I think that it is at least empirically arguable that our daily life, our psychic experience, our cultural languages are today dominated by categories of space rather than categories of time, as in the preceding period of high modernism.
>
> (Jameson 1991: 16)

> The displacement of attention from the temporal to the spatial must itself be interpreted in part as a historical phenomenon.
>
> (Jarvis 1998: 46)

> While national boundaries are increasingly blurred in the new global formation, transnational capitalism has paradoxically given rise to an increasing obsession with place.
>
> (Yoshimoto 1996: 107)

The difference that space makes

In this glimpse, we want to look specifically at notions of space, examining why 'space is in the midst of a renaissance' (Kaplan 1996: 147) and why it is, as it were, back on the map. The reconfiguration and valorisation of space, most obviously noticeable in the proliferating use of spatial metaphors (Edwards and Clarke 2002; Edwards *et al.* 2004), is one of the obvious effects of globalising processes, although it is the case also that the heightened sense of globalised awareness is itself a consequence of new ways of thinking about space.

Peters (1996: 93) argues, rightly in our view, that

> educational theory is dominated by considerations of time, by historically orientated theories, by temporal metaphors, by notions of change and

progress exemplified, for instance, in 'stages of development', whether conceived in terms of individual psychology...or of modernisation theory.

As Soja and Hooper (1993: 197) point out, there is now a general agreement, also increasingly affecting educational theory and discourse, that 'space makes a difference in theory, culture and politics'. There is a consequent bringing to the fore, or replacing, of the significance of 'the spatiality of human life' and recognition of the difference that space makes. Space is now more and more seen as having been under-theorised and marginalised in relation to the modernist emphasis on time and history, almost to the extent where it now seems to hegemonically replace time as the key factor to be considered (Edwards and Usher 2003). As a feature of the valorisation of time, space was constructed as neutral, fixed and immobile, unrelated to the social and without impact on the formation of subject identity and biography. Space was framed as a container or backcloth within or against which activity took place through time. Now as a result of the greater focus on the spatial, there has been a shift from considering it as universal and abstract in favour of conceptions which bring to the fore its hybrid nature, pointing to the ways in which the local is enfolded in globalising processes. Thus, it can be argued that there is movement towards a situation where

> spatial relations are seen to be no less complex and contradictory than historical processes, and space itself refigured as inhabited and heterogeneous, as a moving cluster of points of intersection for manifold axes of power which cannot be reduced to a unified plane or organised into a single narrative.
>
> (Hebdige 1990: vi–vii)

However, it would be inappropriate to conclude from this that time has now been replaced by space. As Jarvis (1998) points out in the quote above, the new emphasis on the spatial is itself a historical phenomenon, the phenomenon of a globalising dynamic. Yoshimoto (1996) argues that we should not think in terms of the primacy of space over time lest we fail to understand the full contemporary significance of spatiality. It is not so much a matter of changes in the relative importance of space and time but more a matter of changes in their relationship. The impact of electronic technology that enables the compression of space–time brings places together in different associations and configurations. To think otherwise is simply to reverse the hierarchy yet remain caught in the binary 'time–space' – a binary which is the problem in the first place. It is more helpful perhaps to think of it in the way Massey (1993: 155) does – 'space is not static (i.e. time-less), nor time spaceless...spatiality and temporality are different from each other but neither can be conceptualised as the absence of the other'. As she goes on to point out, we need to think now in terms of 'space–time', of a conception and actuality of time and space as inseparable and interactively relational. Or as Jones *et al.* (2004) suggest, we may need to consider spacing and timing as actions.

If we accept this, then inevitably we have to consider the impact of information and communication technologies (ICTs) and other media on the way that relationship has been changed. Space–time compression not only makes it impossible to disconnect these dimensions but also treats them as inseparable in relation to understanding cultural politics and the forging of identities and biographies. As Peters (1996: 100) argues, 'it is increasingly in terms of computer or communicated networks that we act and define ourselves as subjects'. These are mediated networks that for many give rise to an immediacy of the other even though they may be at a distance. To each other people are connected absence–presences.

These technologies of space–time compression are many and varied. Their availability and impact are uneven. Their development and use are subject to wider economic, cultural and political influences and strategies. It is not our intention here to map them fully, but, rather, to explore the re-inscription of the importance of space by focusing on the emerging and fast-expanding realm of electronic/digital technologies. The research on these technologies and their pedagogic impact and implications is large and growing almost as fast as the use of mobile phones and home computers (see, for example, Bigum *et al.* 1997; Morgan 1997; Snyder 2002; Lankshear and Knobel 2003). Our intention here is to focus merely on one aspect of current changes in space–time, i.e. the notion and actuality of 'cyberspace', the most obvious manifestation of the emergence of space, itself an emerging (non-)place and an important source of the spatial metaphors currently prevalent.

Cyberspace is itself a controversial topic – in many ways legitimately so. It is subject to both utopian and dystopian analysis (Kenway 1996). However, rejectionist stances ignore the significance of its role in the organising of space – the work that it does or can potentially do. It is because of the controversies surrounding it and the postmodern understandings informing our engagement with globalisation that we have decided upon this particular focus. The ICTs and computer-mediated communication associated with cyberspace have helped to construct new and different relationships between space and time. As Baudrillard (1983: 153) points out, in the hyper-real condition induced by space–time compression the relationship between the real and its representation are unclear, 'the cool universe of digitality has absorbed and won out over the reality principle', and it is the latter which largely is associated with place and bounded space. In the hyper-real, the relationship between the real and its representation or image becomes blurred (less bounded), and time–space and individual identity become more easily unmoored from modernist physical locations. Thus, through space–time compression, ICTs have created a situation where both clock time and physical space can be transcended. This has the consequence of reconfiguring the space–time limitations of modernist organisations and forms of identity. In the process, new forms of interaction without territorial boundaries or physical attributes, decentred and with more limited hierarchy, are made possible (Loader 1997), if not always realised. Although such ideas are suggestive, they need to be treated with caution, for, as we have said before, each spatialisation is itself a manifestation of powerful practices, none of which can be embraced by a single narrative. Yet again, we can only offer glimpses.

Therefore, one of the things that we will do here will be to look critically at the notion of cyberspace. We begin, however, with a more general consideration of space, and new spatial metaphors in relation to issues of identity and some of the debates surrounding space, place, identity and biography. We will use the term 'auto/biography' to more readily indicate the lived and textualised practices through which sense is made of a person's individual and collective identity. The reconfigurations of space and the use of spatial metaphors (Lakoff and Johnson 1980) in relation to issues of auto/biography have been central to a range of feminist, post-colonial and cultural studies. More recently they have played a central role in certain discussions of education (Jacklin 2004; McGregor 2004). It is here that we most readily see the influence of globalisation in terms of the intersection of the global and the local – the associations and translations of globalised space and places of identity – their (en)counters and their enfoldings.

On the move – space, place and auto/biography

> The spatialisation of knowledge and education in the postmodern age is based in the 'soft architecture' of the network which increasingly defines the nature of our institutions and subjectivities.
>
> (Peters 1996: 100)

Globalising practices can be seen as providing the grounds for, and indeed necessitating, a conceptualisation of the current situation in terms of hybridity. As Rizvi (2000: 209) argues, 'hybridisation differs from the earlier modernist requirement for assimilation because its cultural politics does not have a cultural "centre of gravity"'. This does not stop the desire on the part of some for assimilation of course, but it is a constantly failing project. Diverse others and other cultures cannot any longer be subsumed within the single universal narratives of modernity or, for that matter, any other such totalising narratives, for example religion. Nor can they be seen as entirely separate, bounded or distinct. From this emerges

> a politics of location as locationality in contradiction – that is a positionality of dispersal; of simultaneous situatedness within gendered spaces of class, racism, ethnicity, sexuality, age; of movement across shifting cultural, religious and linguistic boundaries; of journeys across geographical and psychic borders.
>
> (Brah 1996: 204)

Globalising processes therefore do not result automatically in a universalising of particular trends and perspectives, but lead precisely to their problematisation. Hybridity rather than homogeneity and the relational rather than the bounded characterise both the contemporary experience and conceptualisation of globalisation. Within this, 'the significance of new hybrid and syncretic identities shows the potential for crossover identities which destabilise old...absolutisms' (Rattansi 1995: 280). Globalising practices and responses to them therefore present us with a number of contradictory positionings that bring to the fore the importance of location and locating practices, and with that the metaphor of the *network*. Similarly, the politics of globalising practices are not unidirectional. Here 'different social groups, and different individuals belonging to numbers of social groups, are located in many different ways in the new organisation of relations over time–space' (Massey 1994: 164). It is perhaps unsurprising therefore that cultural geography and the spatialisation of the social sciences and humanities more generally have grown in importance over the years.

What then are some of the consequences of globalisation for auto/biography? If the contemporary condition is increasingly one of hybridity, de-territorialisation, mobility and disembedding, what can be understood by place and space? In what sense, if at all, can globalisation then be understood as a state of 'homelessness', of insecure boundaries and flux, where a sense of place, meaning and identity become problematic or no longer exist at all? These are themselves complex questions, located in certain traditional assumptions as to the 'proper' relationships among place, meaning and auto/biography, where stability of place is often seen as resulting in stability of meaning and identity. Such assumptions deeply embed 'warm' notions of local community, which at the same time displace the conflicts, oppressions and limitations of such bounded places and readings of 'community', as modern disciplinary institutions, such as the prison, hospital or even the school (Foucault 1979). For Massey (1994), the outpouring about homelessness itself signifies a First World/colonising perspective. For those elsewhere,

> the boundaries of the place one called home must have dissolved long ago, and the coherence of one's local culture must long ago have been under threat, in those parts of the world where the majority of its populations live.
> (Massey 1994: 165)

Homelessness and a sense of a loss of place may be a recent experience for those who have been at the centres of power, but a long-standing one for diverse others and indeed the global majority. Indeed, it may also have been the experience of the colonisers, albeit one that is repressed in the expressions of 'felt' experience.

Globalising processes bring to the surface the problematic element of these assumptions, even as they surface the difficulty of finding a bounded place called 'home'. That is not to say that no such place exists, but rather its bounded nature is now always open to challenge. Rather than the loss of 'home', therefore, it might be more appropriate to reconsider the meaning of home and the possibilities provided when the home is, for instance, networked to the globe through telephone, television, mobile phone, the Internet, fast jet travel, diverse products and services available on a worldwide basis – and subject to the climatic, environmental and political effects of actions taken elsewhere 'at a distance'. Home therefore becomes an effect of the associations which mark a space as a particular type of place. The stable identities of bounded place –

themselves perhaps more nostalgic than actual for many – may need to be reconfigured as 'diasporic identities [which] are at once local and global...networks of transnational identifications encompassing "imagined" and "encountered" communities' (Brah 1996: 196). For Brah (1996: 180), this provides a space that takes 'account of a homing desire which is not the same thing as desire for a "homeland"'. Brah is building on previous work by Hall (1995: 47–8), who argues that diasporan identity signifies

> those who have succeeded in remaking themselves and fashioning new kinds of cultural identity by, consciously and unconsciously, drawing on more than one cultural repertoire...although they are characteristic of the cultural strategies adopted by marginalised people in the latest phase of globalisation, more and more people in general – not only ex-colonised or marginalised people – are beginning to think of themselves, of their identities and their relationship to culture and to place in these more open ways.

It is for these reasons that Brah (1996: 209), like others, has extended the arguments of post-colonialism to suggest that 'the native is as much the diasporan as the diasporan is the native'. In other words, the notion of insiders and outsiders of nation, ethnicity, religion, culture, etc., is unsustainable; the ever strident attempts to create such bounded spaces and places – i.e. through ethnic cleansing – being evidence of the sustained work and exercises of power through which hybridity is fought in the attempt to bound and bind. As Coulby and Jones (1996: 178) argue in relation to Europe, 'plural identities are the reality for most Europeans, despite the desire of many individual European states and their education system to deny this'. Here place rather than being bounded and excluding is conceived as a meeting place, a point of (en)counter (Massey 1999), of association.

It might be imagined then that 'in the global village all participants are likely to be strangers' (Turner 1994: 111), but such a view is overly generalised, already assumes that strangeness and geographical distance go hand in hand, and works in a binary of strangeness–familiarity when the strange can also be familiar and vice versa. We would suggest it is rather that the familiar and unfamiliar are reconfigured and reordered and that increased (en)counters with strangeness – direct or indirect – can result in enhanced understanding and sociality as much as increased alienation and/or hostility. Increasing cultural complexity might be daunting but it cannot be avoided, as 'global influence is strongly circumscribed by the bodies and nation-states which own and control mass media and communications, by the colonial legacies of language and culture, and sometimes by ethnic and religious traditions and tribalism' (Evans 1997: 18).

As we have noted, the problem here is the strength of the assumptions that underpin and structure much of the debate about space, place and auto/biography. In simple terms, we can discern certain binaries at work which valorise a view of space based on a conception of the local as bounded place, and with that a stable and bounded identity as the norm. In many ways, this is a particular view of traditional society disrupted by the modernising process of industrialisation, urbanisation and capitalism and out of which emerged discourses of alienation, isolation and anomie. In itself, this tends to ignore the fact that 'boundedness has not for centuries really been characteristic of local places' (Massey 1994: 170). For some, the contemporary period is signified in the renewed interests in the regional, historical and local in response to the perceived efficiency, functionalism and impersonality of modernism, something particularly noticeable in architecture (Robins 1993). In some ways, this results in a reworked traditional reassertion of the link between place and auto/biography, sometimes associated with a conservative postmodern stance, although perhaps this should more readily be conceived as anti-modern, something one might associate with certain strands of religious fundamentalism. Here, there is an inversion rather than deconstruction of the modern perspective within which '"time" is equated with movement and progress, "space/place" is equated with stasis and reaction' (Massey 1994: 151). As we have already suggested, in modernity it is time which is asserted over space and this is as true for the radical challenges to capitalism as it has been for capitalism itself. Thus 'it is no coincidence that communities for resistance are termed "movements" in much political struggle' (Pile 1997: 29).

The play of opposing notions of the 'traditional' and the 'modern' can be seen in much of the debate about globalising practices and identity. However, what we wish to suggest is that each simplifies the processes at work, constructing the other negatively in order to better valorise itself. It is through a radical postmodern reading that these binaries can be deconstructed, making possible the exploration of the complexity of 'space', 'place' and 'auto/biography'. This is something that is made possible by globalising trends which bring to the fore the complexity and relationality of experience. For some, this places the emphasis on the increased mobility experienced in the contemporary period, giving rise to metaphors that emphasise movement – the 'nomad' (Braidotti 1994) and the 'traveller' (Clifford 1992). As Turner suggests (1994: 113–14), 'it is important for any sociology which wants to avoid nostalgia and *fin de siècle* nihilism to look at the opportunity side of rootlessness, complexity, and diversity'. By so doing, 'the ethnic absolutism of "root" metaphors, fixed in place, is replaced by mobile "route" metaphors which can lay down a challenge to the fixed identities of "cultural insiderism"' (Pile and Thrift 1995a: 10). Here it is the notion of the global cosmopolitan which has emerged in some discourses to mark a positive imaginary of a global identity.

An important distinction here is between those who assert movement in a radicalised modern form, which continues to position space as an inert background, and those who emphasise movement as a spatialisation of auto/biography and the political (Mohanty 1992; Blunt and Rose 1994). This has been central to much feminist and post-colonial analysis, attempting to theorise new possibilities and auto/biographies with which to construct a more equitable global dispensation. Here metaphors of movement are deployed to destabilise the centres of power and provide for new power geometries through different mapping practices. Travelling, then, assumes a political as well as a metaphorical role – 'nomadism consists not so much in being homeless, as in

bounding in globalising conditions. Here, the notion of 'association' is itself problematic with certain assumptions about choice that may not reflect the different forms of sociality and (dis)continuities at play in cultures and communities. As Robins (1993: 312) argues, 'if there is now a revival of interest in community and sense of place, this can only be seen in the context of what is in fact increasing fragmentation of urban [and much non-urban] life'. Perhaps therefore,

> instead of thinking of places as areas with boundaries around, they can be imagined as articulated moments in networks of social relations and understandings, but where a large proportion of those relations, experiences and understandings are constructed on a far larger scale than what we happen to define for that moment as the place itself, whether that be the street, or a region or even a continent.
>
> (Massey 1994: 154)

It is for such reasons that Webster (1995: 141) suggests that 'the trend is towards the world being the context within which relationships are conducted, no matter how localised and particular an individual life may appear to be experienced'. The stretching of social relations over space through space–time compression results in reconfigured, globalised senses of place. Indeed, in certain locations, this can lead to what Benko (1997: 23) refers to as non-places, spaces 'devoid of the symbolic expressions of identity, relations and history: examples include airports, motorways, anonymous hotel rooms, public transport' – and possibly even cyberspace, as we shall see later.

Thus, with the increased interest in space has also come an increased attention to issues of identity and auto/biography, at least for those within globalising practices who are most subject to certain tendencies. While some see these processes and postmodernity generally as inducing a loss of meaning along with the loss of place, it is perhaps, rather,

> not that the world has little or no meaning, but that we should feel the constant need to give it a meaning. In traditional societies, meaning could be taken for granted. Today, we are expected to find a meaning for everything...
>
> (Benko 1997: 25)

One of the ironies, therefore, of the postmodern and of globalising processes is that, even as they may engender a greater volatility and uncertainty in auto/biography that is subject to symbolic exchange, in many significant ways they do also affirm the centrality of auto/biography as a reflexive construct. This is not necessarily either overwhelmed by the traditions of place and the local nor lost completely in modernist alienation and anomie, although in some renditions there is a tendency towards individualisation and a focus on the personal rather than the socio-cultural (for more on this, see Usher 1998). However, the conditions for a heightened engagement with questions of identity and meaning are to be found in and through globalising and postmodern processes, although these never completely displace traditional and modernist concerns and experiences. Thus the concern perhaps for issues of social presence in the discussion of cyber-space and e-learning. The increased importance we have suggested given to signifying practices is thus both a response to and condition for that which it seeks to interpret – which ever way one looks at it, there is reflexivity! There is a heightened 'to-ing and fro-ing' in where one stands.

However, this is not of course a view shared by all. For some, the de-realisa-tion and de-territorialisation of place associated with the intensifying of globalisation and symbolic exchange results in a loss of social meaning and dis-ruption of established senses of community, culture and auto/biography. This provokes what Robins (1993: 320) refers to as 'feelings of dislocation and disori-entation'. However, once again, this tends to assume the authenticity of a relationship between place, meaning and auto/biography. This is certainly dis-rupted by globalising practices, but is also problematic given that to have a sense of place historically has meant 'being kept in one's place'. For instance, in his framing of racism, Rattansi (1995: 253) suggests that 'there are no unambiguous, water-tight definitions to be had of ethnicity, racism, and the myriad terms in between'. The de-essentialising discourses of postmodernity accept, uncover and help to explore and explain this, even if the experience of so doing is an uncom-fortable one. 'A cultural sense of "postmodern" spatial stress and dislocation can thus be grounded in the material framework of new relationships between spatial regions and localities as well as in the "imaginary geographies" and spatial prac-tices of agents' (Shields 1997: 196). Feelings such as those of dislocation, as we shall argue later, are not necessarily or inherently negative. Indeed they can be a springboard for learning and positive forms of change. It is for this reason that we draw upon the notion of diaspora because

> for a meaningful identity and a flexible response to burgeoning opportunities, a double facing type of social organisation is highly advantageous. Just such an organisation exists in the form of a diaspora...[diasporas] have always been in a better position to act as a bridge between the particular and the universal.
>
> (Cohen 1997: 170)

Here, as Rattansi (1995: 253) suggests of racism and ethnicity, but which we believe can be applied to all attempts at firm categorisation and bounded notions of identity, 'all these terms are permanently in between, caught in the impossi-bility of fixity and essentialism'. This draws upon Derrida's argument, summarised by Natter and Jones (1997: 146), that 'the outside of any category is already found to be resident within, permeating the category from the inside through its traceable presence-in-absence within the category'. Dislocation may be a new experience for those previously at the centres of power, but it is as much an unfixed, diverse and contradictory phenomenon as globalising processes themselves. We believe this is something that can be given expression in the for-mulation '(dis)location', signifying that auto/biography is not bounded but framed in relation to diverse others, governed by alterity rather than foreignness.

Even where attempts are made to bound identity, these can only make sense relationally, even if self-understandings may be different – thus, once again the need for a both/and rather than either/or approach to examining globalising processes and their implications for education.

For us then, globalisation surfaces a number of conceptual metaphors and spaces – difference, location, mapping, diaspora space, hybridity, absence–presence, (dis)location – through which to destabilise the binaries which frame much of the thinking about the contemporary and which are themselves destabilised by contemporary processes and practices. In a sense, therefore, globalising processes – including the writing of this text – provide us with the opportunity to enter Bhabha's (1990: 211) interstitial third space, which 'displaces the histories that constitute it, and sets up new structures of authority, new political initiatives, which are inadequately understood through received wisdom'. We, like many others therefore, are trying to 'change the subject', annoying to those who see it as avoidance, encouraging for those who consider the 'subject' in need of change. This is an uncomfortable space, but not in any uniform sense. It is to an exploration of the discomfort posed for pedagogies by globalisation that we will explore within the rest of this text, where we will return again and again to the metaphors we have outlined here in the attempt to provide a particular mapping – topographical and hopefully topical.

Cyberspace – making the virtual real, really!

> Each self exists in a fabric of relations that is now more complex and mobile than ever before. Young or old, man or woman, rich or poor, a person is always located at nodal points of specific communication circuits, however tiny these may be.
>
> (Lyotard 1984: 15)

> *Terminal identity*: an unmistakably doubled articulation in which we find both the end of the subject and a new subjectivity constructed at the computer station or television screen.
>
> (Bukatman 1996: 9)

In recent years, cyberspace has developed rapidly both as a concept and an actuality. The explosive growth, for example, of the Internet as a communication system is indisputable, although its significance and effects are both contested and contestable (Kenway 1996). Part of the key to this growth lies in the Internet's technological structure, which enables costless reproduction, instant dissemination and radical decentralisation (Poster 1997) – as we have noted earlier: no centre, limited hierarchy. However, in mapping the significance of the Internet, due weight must also be given to factors which are not the outcome of technology alone, such as, for example, its accessibility and reliability. Despite some of the ways in which it is represented, e-learning is not a technical fix for all that is wrong with education centred on bounded built

environments. Such other factors are economic and socio-cultural in assumption and impact. This means that the Internet cannot be understood simply in
an instrumental sense as an efficient tool of communication, but more aptly as a
socially and culturally produced space that stimulates new forms of interaction,
helps in restructuring and forging creolised identities and produces in the case of
e-learning new relations of power, for example, between teachers and learners.
Thus, for instance, as Morgan (1999) says more generally of the use of information and communications technologies (ICTs) in schools, they

> have been 'schooled' – and schools are a powerful set of social technologies
> themselves: the tools and techniques for getting things done socially and
> culturally: not only transmitting knowledge but also thereby forming indi-
> viduals and groups as productive social beings.

Following Bigum and Green (1995), she argues that ICTs are both a resource
and context for getting things done. Cyberspace then is a powerful metaphor
through which things get done. Like all spaces, therefore, it has a pedagogic role
in the production of subjects and bodies, giving rise to diverse, but only certain,
possibilities for learning and ways of learning.

The Internet can be understood as the day-to-day expression of cyberspace,
with the latter definable in a number of ways. Featherstone and Burrows (1995:
5), for instance, stress the technological/interactive aspect with cyberspace as a
generic term, referring to 'a cluster of different technologies, some familiar, some
being developed and some still fictional, all of which have in common the ability to simulate environments within which humans can interact'. Rheingold
(1993) puts it rather differently, referring to cyberspace as a conceptual space
where words, relationships and data are manifested through the use of computer-
mediated communication. Kramerae (1995: 38) has another emphasis again:
'"cyberspace" refers to the worldwide computer-mediated communication network where words and graphics are shared, and friendships and power relations
are manifested'. We will return to the significance of these different emphases at
a later point, but for now we want to highlight the fact that there are a range of
ways of framing cyberspace. We take it from this, therefore, that the term 'cyberspace' is not simply a neutral description of reality, but has become now a term
within a discursive practice which seeks to understand, and intervene in, the
world of virtuality and symbolic exchange associated with globalising processes.

Some elements in this discourse construct cyberspace simply as technologically produced, whereas others (of more interest to us) see it as a space that has
emerged where none previously existed, yet a space which is also what Benko
(1997) refers to as a non-space – in this case, constituted through an expanding
range of communicative practices. As we have noted earlier, this is, in a sense, a
(dis)location – something which is both positioned and not positioned, displaced but not re-placed, a diaspora of hybridity and flows where one and many
locations are simultaneously possible. In itself, this is also (dis)locating, producing a range of positionings, some more structured than others. As Bukatman

(1996: 18) notes, cyberspace is 'a completely malleable realm of transitory data structures in which historical time is measured in nanoseconds and spatiality exists somehow both globally and invisibly'. Here, it is important to note, as Featherstone (1995) points out, and as we have suggested above in relation to conceptualisations of space more generally, how frequently metaphors of movement and mobility crop up. Most notably, the metaphor of 'flows' contrasted with those of 'positionalities', originating with Deleuze and Guattari (1988) and their notion of rhizomatic branching networks as a critique of fixed boundaries and identities. These flows with their source in globalisation have a de-territorialising effect – of people, images and information, commodities, money and ideas (Appadurai 1990). Wark (1997), borrowing an image from geometry, refers to them as 'vectors' (lines of fixed length and direction but with no fixed position) and argues that 'we' all now live in a space of vectoral flows not places. A vector is a trajectory along which information (or anything else) can pass and they have become faster and more flexible, in the process potentially connecting anything to anywhere and creating a new space of possibilities. Cyberspace then for Wark is the emerging de-territorialised terrain of vectors; the Internet along which information and images flow being an example of a vector that traverses space and time, abstracting these from the specificities of place and thus simultaneously rendering them into non-space and non-time.

Like others then, Wark (1997: 57) argues that cultural differences are now not so closely tied to the experiencing of particular places – 'vertical differences of locality, ethnicity are doubled by horizontal differences determined not by being rooted in a particular place but by being plugged into a particular circuit'. He goes on to describe this new experience of difference as antipodality – 'the experience of an active trajectory between, places, identities...rather than a drawing of borders, be they of self or place' (Wark 1997: 57). Antipodality then is the experience of (dis)location – the feeling of being neither 'here' nor 'there' yet also of being 'here' and 'there' – that arises as an effect of the vectoral communications of transnational and globalised conditions.

This is suggestive but of course also problematic for there is the danger of constructing a view of cyberspace and space more generally which is transcendental, detached from the practices through which it is formed, the materialities through which it is enacted and the constraints it imposes. Although cyberspace may be malleable, we nonetheless need to be aware of the powerful constraints within it and the forms of regulation to which it is and can become subject. The danger is in the implication that 'anything goes' in cyberspace, but that is only so if it is made to be so and that is not yet, nor likely to be, the case. Thus, as Kenway (1996: 219) says of the related notions of the 'information superhighway', 'those who regularly employ it say little about the direction and quality of its traffic, the different activities in different lanes, who controls the lights or who gets to travel'. In addition, the traffic is traceable with the potential spreading of surveillance over those who make use of the electronic media. This relates to the growth of sophisticated watching, listening, storing, sifting and intrusive devices and to the eventual capacity of full service networks to track behaviour of individuals and to develop digital profiles for various state or market purposes.

(Kenway 1996: 224)

There is a sense in which in some interpretations of globalising processes cyberspace provides metaphorical resources for the reconceptualisation of space more generally – emphasising flows, nodes and networks – even as those notions inform interpretations of cyberspace. There is a flow of ideas in which certain understandings of cyberspace become in some ways paradigmatic of space more generally and there is a naturalising of practices which are subject to exercises of power, contest and change. Like globalising processes more generally, therefore, cyberspace is a space in which there are multiple possibilities, potentialities and enfoldings.

Of course, any account of globalising practices needs to highlight the crucial role of ICTs and their effects in terms of the reconfiguring and patterning of auto/biographies. This is the case generally and more specifically for pedagogy, for, as Morgan (1999) notes regarding a project on new technologies and classroom practice, 'because many teachers are out of touch with the cultural and critical aspects of ICTs, their work can remain ineffective, entrenched in "schoolish" uses'. Poster (1990) argues that in modernity auto/biographies are shaped by production practices, whereas in postmodernity they are shaped by communication practices. In the former, auto/biographies are elicited as autonomous and instrumentally rational, in the latter they are elicited as unstable, multiple and diffuse. (Dis)location or 'dis-place-ment' is an aspect of the postmodern condition in which a sense of auto/biography is marked by the peculiarly postmodern geography of identity – marginality and otherness increasingly figuring as the signifiers of identity. ICTs and computer-mediated communications would seem therefore to provide the means of enhancing postmodern possibilities for different forms of auto/biography, not least in the proliferation of blogs through which people narrate (and indeed construct) their existences.

Kaplan (1996) argues that postmodern spatialisation, the new relationship between place and space enabled by these new technologies, creates new and different networks, communities and auto/biographies as more and more people are connected electronically than by conventional geographic proximity. This is a tendency already in place through pre-existing forms of media and communication, such as the television and the telephone, but it is the possibilities for and levels of interactivity which are increasing in relation to more traditional broadcast media. Even desktop computers are becoming staid for those who desire the mobility made possible by mobile phones, pocket computers and the like. The notion that geographical proximity or 'place' is now not so significant is undoubtedly troubling. A common response to this is to question whether cyberspace is a 'real' place. The way such a questioning is expressed is itself interesting, signifying the difficulty of critiquing in the language of that which we seek to critique, that which it seems we find difficult to do without – in this case the 'reality' of place. However, as Bukatman (1996: 118) points out, 'whether cyberspace is a "real" place or not, our experience of electronic space is a "real" experience'. Furthermore, as Loader (1997) argues, cyberspace has to be understood in relation to a technosocial restructuring that is real enough. There is a materiality to people and objects, which is not overcome in the interactive spaces of cyberspace. However, as Kenway (1996: 224) suggests, it is precisely 'Internet communities and identities [which] have the potential to provoke a new critical discourse about the "real"'.

The discourse of cyberspace also expresses a significant technological and social imaginary for many. One aspect of this was the literary movement of 'cyberpunk' that is now increasingly recognised as having been in a recursive relationship with theorisations of the contemporary condition (Featherstone and Burrows 1995). Poster (1995) refers to cyberpunk as a narrative *of* cyberspace that is also a narrative *in* cyberspace. With both utopian and dystopic elements, it combines speculative science fiction with the actuality of technological change. It is widely thought of as having been the literary expression of certain aspects of postmodernism in conditions of globalisation and flexible capital accumulation. As Bukatman (1996) points out, cyberpunk not only expressed a science fictional ('terminal') world but was actually a product of such a world. For some, cyberpunk fiction engaged more fully with aspects of contemporary cultural practices than more academic studies. Thus, the notion of 'business as usual' in many academic studies – and indeed in the use of ICTs in classrooms – has continued to result in increasing (dis)locations between the 'realities' through which lives are lived.

Cyberpunk presented visions of the future worlds of cyberspace (a term itself coined by William Gibson, the 'father' of cyberpunk, to characterise a 'notional space') – visions encompassing a vast range of technological developments, power struggles, post-human forms and boundary-displacing interzones on- or offline. His science fiction novel *Neuromancer* (Gibson 1984), perhaps the best-known and influential example of the genre, is now regarded not merely as speculation but as presenting a theoretically coherent vision of the near future, a narrative of the not far off now. As Jameson (1991) has said, it was the best literary expression of late capitalism and postmodernism. It has been read as a prefigurative social–cultural theory that presented an instantly recognisable portrait of the postmodern predicament and of the coming direction of contemporary social change. For many, cyberpunk sounded both a hope and a warning – at the very least, it acted as a reminder that technology has a cultural impact, that it mediates social relationships, senses of identity and the wider sense of social life to an extent we are only just beginning to grasp. It is one of the ways whereby the globalised future is 'colonised first by our imagination' (Jones 1995: 11). As Bukatman (1996: 6) points out, 'there is simply no overstating the importance of science fiction to the present cultural moment, a moment that sees itself as science fiction'. And indeed in a 'society of signs' (Usher and Edwards 2007), for some, auto/biography is shaped through the discourses of science fiction.

There is, however, another aspect to this. The language of contemporary science fiction is 'a language of spectacle and simulation, a language designed to be appropriate to its era' (Bukatman 1996: 11). It is hence a language of 'continual linguistic play that resists any totalisation of meaning' (Bukatman 1996: 11). Given that science fiction writing's thematic is spatial orientation and exploration, there is through this a doubling which brings to the fore and mirrors the condition of decentredness. The experience of reading, which resists the totalisation of meaning, is doubled in the experience of cyberspace's hypertextual linkages, which resist through their non-linear potential the closure of totalisation. Each reading has the potential to link you to a next, and next, and next, with a degree of openness beyond that of the traditional book.

The same could also be said of another aspect of the discourse of cyberspace – the notion of the 'cyborg' (or 'cybernetic organism'), a term first coined by Haraway (1991) and defined by Featherstone and Burrows (1995: 2) as 'a self-regulating human-machine system...a human-machine hybrid in which the machine parts become replacements, which are integrated or act as supplements to the organism to enhance the body's potential'. Although cyborgs are associated popularly with the frighteningly 'inhuman' characters portrayed in postmodern dystopias (for example, in films such as *Robocop* and *Total Recall*), it could be argued that in one way or another many people are already cyborgs through obvious things such as the use of prostheses of all kinds to technologies such as iPods, transplants and biogenetic engineering. However, for us, the significant point about the notion of the cyborg is its hybridity, its embodiment (literally) of the breakdown or blurring of boundaries (and therefore of a necessary and interactive relationality) between nature and culture, technology and nature, bodies and subjects, active agents and involuntary machines – 'the osmotic flows between the social and the natural, between biology and technology that constitute new forms of social space' (Lankshear *et al.* 1996: xx). Beller (1996: 194–5) argues that 'the cyborg is the absolute limit figure for the conjunction of the global and the local – the intersecting of the human being from anywhere in the world...and the technology endemic to transnational capitalism'. In the *Star Trek* series, for example, this goes a stage further with the 'assimilation' of organisms and technologies from across the universe by the Borg, who somehow seem more threatening and seductive than an earlier generation of apparently solely mechanical other-worlders, the Daleks from *Doctor Who*.

The cyborg can be seen then as another metaphor for that restructuring of boundaries and associations that characterises globalising processes where hitherto fixed boundaries between subjects, bodies and the world are no longer so stable and impermeable. As Keith and Pile (1993) point out, the modernist conception of a unitary self in a single biological body is rendered untenable. With cyberspace come notions of virtual space, a space that is not a space and therefore navigable but not fully mapped. Turkle (1995) argues that within cyberspace the territory can never be fully mapped because the horizon shifts with every connection made. However, there might also be an ongoing necessity for mapping.

With this comes a challenge to large-scale systematic theory building and an accompanying valuing of a greater range of difference and complexity, a questioning of the analytical categories deriving from fundamental divisions or binary oppositions, such as that of 'technology–nature', which structure the 'reality' of the world. It may therefore be no accident that with the emergence of interest in globalising processes has come a growing framing of the world in socio-technical terms, such as we find in actor-network theory for instance. The spatial–virtual metaphors of cyberpunk and cyborgs are a way of expressing new modes of (dis)located technological being in the world – new subject positions that 'interface with the global realms of data circulation' (Bukatman 1996: 9). Here, cyberspace itself provides a vehicle for widening the debate in social theory from fixed accounts of self and agency. With computer-mediated communication, human and machine are engaged directly, with the consequent requirement to reconsider the 'reality' of self and experience and how we represent the world to ourselves and others.

The space that makes a difference

> The present epoch will be above all the epoch of space. We are in the epoch of simultaneity; we are in the epoch of juxtaposition, the epoch of the near and far, of the side-by-side, of the dispersed.
>
> (Foucault 1986: 22)

As Peters (1996: 93) points out, 'modern educational theory has all but ignored questions of space, of geography, of architecture'. In this glimpse, we have argued that with globalising processes this is now an untenable position. Spatialising metaphors, both an outcome of these processes and themselves contributors to globalised awareness and reconceptualisation, have assumed an increasingly significant currency in social theory and educational discourse (Paechter 2004).

We have argued that these metaphors provide the space for new modes of action and identity formation in bringing to the fore dimensions such as relationality, virtuality and reflexivity. We have attempted to show how cyberspace, itself both space and non-space, both locating and dislocating, stimulates, facilitates and is itself a significant aspect of the contemporary changes associated with globalisation – 'a new spatialisation of knowledge and education based upon the mode of information' (Peters 1996: 100). We have argued that the vectoral nature of cyberspace makes it a (dis)locating medium for those finding themselves within it – and it is not simply information that is at stake here but auto/biography too. Whereas naive technophilia and/or technological fetishism construct cyberspace as a transcendent location, and in so doing reintroduce space as fixed and bounded, a space of enclosure, it is in the work it does to give expression to flows, networks and relatedness that we find cyberspace productive, if problematic.

In educational terms, what seems to be implied by the spreading use of spatial metaphors is a questioning, and the possibility of a restructuring, of those hitherto

Glimpse three
Globalisation, pedagogy and curriculum

Discussions of the impact of globalisation on curriculum and pedagogy are concerned increasingly with two areas. One is those matters that need to be covered in learning encounters where the aim is to enable learners to engage as global citizens or consumers – covering, for example, issues such as global values, social justice, sustainable development and environmental education (Gough 1998). The second is an examination of the impact of information and communication technologies (ICTs), of space–time compression, and of emerging forms of global education enabled by these developments (Mason 1998). Significant though these issues are in themselves, there is a danger that they can be constructed as encompassing all that there is to be said about the implications of globalisation. We would argue that it is just as, if not more, important to be able to locate the full range of contemporary and emerging curricular and pedagogical practices in relation to the play of globalisation. Thus, we would argue that attempts to tighten control of the curriculum at state level do not, as it is often suggested (Power and Whitty 1996; Green 1997), undermine the globalisation thesis but can be understood as a dimension of the contemporary interrelationship between the global, regional and the local. In this sense then it is not simply formal institutionalised practices which are subject to examination but also the location of those practices within a range of globalising processes and influences which include trends towards regionalisation, localisation and particularity. The emergence therefore of national curricula is as significant in a context of globalisation as the development of ICTs in pedagogic practices, and the role of media and cultural changes more generally. This illustrates that globalisation is no single unidirectional and mono-valent trend. As we have pointed out previously, the global and the local cannot be separated.

The more general point furthermore is that no single development can be made transparent within a single overarching and transcendent explanation or narrative, but rather rests more readily within the differences and diversity that are both a feature, and an outcome, of globalising processes. As Gough (1998: 1–2) rightly points out,

> in the apprehension of complex, multiple, proliferating and immanent realities there is no unitary 'reality' of globalisation...whatever 'awareness' may

be increasing is somewhat inchoate, overlaid (and further complicated) by our own reflexive 'awareness' of the need to be – and to be seen to be – aware that globalisation is indeed worthy of our attention.

In this part of the text, we will examine some of the current changes that challenge education's modernist 'spaces of enclosure' – changes in what constitutes knowledge, how it is organised (curriculum), presented and disseminated (the book), delivered (pedagogy) and justified (democracy). We will then relate this discussion to the possibilities – and problems – opened up by cyberspace as a space of learning and participation. From this, we proceed to an examination of the emerging practices of distributed and e-learning, where globalising processes based on space–time compression can create active learners and where there is at the same time the possibility of an extension of disciplinary practices beyond the walls of the educational institution and the physical presence of the teacher.

Globalisation and the reconfiguring of pedagogy

Lankshear *et al.* (1996) argue that education as a modernist institution is characterised by the 'spaces of enclosure' of the book, the classroom and the curriculum that work to enclose meaning and experience. Here the learner's task becomes one of extracting and re-presenting a singular canonical meaning, and the teacher's that of being the authority in terms of interpretation and accuracy. The implication of this is that there is a single definitive meaning waiting there to be found.

They maintain that developments made possible by the use of ICTs in education – developments captured with the notion and actuality of cyberspace – work in ways that call these spaces of enclosure into question. There is a questioning of underlying assumptions about the fixity and stability of the word, the linear text and the teacher as authoritative bearer of meaning. This opens up possibilities for learning to be more diverse, purpose driven, self-imposed and self-monitored than that normally found in current mainstream educational practices. The claim is that cyberspace creates an environment where the distinction between readers and writers becomes blurred and where, consequently, textual production and interpretation become less bounded. In cyberspace practices, there are no authoritative meanings waiting to be found by the suitably trained mind. By contrast, meanings are negotiable and more readily negotiated by users. Image and text, multimodality and semiotics come to the fore in this respect (Snyder 2002; Kress 2003; Jewitt 2006). Hence, this is a possible situation where learners do not simply interpret meanings but actively collaborate in creating meanings, and thus are more able to determine their own paths of learning. The emphasis shifts from meaning to meaning-making, from canonical knowledge to transferable skills.

This of course is over-generalised, but there seems to be a considerable degree of agreement that the incorporation of ICTs and its associated mode of communication into pedagogic practices is more likely to encourage independent and lifelong learning skills (Cunningham *et al.* 1997). The hypertextual capacity of cyberspace allows learners more scope to construct knowledge rather than just passively receive it. Meaning-making takes on a different form.

Cyberspace both as concept and actuality seems to be productive of a questioning of modernist systems and frameworks. Practices based on multilinearity, nodes, links, flows and networks seem more appropriate. Furthermore, by undermining the stability and coherence of the book, cyberspace contributes to a questioning of the modernist subject with its assumption of a core, fixed identity. Lankshear *et al.* (1996) argue that new forms of textuality, intertextuality and hypertextuality necessarily imply a reconfiguration of the subject – in terms both of knowledge and identity. Thus, as Scrimshaw (1997) suggested in relation to the UK government's then Superhighways Initiative,

> the introduction of ICT overcomes or blurs many different boundaries. These include boundaries between subjects, between the academic and social aspects of a topic or problem, between learners of different ages and abilities, between different categories of teachers, between teachers and other adults as co-workers in supporting learners, between home and school, school and work, and between schools and colleges...Very few of these effects are entirely new, but what is new is that the same set of technologies can produce them all, and in a stronger and increasingly more convergent form than previously.

With this comes the need to rethink pedagogy in terms of relationality and multiplicity, of multiple paths and of nonlinear forms of learning and teacher–learner transactions.

All this would seem to suggest more opportunities for learner-centred pedagogies in shifting the emphasis from teaching to learning, from a pedagogy of transmission to the pedagogue as creator of a learning environment and learning as design (Kress 2003). But this learner-centredness is different from that of humanistic experiential pedagogy since the emphasis here is on a pedagogy which is self-directed and purpose-driven – and therefore can encompass a multiplicity of changing goals and purposes – rather than on a pedagogy orientated to achieving the externally imposed and predefined meta-goals of modernist education. It is suggested that in the virtual classroom the focus moves from teacher as the central authority transmitting knowledge through the written text, responsible for validating input and encouraging consensus, to the learner pursuing a multiplicity of locally defined educational/educative goals in a variety of ways. This process is facilitated by a reconfiguration of the teacher–student relationship, where all can be experts given the abundance and availability of information in the sites and networks of cyberspace.

Of course, as always, words of caution are necessary since there are binaries at play in this scenario which it is necessary to question. First, there is the binary of enclosure–openness which confers an emancipatory value to learning in cyberspace. It may well be that in both historical and contemporary classroom practices a pedagogy of transmission remains to the fore, but the learning within those spaces may draw on experiences beyond the walls of the institution. Cyberspace may intensify and highlight the ways in which learning is not confined to the classroom, but whether it is necessarily more open and egalitarian is another matter. The panoptic surveillance of online learning and online learners may actually close possibilities. Birketts (1994: 27), for instance, lists a number of possible cognitive losses with electronic culture:

- fragmented sense of time and a loss of the so-called duration experience, that depth phenomenon we associate with reverie; reduced attention span and a general impatience with sustained enquiry;
- a shattered faith in institutions and in the explanatory narratives that formerly gave shape to subjective experience;
- a divorce from the past, from a vital sense of history as a cumulative or organic process;
- an absence of any strong vision of personal or collective forms.

We shall return to some of these points later in this glimpse when we discuss cyberspace in relation to democracy and community. At this point, it could be argued that this critique is clearly and problematically based on a modernist, institution-based view of education and learning. However, there is obviously merit in the more general argument that the presentation of cyberspace as necessarily and universally more open and egalitarian is as totalising in its critique of modernist education as modernist constructions themselves. There is a need, therefore, for caution with arguments for cyberspace that are subsumed within a binary logic that is itself challenged by intensified globalisation.

Second, the binary logic of ICTs needs itself to be taken into account. Although the possibilities for communication may grow, interactions with software work within the logic of either/or and may therefore restrict the range of meanings that can be generated. The proliferation of information may provide greater possibilities for diverse meanings, in itself raising questions of the quality and validity of resources to be drawn upon – what authorises information as knowledge? – but the training in rationality may remain one of either/or. This is a tension at the heart of many pedagogic practices, ones that are not resolved at a stroke through the mere existence of cyberspace. Furthermore, it is worth remembering that ICTs are equally deployable for programmed learning that fixes the learner in space–time as for providing a space for curiosity driven and exploratory enquiry. Even hypertext is 'predetermined by a programmer/designer – the student merely chooses whether or not to follow the link but does not create it' (Cunningham *et al.* 1997: 155). And, of course, this is a situation highly reliant on access. We would not then wish to deny the (dis)locations – the openings and closures – of more conventional pedagogic practices. Thus, it is not the fact of cyberspace as a space of openings which is most significant, but the ways in which (dis)locating practices play out in all learning settings, including those of the face-to-face classroom.

However, while we are critical of overly simplistic readings of cyberspace, we nonetheless find that a view of teaching and learning reconfigured in terms of links, flows and networks resonates with our concerns, not least as this inevitably must involve a redefinition of the role of teachers. It does not necessarily mean, as has sometimes been argued, simplistically in our view, that teachers no longer have a role. At one level, a very obvious new role for teachers is in helping learners to access and use information. However, this particular role is one that teachers have to share with learners given that the latter may often be more knowledgeable and skilful in cyberspace environments. Furthermore, the very quantity, availability and accessibility of information may also help to release teachers from their traditionally dominant role as providers of content to a role that is more concerned with making the learning process explicit and transparent by, for example, helping in the framing of questions and ensuring that learners critically interrogate that which they (en)counter in cyberspace. As Tabbi (1997: 239) points out, 'the digital medium encourages a branching discussion in which students link up to a network – the pedagogical dynamic is more provisional, not question–answer but comment–elaboration with cues coming from a number of centres besides that of the teacher'. Lankshear *et al.* (1996: 172) emphasise the greater possibilities for teachers and learners in developing understanding or meta-level awareness through 'communicative practices [that] presuppose openness, self-monitoring and constant reflexivity on the part of participants'.

Furthermore, as Cunningham *et al.* (1997: 155, emphasis in original) drawing on Birketts again point out, there is a strong argument to the effect that

> the move away from the linearity of print text has undoubtedly led to changes in the very *nature* of cognition. The benefits of those cognitive changes are 'an increased awareness of the "big picture", a global perspective' and... 'an ability to accommodate a broad range of stimuli simultaneously'.

A similar point is also made by Green (1993) in relation to learning. He argues that learning has traditionally been conceived in terms of 'interiority', a particular kind of cognition and mental development, linked to a normative view of rationality. He suggests that, in postmodern conditions of knowledge, we perhaps need to think in terms of how forms of learning and cognition are themselves changing in ways which question the very assimilation of learning to cognitive interiority – thus the increased interest in the semiotic or communicative aspects of learning (Usher and Edwards 2007). We could perhaps then see new technologies as 'amplifiers of human attributes and capacities, and hence of human potential; as prosthetic devices which enable learners to operate differently' (Green 1993: 28).

As we have already noted, the globalised world of vectoral flows has already begun to reshape subjectivities, and here we are presented with the interesting notion of the learner as a cyborg. This is an argument which, although provocative, does remind us that cyberspace affects not only pedagogy per se but the identity of learners too, and with that changes in perceptions of what learning is.

Here, then, it is not simply a matter of increasing the transactive efficiency of the learning (en)counter but also of a change in culture about what a learner *is*. Any critical understanding of the effects of the new communicative practices engendered by ICTs requires therefore an evaluation of the type of subject it encourages. This is not the foundational subject of consciousness but a subject with hybrid identities shaped through these communicative practices. Bigum and Green (1993: 4–5) refer to the need for a critical assessment of what they term the 'cyborg curriculum', 'the increasing significance of technology in educational practice, particularly those technologies bearing directly on knowledge production and the relationship between language and subjectivity'. When information can be taken up and used freely, the identities of learners (and their identities as learners) are shaped without the policing of a traditional external epistemological authority. In cyberspace, the disciplinary boundaries and legitimations of knowledge and information, undermined already with the widespread use of computers, becomes even more difficult to maintain. Legitimate or worthwhile knowledge becomes anything generated and used in the self-directing and self-monitored practices of cyberspace's virtual communities.

Globalisation, distributed learning and the demise of discipline?

Space–time compression and new media technology have been an important influence in the contemporary development of distributed learning in its many forms (Lea and Nicoll 2002). The latter is itself held to be both a key effect of, and a contributor to, the globalising processes currently impacting on pedagogy and curriculum. The very notion that learning can be distributed across space–time is itself significant. Nor is the increasing role of distributed learning restricted to higher education, as the technologies and approaches associated with it are more and more found in certain parts of the globe in schooling and in vocational education and training.

In principle, distributed learning institutes the ideal of an education available anytime and anywhere. In following a 'dispersive logic based on the circuit or network' (Peters 1996: 106), it undermines the necessity for attendance at specific places for education at set times. This challenges the spaces of enclosure of the classroom, the institutional timetable and face-to-face teaching, while bringing to the fore the learner's own space as the place of learning, even when this might be using a laptop in an airport lounge. It therefore contributes to contemporary forms of geographical dispersal, as learners, teachers and educators no longer need to be in the same place, locally or nationally, but potentially are available on a global scale to each other. Of course, this situation is still rare in actuality (Mason 1998) and most often what is found is a mixture of technologically mediated learning and conventional face-to-face teaching – blended learning. Nonetheless, distributed learning can have paradoxical effects. On the one hand, as Evans and Nation (1992: 10) suggest, 'distance education and open learning have been key dispersal agents' in the movement towards a post-industrial period. On the other hand, people can still be kept 'in their place' while at the same time communicating and (en)countering others across great physical distances.

Evans (1989: 181) has suggested that 'distance education is partly about "choreographing" a myriad of personal and collective movements in time–space' and that this is part of the hidden curriculum. The notion of choreographing is an attractive one, reflecting the looser organisation of space–time within distributed learning rather than the more conventional notion of the institutional timetable. It implies a lessening degree of control over where and when people undertake their learning. However, it is important to bear in mind that a space–time relationship is already being assumed, as different forms of distributed learning may be organised around categories other than choreography. In other words, the categorisation of space–time in this conceptualisation of distributed learning itself becomes subject to the processes it attempts to describe. Choreography, therefore, may only be appropriate for certain forms of distributed learning rather than serving as a generalised conception.

There is a need to situate conceptions of learners within the experience of space–time compression and the forms of identity associated with that experience. Certain assumptions that transcend space–time may be made about learners that are not consistent with the forms and ways of experiencing with which they are familiar. At a time when learners are themselves subject to great changes in their sense of identity under the influence of economic, political and cultural change and migrations, there is therefore a question as to whether, for instance, the humanistic notions of learner-centredness provides us with the categories to make sense satisfactorily of learners. As with learners, so with learning. If identity is becoming subject to different forms of experiencing with the influence of globalising processes, then the ways in which learners are engaged may also need re-evaluating. For instance, Moscow managers on a business course for IBM were reported to have been unimpressed and did not enjoy participating in interactive web-mediated lectures (Mason 1998). However, with the proliferation of ICTs and associated media, it may well be that future cohorts of learners will not be addressed primarily through a literacy of the written word, but through a computer and media screen literacy that will assume a far greater significance. Thus emerges the argument for multi-literacies (New London Group 1995; Kellner 1998) – 'in addition to...critical media literacy, print literacy, computer literacy, and multimedia literacy...multiple literacies involve cultural literacy, social literacy, and eco-literacy' (Kellner 1998: 119). We will return to this issue in a later section of this chapter.

However, at this point, we wish to turn to a discussion of the relationship of distributed learning to disciplinarity and to pose the following questions. Does distributed learning result in the demise or reconfiguration of discipline? – in both senses of the term 'discipline'. How do the practices of distributed learning act upon discipline as both a body of knowledge and an exercise of power? Is distributed learning itself part of a new disciplinary technology embedded within globalising processes at the societal level? Increasingly, these are issues which are impacting on the educational domain.

The idea of disciplines as disinterested and bounded bodies of knowledge is at the heart of the modernist idea of the liberal university and liberal education more generally. It is central to the legitimacy of universities as above, or detached from, the exercise of power and, with that, the rationale for the consequent necessity for academic freedom. Disciplinary boundaries demarcate what is considered to be knowledge within a particular domain, and through the discursive practices of disciplinary communities the criteria by which claims are established as true or false, legitimate or illegitimate. 'Disciplines are a way of carving up areas of study and regulating what constitutes proper investigation in each area' (Elam 1994: 95). As Usher (1993: 17) suggests, we educators are 'enfolded in an implicit conception of disciplines as neutral bodies of knowledge with enlightening and empowering effects that enable us to act effectively in the world'. Questions of power – the conditions for their own existence and possibilities as bodies of knowledge – are excluded from disciplinary discourse. And disciplinarity becomes the regulatory mechanism which 'assures the continued success of the academic institution itself: by carefully controlling what gets included and excluded at any given point, the academy is able to guarantee its own reproduction' (Elam 1994: 97).

The critique of disciplinarity draws extensively upon the work of Foucault (1979) to examine discipline both as a body of knowledge and an exercise of power. The social practices through which disciplines are formed, particularly in relation to the experimental sciences, has also been the subject of much study (Latour 1999, 2005). Foucault's work challenges modernist assumptions of the separation of knowledge from power. For him, 'power and knowledge directly imply one another...there is no power relation without the relative constitution of a field of knowledge, nor any knowledge that does not presuppose and constitute at the same time power relations' (Foucault 1979: 27). Power and knowledge are therefore correlative – always found together in power–knowledge formations, or regimes of truth. Disciplinary power is exercised effectively through the labels of 'educated' or 'uneducated'. Learners are required to bring forth their subjectivities for disciplining (a training of the mind and the body), and through this, to become a particular type of disciplined person. Through the process of becoming 'subject' to particular disciplines, people are also created as active subjects. In other words, disciplines as systematic bodies of knowledge function as regulatory regimes of knowledgeability – knowledge and ability – through which power is embodied and exercised. People are constituted as active subjects with certain capacities to act. Agency then is not a matter of autonomy in the sense of an escape from power, but a specific exercise of it. Capacities are evaluated through the processes of observation and examination, the criteria and methods which are provided by the disciplines. As knowledge changes, so do the practices aimed at framing behaviour. Thus,

> the chief function of the disciplinary power is to 'train', rather than to select and to levy; or, no doubt, to train in order to levy and select all the

more...Discipline 'makes' individuals; it is the specific technique of a power that regards individuals both as objects and instruments of exercise.

(Foucault 1979: 170)

In this sense, educational discourses can enact a range of embodied subjectivities, including 'the self-actualising, self-directing subject of humanistic psychology or the adaptive, information-processing subject of cognitive psychology' (Usher 1993: 18). Rather than being regulated externally, active subjects come to regulate themselves through the principles of autonomy and self-reflection, themselves disciplinary effects in which power is expressed in and through the lifelong learner. The reflective lifelong learner, a notion that has taken hold around the globe as a feature of globalising processes, is not therefore a natural given, but is itself an effect of discursive practices.

For Foucault, the modern disciplined social order is underpinned by a set of contested pedagogies – of, for example, self-actualisation, autonomy and adaptation – which are explicitly the concern of education and which are practised through educational and other institutions. Shifts within education, such as shifts towards distributed learning, outcomes-based assessment, etc., therefore provide the possibility for disturbing the pedagogical practices for the formation and maintenance of other disciplines and, with that, the subjectivity of learners. Thus, we would argue that the autonomous/self-directed/flexible lifelong learner is displacing the enlightened student disciplined through the practices of education.

This then is of particular significance for the emerging practices of distributed learning and the use of ICTs that extend disciplinary practices beyond the walls of the educational institution and the physical presence of the teacher/lecturer. One does not have to be enclosed within an educational institution to be disciplined. Thus, extending access and opportunity through new forms of teaching and learning may also signify a more extensive achievement of an active, productive and governable positioning of subjects where learners may literally and metaphorically be 'kept in their place' – a different place perhaps but nonetheless a maintenance and possibly an extension, albeit a reconfiguration, of discipline.

What then are the practices through which discipline is exercised? According to Foucault (1979: 170), 'the success of disciplinary power derives no doubt from the use of simple instruments; hierarchical observation, normalising judgement and their combination in a procedure that is specific to it, the examination'. Within the traditional institution, a network of hierarchical observation is based on the physical presence of individuals at particular times in specific places, and disciplinary practices are built on the assumption of that presence. However, within distributed forms of learning, it is precisely that presence which is lacking. It would be understandable to assert from this – as is often done in the discourses of learner-centredness – that the individual is therefore freer, has more autonomy, and is less subject to discipline. However, this lack of physical presence does not necessarily mean that discipline is absent. Foucault talks about the increasing social requirement for 'self-discipline' as a 'self-surveillance'. Evans and Green (1995) refer to the 'absence–presence' in the pedagogy of specifically distributed learning – itself a spatial relationship. From this perspective, it can be seen as an aspect of the moves towards the further disciplining of the subject and not an achievement of freedom, choice or emancipation for the individual as a humanist discourse would suggest. Rather than power being exercised through the direct presence of lecturer and learner, the power of observation becomes exercised by learners upon themselves, embodied in, for example, learning materials, timetables for assignments and the explicit achievement of certain outcomes. It is also perhaps instructive that the bodily absence of learners and teachers from each other has been problematised as an aspect of distributed learning that needs to be addressed. Thus pedagogically we find the development of social presence in online environments to be a significant area of activity. In other words, how to mitigate the disembodiment that globalising processes in education make possible itself becomes a pedagogical challenge. Thus in communicating online, a range of strategies for making oneself present, such as providing contextual details regarding physical location and emotional state, are constructed as ways of making connections beyond the virtual of the electronic.

In some ways also, the increasing use of computer-mediated communication (CMC) offers the opportunity for an extension of observation unavailable through practices mediated by the post and by telephone. For instance, computer conferencing brings lecturers and learners into a virtual presence with one another. Here, discipline may be exerted not only by the lecturer but also by peers, as it becomes possible to spread the practices of observation throughout the networked learning body. In addition to hierarchical observation, therefore, learners are also subject to horizontal observation, even when learning autonomously and individually. However, this in itself may result in a greater range of perspectives within the (en)counter, which may then challenge the pedagogic authority of the gaze embodied in the lecturer. Group work, collaborative learning and learning from peers may therefore be a positive resource and benefit in creating active learners. Mason (1998: 51) talks of the possibility of web-based learning in particular becoming 'a theatre where an active performance is always going on in which students and teachers are both actors and audience, collaboratively constructing the story of the discipline'. This is only one possibility of course and dependent upon many assumptions as to the democratising potential of the Internet and its technological infrastructure.

The development of distributed learning would certainly not seem to undermine practices of normalising judgement. The categorisation and processes of inclusion and exclusion still maintain the distribution of individuals according to ranks or grades, enabling a marking of the gaps and hierarchies of knowledge, skills and aptitudes. The extension of opportunity through distributed learning can be seen as an extension of normalising processes within the social order where more people become subject to disciplinary practices, embraced in the human resource development of lifelong learning in which their very life becomes an enterprise (du Gay 1996). Access to opportunity may well involve therefore the extension of discipline and the spreading of the influence and power of certain norms.

Foucault's (1979) analysis of discipline focuses on the institutional practices through which power is exercised. Choice within the specific institutional contexts does not tend to be encompassed within this. Yet a greater degree of learner choice and autonomy is one of the aspects associated with distributed learning. Learners are not bounded by the arrangements within a single institution nor, and more centrally for the argument here, within that of a single discipline – given the more multi- and interdisciplinary nature of curricula within it. While such approaches are sometimes criticised for lacking depth, they provide the possibilities for new bodies of knowledge to emerge, as disciplinary boundaries become increasingly fuzzy and indefensible. Here, the very conventions of discipline are challenged, as the defence of boundaries and the very possibility of boundedness lose their centrality in the exploration of different possibilities for knowledge production, mobilisation and transfer. Thus the globalising of pedagogy has implications for the curriculum and vice versa. Through distributed learning, learners may engage with a range of bodies of knowledge and be subject to different norms. This provides the possibility for a range of learner identities, and identity as a learner, which can be both troubling and pleasurable (Edwards 1996). This situation could be characterised as one where the modern bounded subject is displaced by the postmodern multi-centred subject, where the identity of 'student' is displaced by that of 'lifelong learner'. It may not be mere coincidence therefore that there has emerged an interest in the cross-curricular outcomes of education, in the form of capability statements and transferable skills, as conventional notions of disciplinarity have been challenged. The lifelong learner is considered as requiring transferable, mobile practices more centrally than conventional disciplinary expertise. In many contexts, research, inquiry and problem-based approaches have all become more central to the aims of education – 'formerly, secondary, largely multidisciplinary, competencies were added on to primary, largely disciplinary identities. This pattern will have to be abandoned. A portfolio of identities and competencies will have to be managed, none of which need to be pre-eminent' (Gibbons *et al.* 1994: 165).

Mason (1998) suggests that one such competence is knowledge management, the capacity to find and use information rather than to simply absorb and memorise it. However, she also indicates that this is easier to develop in some disciplinary areas than others. Whether these capacities can best be developed through disciplinary practices at all remains a question for, as Stronach and MacLure (1997: 84) suggest in relation to the school curriculum, 'if the young in postmodernity are to have "flexible bodies"...better to give them flexible foundations for their self-making than the super-structural fantasies of "adaptable skills" schooled into the supposedly stable "base of their beings"'.

The techniques of observation and normalising judgement, combined in examination, constitute the institutional mechanisms through which learner and teacher are formed as subjects and objects. Within distributed learning, there would appear to be a reconfiguration rather than a straightforward decline of discipline, and with ambivalent significance. Observation of the learner becomes increasingly a matter of self-surveillance and the power of normalising judgement more diffuse, embedded within a variety of relations. However, the power of the examination in the contemporary social order is not diminished, as witnessed by the fetishism of certification and qualifications in most parts of the globe.

From the regime of truth of the traditional disciplines, this looks like the demise of discipline, as subjects lose their rigour, standards fall and individuals become less governed by the rules of the discipline. Knowledge may become multiple with different subjects and subjectivities, but power is reconfigured and its exercise may be ever more subtle as well as extensive. The reconfigured disciplinary practices of examination, observation and normalisation continue, although becoming increasingly mediated outside the walls of the university. Disciplinary practices are objectified in the absence–presence of course materials and technologically mediated tutoring rather than through the direct gaze of teachers. As part of these processes, power over the constitution of knowledge shifts. Thus, distributed learning may be contributing to the demise of the traditional power–knowledge formations of the university, and in this sense it can make a significant contribution to the development of lifelong learners. However, at the same time, it seems to be signalling a power to constitute a self-disciplining and confessional social order of multi-centred subjectivities with the potential to legitimate different knowledges – as much a counselled society as a learning society. However, we are also a long way from global education for, as Mason (1998: 102) argues,

> access to the Web is still problematic on anything resembling a global scale; many course providers have little experience in writing materials for this new environment or in designing and running online interactive courses; students who enrol in professional updating courses have not developed the study patterns or discipline to sustain participation in courses with 'undemanding media'; if cultural and linguistic differences are not addressed specifically by the course designers, Western English mother tongue students will invariably dominate online discussions; institutions need to acquire expertise in the new media...

Education, democracy and virtuality

Along with the impact on pedagogy and teacher–learner interactions, cyberspace also seems to imply enhanced possibilities for a greater degree of democracy both in the classroom (even where it is virtual) and in education generally. There are two issues involved here. The first is to do with access and equity. One of the respondents in the survey conducted by Cunningham *et al.* (1997) puts it this way:

> I'm an information democrat like most people. Having gone beyond trying to create equality through redistribution of income and education, we're now looking at information access as our new democratic project. So I'd be

very optimistic about the potential of global technologies to create information democracy and low cost access to a whole range of knowledges.

(Cunningham *et al.* 1997: 160)

Others, however, take a less optimistic view about access. Clear concerns are
expressed about the creation of an ever-widening gap between 'IT-haves' and 'IT-
have nots', the information rich and information poor, because of the cost of
purchasing and maintaining equipment and the sophisticated infrastructure
needed to provide globalised education. Furthermore, the increasing influence of
corporate media networks with a global reach is seen as posing a serious threat to
equality of access.

The second and not unrelated issue is to do with participation. Whereas it is
necessary to question a priori assumptions about the liberating potential of new
technologies and media, it is nonetheless seen by many as an environment where
the skills and attitudes necessary for engaging in democratic decision making can
be more readily cultivated. Tabbi (1997) argues that while the Internet tends to
be perceived mainly in terms of enabling learners more readily to exchange information it can also function as a forum where differences among learners can be
articulated and where a greater equality of participation and interaction can be
established. It has been argued that cyberspace has the potential to equalise and
empower all voices and to enable a multiplicity of knowledges to be disseminated
and valued. Lankshear *et al.* (1996) believe that, in enabling access to continuously available online information and participation in a range of activities and
experiences, cyberspace's virtual communities make democratisation of education a real possibility.

However, although these virtual communities may well have a democratising
potential, cyberspace, although participative, is not inherently democratic.
Participation can take many forms, not all of which are democratic. Disciplinary
power could well be reinvested from the transmission of inputs to the examination of outputs. Furthermore, any democratising impulse could remain unrealised
if learners are not stimulated to think critically about the impact on their learning of different technologies and the mediating processes that come with them –
learners need to be inscribers lest they only become inscribed. In relation to this,
Kramerae (1995: 43) points out that 'cyberspace like earthspace is not developing as a viable place for women'. She notes that there has been a singular lack of
support for those studying gender issues and the gendering of computer studies
and programs both inside and outside the classroom.

It is clear then that what is involved here is not just a straightforward matter
of bringing in democracy by deploying new technologies. Although a decentred
and interactive classroom experience can have potentially democratic effects,
whether these will still be present depends on the wider social context.
Cyberspace produces new formations of social and economic power and it is
against these that its democratic actuality must be judged. In a sense, cyberpunk,
with its dystopic projections, could be read as an attempt at a politics oppositional to the corporate manipulation of the Internet and the potential danger of

cyberfascism (Featherstone and Burrows 1995). As Gabilondo (1995) rightly points out, there is a need to guard against utopian and libertarian technophilia. However, we would also agree with her that these new orders should not be seen as always fixed and hegemonic. Although contemporary corporate capitalism has a global reach, it does not wipe away everything it (en)counters. What is more, there is more to globalisation than the purely economic.

It is undoubtedly the case that the world that the discourse of cyberspace stories came into being is one that many would regard as highly problematic. The rapid spread of the Internet and its seepage into everyday life raises fears of the social effects of online existence as people become disconnected from 'real' life and simulacra take over from 'reality'. As Macrae (1997: 74) points out, 'virtual existence has become so immediate that what constitutes the real is called into question'.

Underlying this is a question productive of hotly contested debate. Can cyberspace ever be universally accessible and can it replace face-to-face interaction; can it ever be a true public sphere, and thus both educational and educative, in the way that the enthusiastic proponents of virtual communities argue? The fact is of course, as we have just noted, that cyberspace is not universally accessible and perhaps never will be, although a counter-argument would be that potentially it could be. But, even accepting that potential, the problem is that virtual communities are virtual in the sense that they are often fleeting and anonymous, with connections that exist only online. Tabbi (1997) argues that it is precisely the disembodiment, disembeddedness and decontextualisation (no bodies, no history, no place), or dislocation, of electronic interchange that will always limit the democratic, and hence educational, potential of cyberspace. In pedagogic terms, this tends to be expressed in terms of learner preferences for the face-to-face form: 'there is a tension between the isolated, self-paced learning facilitated by some technologies and the interactive, collaborative social climate necessary for rich learning' (Cunningham *et al.* 1997: 164–5). The respondents in the survey carried out by Cunningham *et al.* were almost unanimous in claiming that cyberspace-mediated education was inappropriate at undergraduate level and that there was a need for learning to have 'a physical dimension in place, time and space' (Cunningham *et al.* 1997: 149). There seemed to be a general agreement that the total quality of the learning experience is diminished when the dynamics of face-to-face interaction are absent. More fundamentally, Castells (1999, vol. I: 397), in a point which echoes the argument of Bigum *et al.* (1997) on the enclosed character of schooling, argues that

> schools and universities are paradoxically the institutions least affected by the virtual logic embedded in information technology, in spite of the foreseeable quasi-universal use of computers in the classrooms of advanced countries...In the case of elementary and secondary schools, this is because they are as much childcare centres and/or children's warehouses as they are learning institutions.

In addition to the pedagogical question, there is also the wider question as to whether, given its characteristics of disembodiedness and disembeddedness, cyberspace can ever be a site of culture, although, as Porter (1997) argues, being able to construct and exhibit mobile, multiple and made-up identities may not necessarily be a bad thing. Perhaps what this implies is that we need to rethink our notions of culture as a homogeneous social sphere and as a means of realising a core identity but see it rather as 'the collective response to this experience of ambiguity, the gradual process of adaptation to the semiotic universe of free-floating electronic alibis' (Porter 1997: xii). This is perhaps what constitutes cyberspace as a unique cultural site. Here what is being suggested is the possibility of different post-Enlightenment conceptions of identity, identity formation and what it means to be educated, certain aspects of which are manifested in the burgeoning phenomenon of blogging.

What is very clear is that cyberspace brings to the fore debates about the meaning and effects of culture. This bringing to the fore of the cultural takes us back to the point about the problems of virtual existence. It could be argued that a way of understanding the Baudrillardian simulated real is the most recent example of how the real is made into reality. This is not the place to enter into a debate about the truth or otherwise of Baudrillard's (1983) theories. What is more significant here is to look at the way such theorisations function as a contemporary discourse whose effect is to provide provocative insights about how the real is understood; in effect, how it is storied or narrativised into a plausible reality (Law 2004). We would argue that Baudrillard's (1983) discourse of the simulated real brings to the fore the significance of the cultural in a postmodern condition of globalisation. Here it is important to note that we are not arguing for a single universal culture as the most significant effect of globalisation. Some of the contemporary boundedness of cultures in terms of locality, nationality, ethnicity and religion are themselves a reaction to globalisation and the universalising homogenising culture flows it engenders, but they are at the same time a manifestation of the global–local nexus. In any event, the achievement of boundedness is pursued in part through processes of curricular selection which brings to the fore, and seeks to secure, that which is considered valuable.

The implication of all this is that it is too simplistic to attribute the problems of virtual existence solely to the effects of ICTs in a purely technological sense because the issue is essentially a cultural one. The valorisation of direct face-to-face communication is after all a cultural artefact, an example of what Derrida (1981) calls the metaphysics of presence – itself a narrative of the real. Embedded in this narrative is another structuring binary opposition, i.e. that between 'virtual' (in the sense of 'unreal') and 'real', with its valorisation of the latter. This becomes particularly significant in looking at the issue of virtual existence in cyberspace's communities and helps to frame much of the debate about social presence in e-learning. As Poster (1995: 89) points out, the new kinds of interactivity that develop in cyberspace cannot be adequately specified by this binary and to think this way only serves 'to obscure the manner of the historical construction of forms of community'. He goes on to argue that what makes a community vital to its members is 'their treatment of communications as meaningful and important' (Poster 1995: 90), which is exactly what many virtual communities signify to their participants. As Burbules (2000: 352, emphasis in original) argues, 'the traditional associations of community with proximity, homogeneity, and familiarity can be an impediment for forming *actual* communities – including online communities'.

Notions of an essential community and privileged modes of interaction are themselves practices constituted within particular discourses and cultures, practices we would argue that no longer necessarily have the purchase they once did. This is not to say that we have to embrace wholeheartedly cyberspace-mediated pedagogy to the exclusion of face-to-face forms, nor that we should move totally from campus-based to online education. This would in itself be a totalising and oppressive gesture, a mere reversal that translates the worst features of the modernist educational project. The dynamic and embodied interactivity of the face-to-face is part of a certain cultural heritage and needs to be respected as such. As long as it is not considered exclusively valuable and the dominant mode of interaction, it has its place in the pedagogical diversity of education in globalising processes (and parenthetically we would add that it is the growth of significance of the virtual that has brought to the fore the value of the face-to-face). At this stage, all that can be said with any degree of certainty is that the globalising effects of ICTs and their associated modes of communication bring to the fore the need for thinking anew about what constitutes community, interaction and learning in virtual times.

Rethinking learning in globalised interconnectedness

> Globalisation is expressed in our apprehension of new and increasingly complex patterns of interconnectedness.
>
> (Gough 1998: 2)

Questions then about what now constitutes community and authenticity are key in examining the enfolding of curriculum and pedagogy within globalising processes. Nowhere is this raised more acutely than in discussions of the relationship of globalisation to the post-colonial, itself an expression of new and complex patterns of interconnectedness. The question usually asked is: does the spread of certain forms of Western curricula and pedagogy around the globe, accelerated through the use of ICTs, constitute a form of new and more subtle cultural colonisation that replaces the more complete forms of economic and political colonisation from which arguably so many parts of the globe have only so recently emerged?

> Generally speaking, globalisation is not about military battles fought over borders...but rather it is about a colonisation of signs, symbols, language and culture. Eventually it becomes a matter of identity, as people begin to

identify themselves in ways which transcend their traditional cultural borders and engage with global entities.

(Bartlett *et al.* 1997: 3)

As Evans (1997: 18) puts it, nation states are now presented with a dilemma wherein 'they access the world but the world invades them'. The very access creates the conditions for possible new forms of colonisation and ones that are less visible than previous forms of colonisation but no less powerful for that.

Of course, it could be argued that this analysis is itself a simplification that ignores the complex patterns of interconnectedness because it rests on a modernist liberal view of the world, expressed in the emotive language of invasion. The discreteness and boundedness of languages and cultures has always been more ideological than material. And the relationship between language, culture and nation state has never been simple. This is not to deny the dilemma that Evans points to, but implicit in the way in which the dilemma is expressed is an assumption that nation states have an *essential* cultural identity, language, stability and coherence. Against this, it could be argued that this is no doubt something they have aspired to, but the historical record seems to show it is not something that they have often achieved. But, perhaps more significantly, the argument assumes an inside–outside binary, whereas a more useful way of looking at nation-state formations is in terms of a process of interaction, for example trade, war, migration and communications, through which they have emerged. Furthermore, within nation states, given the multiculturalism that prevails, the dilemma may be as great as between nation states. Thus, it is not a matter of denying the dilemma but rather of suggesting that it may not be of the form Evans argues. Indeed, the influences of post-colonialism that inform this text – an invasion from the margins – is both suggestive of the complexity and hybridity of cultural influences and itself indicates different possible readings of invasion.

To take one educationally pertinent example: forms of distributed learning offered around the globe by institutions within English-speaking (over)developed nations might be said to constitute an invasion that colonises and denies the culture, knowledge and understandings of local learners.

> Recent and future advances in their electronic media would mean that in our region [the South Pacific] multiculturality, people's sense of situational geography will become disorientated and it is possible that where people are physically will no longer determine who and where they are socially...This trend may have serious implications for Pacific people's sense of identity.
>
> (Thamen 1997: 31)

On the face of it, this seems a reasonable argument and it raises the larger issue of cultural imperialism through globalised education, particularly in an era of greater international commercialisation of education. As Cunningham *et al.* (1997: 163) point out, 'there appears to be a rising level of concern in Asia that both exporting students and importing courses presents a very real threat of students' loss of identity, culture and family values'. At the same time, however, it is also not unreasonable to question whether it is always desirable for place to determine who and where people are socially. Clearly, place is an important factor, but it now makes more sense to look at place as globally mediated space. Furthermore, the developments being pointed to here after all occur where there is a demand for such learning. As Mason (1998: 54) rightly points out, 'there is a mismatch between the hype about resource-based learning and students' stubborn interest in taking advantage of such resources'. Mason (1998: 45) also makes the relevant point that what is involved here perhaps is 'not so much an exporting as a re-engineering of the educational paradigm'. Should it always be assumed that those in the West who oppose colonisation are always in the best position to prescribe what is best for those elsewhere – an invasion of good intentions – and is it a colonisation in the way suggested? As one of the respondents from Malaysia in the survey carried out by Cunningham *et al.* argues, globalisation can be welcomed if it means 'we build bridges together' and is 'only a threat if it is used for a one-sided victory' (Cunningham *et al.* 1997: 163). And, as Rizvi (2000: 221) argues, based upon his study of Malaysian students in Australia, 'the suggestion that international education represents an accelerating trend towards Westernisation is unfounded'.

Even where it is suggested that processes of colonisation are in play within nation states, there seems to be the assumption of a bounded traditional culture which is in some ways more authentic than that acquired through education and training (Thamen 1997). However, what constitutes this culture is itself open to debate (Wah 1997), which of course only serves to illustrate the difficulty of such positions. Alternatively, however, it could be argued that the possibilities for learners to access opportunities globally provides the opportunity for them to operate in different learning, cultural and economic contexts, an experience that is enriching rather than simply depleting. Although this is obviously a matter for empirical investigation, certainly the notion of globalisation with which we work suggests that even with globalising processes there are alternatives to the collapse of the nation state and the eradication of local cultures and languages (Mayor and Swann 2002). In many ways, it is precisely in attempts to oppose and counter globalising influences that we witness some of the most oppressive contemporary practices carried out in the name of the particular nation, religion and ethnicity.

Thus, the colonisation–anticolonisation binary can work to produce an essentialism in explaining the effects of trans-cultural learning, an essentialism which we would want to challenge. We are arguing instead for a conception of globalisation that is active in producing different forms of hybridity. The consciousness of the globe as one place is the very consciousness which heightens a sense of the relativity and value of particular location(s). In some ways, this paradox is at the heart of education as a practice centred on those fixed 'spaces of enclosure' we (en)countered earlier – the book, the classroom and pedagogy founded on the transmission of canonical and bounded bodies of knowledge.

These spaces of enclosure are located within the educational practices which are both primarily formulated within, and are a concrete manifestation of, the grand narratives or universal legitimising discourses of modernity (Lyotard 1984). These are narratives of individual and social betterment and emancipation that result from the application of reason and the development of scientific knowledge. They function to justify the work of producing bodies of knowledge of a particular kind held to be universal in scope which, transmitted through certain pedagogical forms within educational institutions, provide a training in a particular rationality which is yet held to be universally applicable and appropriate.

The export or internationalising of such practices and their continuing influence in the post-colonial era are evidence of the power of these universalising tendencies. At the same time, these practices have been fundamental in a very specific nation-state building role for education, where it has functioned as the means of transmitting the dominant messages and values of a specific and bounded national culture.

> Through national education systems states fashioned disciplined workers and loyal recruits; created and celebrated national languages and literatures; popularised national histories and myths of origin, disseminated national laws, customs and social mores...National education was a massive engine of integration, assimilated the local to the national and the particular to the general.
>
> (Green 1997: 5)

One outcome of this, not always acknowledged, has been the suppression of oppositional messages, where only certain forms of knowledge and knowledge production have been privileged while others (both bodies of knowledge and bodies of people) have been excluded by institutional and curricular practices, such as selection, assessment and accreditation.

Thus, the privileging of certain positions as universal has functioned as a legitimating device, a means of drawing and maintaining boundaries of the valuable and the useful. Arising from this is an inherent tension between the universal and the particular, the global and the local, between the universal messages of education, the particular bodies of knowledge transmitted and their development in, and mediation through, specific national cultures. A similar dynamic can also be seen in the increased emphasis given to discourses surrounding the development in many countries of competencies for labour market participation. Here the grand narratives of truth and emancipation are left behind, displaced by the logic of performativity or systemic efficiency. Yet at the same time, central to the prognosis of economic competitiveness in the global economy as a universal condition for all are the assertions of regional, national and sub-national economic interest that bring to the fore particular competencies and their framing in specific ways.

As we have noted on several occasions so far, globalisation therefore results in, and to some extent arises from, an increased integration within a framework of economic competitiveness. With this, the emphasis on education transmitting a national culture becomes either displaced by one of education's roles in servicing a global economy where each nation state is embraced by the logic of competitiveness, or its role is integrated into a reframed national culture to which economic competitiveness is integral. Educational practices therefore come to both service and contribute to the intensifying processes of globalisation. There are many relevant examples here – the attempt by educational institutions across the board to develop international markets and attract overseas fee-paying students (Henry and Taylor 1997); the growth and development of distributed learning and the increasing emphasis on computer-mediated learning; the emphasis on non-subject-specific generic and transferable capabilities; and the prevalence and spread of English as the medium of curriculum transmission. Yet, at the same time, we also witness the other side of globalisation in the reassertion and renegotiation of, for instance, religious, ethnic, regional and gender identities and the proliferation of 'Englishes' (Warschauer 2002). Both strands subvert and cut across specifically national identity, even as some continue to assert the primacy of the nation state and attempt to re-embed it through centrally controlled national curricula.

A lot of course depends upon the particular curriculum and pedagogy under discussion. If curriculum is taken to be a selection from the dominant culture and if the pedagogy is one of transmission, it could be construed as an attempt to impose a certain order, engendering dislocations of its own. For instance, writing of Pacific communities, Wah (1997: 76–80) suggests that

> in the learning situation the teacher is looked upon as an elder, full of wisdom, and certainly not to be questioned. Often however, when students in the formal education setting do not ask questions or debate, they are labelled 'stupid, ignorant, not capable and uninterested' by their Western (influenced) teachers...the education provided tends towards competitiveness, individualism and excellence, conflicting with the cultural norms of mediocrity and communalism.

This is as true within countries as between them, one response to which has been more student-centred or student-led practices. Yet this can be problematic, as the very focus on the learner might itself be a form of cultural dislocation in certain cultures and subcultures. Putting the learner at the centre – a spatial positioning – as a necessary way of developing autonomy in education has proved to be a powerful metaphorical resource for a particular set of pedagogical practices. Yet, although this has been constructed as universally applicable, it is nonetheless culturally specific and in this way its metaphoricity has been submerged or even naturalised. These practices have therefore become heavily prescriptive and normative, dimensions which themselves need subjecting to critical engagement. Thus, rather than retreating into a certain cultural essentialism, liberal guilt or radical emancipatory posturing, what would be more useful is a more detailed analysis of particular curricula and pedagogic practices, their locations and dislocations.

In his analysis of some of the limitations in post-16 education in the UK, for instance, Bloomer (1997) examined what he refers to as the prescribed curriculum (that which is laid down), the described curriculum (that which teachers say they do), and the actual learning of students. He provides strong empirical evidence for the familiar argument that what is prescribed and described does not reflect what is learnt, and that teachers and learners, through their practices, play an active role in curriculum making. In particular, Bloomer (1997), in illustrating the inevitable failure of prescription and transmission, identifies a number of forms of studentship or dispositions to learning – conformity, retreatism, rebellion, strategic compliance, innovation – in which learners engage in response to the curriculum, pedagogy and teachers.

From this and from some of the more general literature on studentship and learning careers, he seeks to draw more general conclusions. He suggests that a theory of learning for the future needs to have a number of founding principles, as follows:

- Knowledge is socially situated and socially constructed.
- Learning is socially situated in the sense that it is always a social act.
- At the same time, it is also a personal act, an expression of human agency.
- Learners' disposition to learn is visible in their studentship.
- Through their studentship, learners construct their descriptive curricula, thus delimiting what is actually learnt and how.
- Learning and being are mutually constitutive, continually in a process of transformation within the context of learning careers.
- Becoming a person and transformation of a learning career are inextricably linked. Both are to be understood as constituents of a partly unpredictable but powerful dialectic between agency and structure and are not simply the outcomes of prescriptive intervention.

He then goes on to sketch some of the aims, values and organising principles for the curriculum, concluding with the claim that 'the main overarching aim of the curriculum for post-16 education and training must be the liberation of human agency in learning' (Bloomer 1997: 204).

Useful though this analysis is, there is a sense in which it falls into a narrative trap commonly found across a wide range of educational and related literature. This trap is a function of the logic of identity which underlies such narratives. Having explored the complexity of a particular phenomenon, general conclusions are then sought. However, the very complexity uncovered suggests the inappropriateness of such conclusions. This is illustrated in relation to Bloomer's (1997) text in two ways. First, if knowledge is socially situated and constructed, this must also be true of Bloomer's own text, yet there is no indication of the reflexive difficulty this raises for his position. The very fact that he constructs his theory of learning as having 'founding principles' might be argued to point away from the situatedness of the very position he is advocating. Second, having argued that curriculum making by learners undermines the prescriptive assumptions in curriculum texts, to provide a prescriptive overarching aim for the curriculum seems both contradictory and futile.

Even where curricula are not explicitly a selection from dominant culture, such as in forms of skill development or where there is a selection based upon less bounded notions of culture or where pedagogy is more interactive, there can be no escaping that 'texts are not neutral carriers of ideas; rather they are particular re-presentations of the world which are based on specific cultural and social values and positions' (George 1997: 43). They will be worked on and against in a diversity of forms by diverse learners in particular locations. Even here, there are simplifications at work as the very location of learners is traversed by globalising influences other than education – whether it is the media or global warming – and, indeed, many learners are increasingly mobile, from children of itinerant families to business people studying for an MBA. Thus, as Fitzclarence *et al.* (1995: 146) suggest of the relationship between schooling and the media, they

> are to be seen as competing mass-communications systems, or discursive fields, each with its own projected subject. Increasingly there is a struggle underway between them for the hearts and minds and bodies of the young: the citizens and/or consumers of today and tomorrow. Each clearly has an interest in constructing and securing the future...

Here the complexities of globalisation for pedagogy are brought to the fore, as pedagogy is not confined to schooling or education more generally.

With the importance attributed to questions of location as both a result, and a condition, of globalising processes, it is therefore no wonder that spatial metaphors have come to the fore in discussions of pedagogy. We have already made mention of those emerging from within critical, feminist and post-colonial pedagogies. Some of these, such as Giroux's (1992) notion of border pedagogy, have themselves migrated into more mainstream discussions (Study Group on Education and Training 1997). Rather than providing a basis for an analysis of curriculum and pedagogy, there is an attempt to formulate a pedagogic practice in response to contemporary challenges. Thus, in their report to the European Commission on strategies for economic competitiveness and social inclusion, the Study Group on Education and Training write the following:

> Border pedagogy is a strategy for learning about the cultural Other, by looking critically at how images, representations and texts are constructed and at their hidden messages. This approach facilitates learning how to identify one's own borders, those of others, and the borders of the external social world.
>
> (Study Group on Education and Training 1997: 19)

From another context – Australian-based discussion of open and distance learning – Rowan and Bartlett (1997: 127, emphasis in original) suggest that 'what is important is that individuals are allowed space within an educational framework to locate themselves, *however that sense of self is defined*'.

The spatial is not therefore at the margins of discussions of pedagogy, even though there are attempts to disrupt the mainstream of teacher-centred and student-centred concerns and explore those margins. Furthermore, not all of these are concerned with emancipatory practices. In their influential study of learning as a social practice, Lave and Wenger (1991: 94, emphasis in original) argue that learning

> depends upon *decentring* common notions of mastery and pedagogy...To take a decentred view of master–apprentice relations leads to an understanding that mastery resides not in the master but in the organisation of the community of practice of which the master is part: the master as the locus of authority (in several senses) is after all as much a product of the conventional centred theory of learning as is the individual learner. Similarly a decentred view of the master as pedagogue moves the focus of analysis away from teaching and onto the intricate structuring of a community's learning resources.

It is on this basis that they formulate a notion of learning as 'legitimate peripheral participation'. Rather than the focus simply being on individualised cognitive processes (the interiority which we noted earlier), it is instead on the full range of resources available to learners within communities (or spaces) of practice that are signed specifically as learning places. Increasingly these communities are globalised in their location. Here, learning becomes a process of '"boundary crossing" mediated by access to different "communities of practice"' (Guile and Young 1998: 177). Lave and Wenger (1991), like Bloomer (1997), see learning as distinct from teaching and with this comes an increase in the range of pedagogic spaces and curricula which could be valued. These are not enclosed by the practices of formal and institutionalised education, although control over the practices of assessment and accreditation may still mean that educational institutions have a pedagogic power beyond that which is legitimised by a concern for learning in all its forms. However, the policing of assessment itself becomes more difficult with the increased possibilities for plagiarising that comes in the wake of increased reliance on the use of ICTs and their associated modes of communication. This raises issues about the processes of social selection through reliance on educational qualifications, something already voiced by many employers in their concerns over the knowledge and skills of 'qualified' people.

There are other aspects that also need to be emphasised. One is to do with the very notion of communities of practice and the extension of these into communities of learning through the use of ICTs. As Guile and Young (1998: 177) point out, 'such communities would enable their members to extend the sources of information to which they had access, expand their socio-cultural basis and develop new forms of "knowledgeability"', this being the particular repertoire of knowledge and skills developed through learning within a community of practice. The other is that theorisations of learning such as those of Lave and Wenger (1991) are in a sense not only a different way of understanding learning – for example, in their emphasis on the social and participative – but also a mark of the increased significance given to relationality and reflexivity, which, as we have already noted, are key features of a globalised awareness and bring to the fore the social location and construction of learning rather than seeing it as an individualistic and bounded cognitive process. As Guile and Young (1998: 185) point out, reflexive learning is 'the "micro" expression of the "macro" process of reflexive modernisation'. The bringing to the fore of relationality by these new theorisations is a mark, at the level of micropractices, of the macro-level interconnectedness of globalisation. Thus we witness the increased importance given also to activity theory (Tuomi-Grohn and Engestrom 2003) and actor-network theory (Nespor 1994) in framing the understanding of learning where both in different ways focus on relationality.

New spaces

> We are in a period of crisis in relation to all environments of enclosure.
>
> (Peters 1996: 105)

We would argue that, at the very least, the changes discussed resonate with the move from the fixed institution-based space of education to the more emergent terrain of learning. The re-conceptualisations of learning examined in this glimpse are in themselves suggestive of different forms of pedagogy in which notions of teacher-centred and student-centred learning positioned as opposite locations and locations of opposition are put to one side in the engagement with the ongoing performative yet ambivalent question of 'what works' in a philosophically pragmatic sense. The answer to this can never be bounded by a single pedagogic strategy but only with ongoing approximations, where teachers themselves have to be mobile.

What this would seem to suggest, therefore, is the need to move from a focus on teaching and learning as bounded practices to an examination of new and complex patterns of interconnectedness, and the pedagogic spaces and socio-cognitive, socio-practical, socio-semiotic and socio-affective possibilities that are both opened up and excluded by the multiple interconnectedness of globalisation. Here, pedagogic spaces suggest a learning that is not simply mediated through a teacher but also through hitherto marginalised others, for example learners, teaching assistants, technicians, parents in classrooms and media and artefacts, icons and texts. Such an approach brings to the fore the social nature of learning, something we can see illustrated in the current interest in collaborative learning, itself a possible analogue of moves towards inter- and trans-disciplinarity and team working. This challenges the individualising practices of much education, assessment and accreditation, although there is a need to recognise that globalising processes do themselves induce individualising effects. Furthermore, the pedagogic spaces of the educational institution cannot any longer be isolated from those of the home, the street and the workplace, etc. Each encompasses a range of pedagogies through which people learn to be and become in specific ways.

Spatialising pedagogies therefore result in an increased focus on pedagogic spaces as the condition of possibility for certain forms of learning and the idea that 'different ways of being in place are connected with different ways of meaning' (Game 1991: 148). Furthermore, as we have noted in this and previous glimpses, pedagogic spaces are themselves changing. Deleuze (1992) has argued that our modernist society is characterised by a situation where people are passed from one closed space to another – the family, the school, the university or the factory. However, with the development of control mechanisms based on the network, these bounded spaces have become open and flexible. This is not to say that discipline (in both senses) has disappeared, but we have seen that it has been reconfigured. Although there is much in this that is rightly problematic, it is nonetheless the case that new spaces are being opened for pedagogy and curriculum.

Glimpse four
Working and (l)earning

No one can doubt the significance of globalising processes for employment, work-places and work over recent decades. This significance is often represented under the sign of the 'knowledge economy' or 'post-industrial society', where the role of information and knowledge is now given a greater economic significance than ever before. In many spaces around the globe, the nature of work and employment has been transformed over the last twenty to thirty years. One need only look at the industrialisation of China as it has opened its borders for trade, the commercialisation of parts of Kenya as it has responded to International Monetary Fund and World Bank conditions in relation to its debt and the deindustrialisation of large parts of the UK and USA due to declining competitiveness. There are many such examples, not all of which can be explained totally by globalisation processes, but to which the latter has certainly contributed in significant ways. As a result, traditional models of economic development and modernisation with their notions of stages which national economies have to undergo to become developed have been thrown into doubt. The economic order has become both global and more globally competitive and intense through the connections and interconnections which have now become possible. Thus the spaces of work, the types of work and the forms of connection both between workplaces and between workplaces and consumers/clients have become more complex and in many cases stretch across greater distances.

Inevitably communication and transportation networks have a role to play in these processes, as they have enabled the flows of data, information, services and goods at a level and intensity that we have not previously seen. This has changed both the spaces of employment, for example Scottish call centres located in India, but also the nature of workplaces themselves. How many workplaces these days are not digitalised and informated in some way? These developments have changed the nature of work and with that the sorts of learning that people are required to have both for and in employment. Changed also are the ways in which they learn in and about work. Workplace learning, work-related learning and work-based learning have all become familiar framings within the contemporary discourses of education. The current strong support for policies of lifelong learning in many parts of the globe is a feature of these discourses where it is articulated as a necessity arising from a changing economic order influenced by globalising processes. While, once again, this is a too simplistic and reductionist argument to be a complete explanation, there is certainly no denying the importance of economic globalisation to education and learning.

In this chapter, we explore two aspects of this situation. First, we will explore the issue of the global reorganisation of work and the types of pedagogic requirements that emerge as a result. This is supported by the growing practices of daily and weekly commuting in many parts of the world that have become part of the mundane practices of work (Moran 2005). Globalisation and, in particular, global competition have been positioned as key drivers for workplaces in recent years, impacting upon the nature and organisation of work and the requirements placed upon workers to more readily adopt, in the cause of 'flexibility' and multi-skilling, a learning disposition to their work. Learning and earning have now become equated in many discourses, such that to be able to earn requires the capacity, opportunity and necessity to learn – thus our use of *(l)earning* in the title of this chapter. These messages are carried in the policy-led discourses of lifelong learning, as well as the hyperbole of business gurus and in the popular media. They are not without opposition, of course, in both academic and political circles, but this has not prevented them from being powerful. The movements of globalisation from below, which attempt to organise through political globalisation in opposition to economic globalisation, themselves create powerful media presences and images, but hitherto these have had a more limited impact in shaping the processes in play. This is fairly familiar terrain, so we will not rehearse the full range of previous discussion on this issue.

Less familiar, and building on work by Edwards and Nicoll (2007), we will discuss after this the ways in which the new forms of connectivity associated with globalising processes actually bring learning with them. Here we will draw upon actor-network theory (ANT) to sketch some of the 'actants', relationships and performances that make these globalised practices possible and consider the learning enmeshed within the practices of these workplaces. In the process, we will explore the ways in which these practices become realised within globalisation itself as an actor in, rather than simply an outcome of, certain technologically enabled practices and some of the implications of this. We will point to the ways in which globalising processes are realised through the entanglement of human and non-human actors, in particular information and communication technologies (ICTs), in the performance of work through the aggregation and distribution of data. Here globalisation becomes realised through globalising processes with people learning the practices of globalisation through their very engagement in work. Following Derrida's (1994) reading of Marx then, our exploration is based upon a hauntology exploring the *spectre* of globalisation. The metaphors of the ghost and of haunting are derived loosely from Derrida, and in this text we want to argue that two things are suggested by these. The first is that globalising practices, like all ghosts, have a troubling and unsettling effect on existence, with work and learning no exception to this even though this is not so fundamental that all that has gone before is annihilated. Just as the ghost paradoxically can never fully realise its past within the present – it remains a ghost after all – globalising practices are never able to be fully realised. Thus while its effects are real in the sense of material, glob-alisation never fully relinquishes its 'ghostly' existence. This relates to the second aspect suggested by hauntology. The latter, as articulated by Derrida, plays on the homophony in French of *hauntologie – ontologie*. In other words, the 'is' (ontology) and the 'is not' (hauntology) cannot be divorced from each other. This presents a resonant means of characterising globalisation as globalising processes since glob-alisation can be said to be both here and not here, present yet also absent – or to put it another way, globalisation is itself (dis)located. Globalising processes 'haunt' the contemporary workplace and the learning that people engage in through their work but this haunting goes on in an often invisible way – 'behind the backs' as it were of those upon whom it impacts.

The arguments concerning the global reorganisation of work and the types of pedagogic requirements that emerge are to do with the contemporary rationale for learning. The arguments about new forms of connectivity associated with globalising processes and the kinds of learning they bring with them can perhaps be referred to as part of the hidden curriculum of globalisation, the learning car-ried in the very practices through which globalising processes emerge. It is the latter, given the pedagogic focus of this text, which is of particular interest to us.

Changing spaces of work

The changing spatial organisation of work has been of interest to economic and cultural geographers for some time. In earlier chapters, we drew upon some of that work to help us formulate our own understanding of the complexity of glob-alising processes. Here we focus on this as the basis for discussing how globalisation has become a key exigency for learning. Part of what we want to do, however, following Massey (2005), is to suggest some of the ways in which the changing spatial reconfiguration of work can also reconfigure boundaries between work and home and, with that, gender and family relationships. Thus the learning associated with, and required by, the changing nature of work and employment is not simply bounded to that domain, but also flows through the wider social order of which these are part. Here then there is a pedagogy where new identities and relationships are learnt in the very process of becoming a globalised and globalising (l)earner.

The workplace as a site for learning and the interface between educational institutions and the workplace have always been an important part of the peda-gogic landscape. However, globalising processes reconfigure the geographies of those spaces and places. As we have already indicated, this is often put forward as a situation where the institutional spaces of enclosure such as workplaces and places of education are now more open, with greater flows through and between them. Thus both the range of learners and of pedagogic relationships have grown and diversified. For example, teachers from South East Asia, in order to advance their careers, now come to Europe to do courses in Education through the medium of English. Different languages, cultures and identities flow through ped-agogic spaces. To address economic competitiveness, science and innovation parks that enhance knowledge transfer are established alongside or close by universities. Within workplaces, open plan offices are built with no set and compartmentalised desks, to allow staff to come in with their laptops and work wherever a space exists. People work from home and are programmed through their online and mobile technologies to the tasks required of them.

Thus, the notion of the mass of the workforce organised within enclosed spaces is displaced by more mobile individualised workers in more fluid or virtual spaces. The images are familiar ones. Enclosed and collectivised masses of labour are replaced by more open, mobile and individualised workers. Yet, these individualised workers cannot be said to be disconnected from their workplace – indeed they are often more connected communicatively than might have previously been the case. One has only to take a train journey to find evidence of this, with many a business conversation starting with 'I'm on the train'. These workers may be individualised but they are not alienated in the same ways as their industrial counterparts are purported to be. However, it is also easy to overstate the extent and significance of such shifts, especially when looking at the hugely diversified work practices, including the continued forms of slavery that exist around the globe.

This is a point made by Massey (2005) in her important study of a science laboratory and the ways in which the ostensible flexibility and openness of this workplace, which at first seemed so illustrative of the emerging globalised economy, began to look somewhat different when subject to closer scrutiny. At first glance, the laboratories appeared to live up to the image of openness and flexibility:

> Every day the activities here were hooked up with activities on other continents: conference calls, emails, intellectual exchange and contract negotiations. Trips abroad were routine. Truly globalised places, nodes of international connectivity even more than local (and mirroring in part their own globalisation, indeed producing it in part, the structural inequality within the wider phenomenon). In these senses, then, these high-tech workplaces were the epitome of openness.
>
> (Massey 2005: 177)

At the end of the day, however, these globalised practices of the mostly male staff were replaced by a return home to a bounded local place, often literally a country cottage in an English village. Thus openness and closure, fluidity and boundedness, the global and the local – we see here once again some of the binaries as they are utilised in relation to framing changes in workspaces that have helped to shape the discussion of globalisation. However, Massey's analysis begins to show something more at play. In relation to the laboratories, she identifies the ways in which they are open in certain ways, but also closed both materially and symbolically in others. Security guards, one of the growth forms of employment in service economies, protect the laboratories, as they do the shops in the mobile consuming spaces of the mall. In terms of the relations between the workplace and the home, the fluidity between the two, symbolised by the setting aside of a room in the latter as an office, was more suggestive of a colonisation than a two-way process – 'there was a decidedly one-way invasion (one which rather casts in a different light the usual rhetoric of some unspecified blurring of the boundaries of home and work); an invasion of home by work but not *vice versa*' (Massey 2005: 179, emphasis in original). Thus the binaries that frame the way in which the changing nature of work is understood and articulated themselves start to break down on closer examination.

When we examine therefore the changing practices associated with work both as a response and a contributor to globalising processes, we need to be cautious about the assumptions we build into our analysis. The spaces and places of work and employment are being reconfigured in response to the requirements of competitiveness and higher productivity associated with globalising processes. In the very process, they are themselves contributing to and enacting that reconfiguring of space–time and place to which they are also a response.

It is easy to focus on economic globalisation and the requirements associated with it. Indeed there has been much initiation of policies associated with vocational education and training around the globe over the last thirty years that is precisely aimed at identifying and anticipating the requirements to raise productivity and skills in order to compete globally. Economic development at national, regional and local levels has been a major factor in this and more recently interest in the development of learning regions has grown. Here learning, innovation and economic development are literally embedded in the built environment. This extends the notion of the learning organisation to a learning area – most commonly a learning city or region. Many such developments attempt to replicate Silicon Valley in the 1990s, where the concentration of workplaces, research and development and educational spaces arguably provided the basis for the surge in innovation associated with the development of ICTs.

Within this context, the emphasis tends to be on the development of vocational and problem-solving skills, knowledge management and knowledge transfer. However, precisely because these practices are now increasingly globalised, there are also important cultural, language and literacy issues associated with enabling the forms of intercultural communication so that these workplaces become and remain competitive. This is particularly marked in those companies which operate around the globe, wherein through the (en)counters engendered the complex intercultural mix of workers and consumers both requires and supports forms of communication and learning.

Here economic globalisation cannot be separated from the cultural, technological and social. And indeed, to articulate these as in some ways separate, bounded and discrete categories through which to analyse the changing spaces and connectivities of workplaces itself becomes problematic (Bowker and Star 1999). This is an insight shared with actor-network theory and it is to an initial attempt, following Edwards and Nicoll (2004, 2007), to consider globalised and globalising workplaces from an ANT perspective that we now turn.

Connectivity and learning

Actor-network theory is part of the shift from individualised, psychological approaches to the understanding of knowledge-production to more social and cultural interpretations. Here the focus is on ontology rather than epistemology, wherein 'reality *is a relational effect*. It is produced and stabilised in interaction that is simultaneously material and social' (Law and Urry 2003: 5, emphasis in original). ANT articulates the social as both enacted yet nonetheless real or material; it is *realised*, it is an achievement. Thus, rather than drawing a distinction between the enacted and the real, as is often the case in ontologically oriented discussions of the social in the social sciences, in ANT the enacted is precisely the real and vice versa. Learning then can be taken to be a joint exercise by actors or actants within a network that is spread across space and time and includes inanimate – e.g. tools, pens, computers, software, mobile phones, charts, machinery – as well as animate objects. The symmetry between inanimate and animate objects is recognised in ANT because 'human powers increasingly derive from the complex *interconnections* of humans with material objects...This means that the human and physical worlds are elaborately intertwined and cannot be analyzed separate from each other' (Urry 2000: 14, emphasis in original). To talk of the social then is to talk of the (en)counters of the human with the non-human. An important consequence is that ANT enables a deconstruction of the traditional boundaries between society and technology, nature and culture, etc. and, with that, the distinctions between the natural and social sciences (Law 2004).

With this perspective we can see that what happens in any workplace is not simply the result of human intention (voluntarism) nor is it determined simply by the operation of impersonal forces (determinism), but rather is the result (achievement) of forms of connection, interaction and translation between different actants, connections that at the same time always have the potential to fall apart. In this, ANT shares much metaphorically and intellectually with complexity theory in the natural sciences and chaos theory in mathematics (Urry 2003) in the sense of attempting to elaborate understandings of the messiness that characterises the social order. Workplaces are realised through the (en)counters of the human and non-human and, in particular, those actions at a distance of globalising processes that haunt particular spaces – that are, in other words, both present and absent.

We see immediately the heuristic usefulness of ANT in considering globalisation and workplaces, since workplaces are work*spaces* to use Farrell's (2005) distinction – 'physical work*places* [form] local nodes of a complex network of people, technologies and practices that constitute a potentially globally distributed work*space*' (Farrell 2005: 5, emphasis in original). In other words, the workplace is inseparable from the interconnections which make the performance of work possible and it is constituted by those actions at a distance for which it is a node in a global space. These spaces of work are distributed across time and distance and are both manifestations of globalisation and a contribution to its realisation. They involve humans and non-humans being both connected and 'translated' in order that a specific workplace can continue to thrive.

> According to [the model of translation], the spread in time and space of any-thing – claims, orders, artefacts, goods – is in the hands of people; each of these people may act in many different ways, letting the token drop, or mod-ifying it, or deflecting it, or betraying it, or adding to it, or appropriating it...When no one is there to take up the statement or token then it simply drops.
>
> (Latour 1986: 267)

It is on the effectiveness of interconnection and translation that a workplace may then be evaluated in the production of information, knowledge, goods and services. A workplace only becomes such because actors are interrelated in ways that can be signified as work; it is a network effect.

Networks 'expand, contract and shift configuration over time, and even the most stable and predictable of them are constantly being re-appropriated and rede-fined by the nature of the flows that animate them...' (Nespor 1994: 12). Workplaces therefore can be seen as actor-networks constituted by the participa-tion of actants and which are ordered in time and space, and increasingly *across* time and space. A range of working practices are embedded in the very ordering of space and time and the actants mobilised. With that comes the learning present in those practices. Thus we can discern an architecture or 'built' environment of workplace learning starting to emerge for consideration, one that extends beyond the workplace as a container of work practices to embrace the complex networks and uptakes through which those practices become possible. These may reside partly in the workplace, in the internal relations within organisations, but also coexist in their external relations to, for instance, markets, providers of materials, service clients and funding bodies. The marketing websites of organisations, for example, are powerful actants within globalising processes, acting as a conduit for flows between actor-networks that are potentially global in reach. They participate in the connecting up of actor-networks as people do business together and between institutions, whether this be a one-off purchase of objects that will become embed-ded within networks or the stabilisation of business relations that are made possible by the compressing of time and space. We can say therefore that workplaces are complex and contested organisational forms, which have to be constantly *per-formed* in order to continue to exist, and thus within which there will always be many tensions and contradictions. ANT therefore emphasises the performative nature of work as a network effect. It is in exploring it as such that we start to find the spectre of globalisation and the hauntings of globalising processes.

Networks are formed through translation or mediation since without these practices and their effects there is literally no network. ANT emphasises the dynamic nature of practices and actions and, given the focus on the spatio-temporal and on mediation, provides also a means of examining the ways in which action at a distance occurs. As such, it is useful for examining the dynamics of workplaces in relation to globalisation as an actant, where 'the global comes to constitute its own domains...continuously reconstituted through material-semiotic processes' (Law and Urry 2003: 7).

Workplaces have to a greater or lesser extent porous boundaries through which connections are possible. '[P]eople...aren't simply interacting with the other people and objects physically present in settings. They are also interacting with all the distant spaces and times that they carry with them and that went into the constitution of those actors and objects' (Nespor 1994: 22). The worker/learner is an element within networks, whereby 'each element of a setting...are "mobilisations" of other spaces and times moving along trajectories and intersecting' (Nespor 1994: 22) within that setting. The compression of space–time that is realised and realisable through, for instance, the networking, with electronic communications technologies, of people as actors compresses and intensifies networks making them ever more realisable virtually. Here there is no firm boundary between the real and the virtual, but, as we suggest elsewhere in this text, the virtual is itself real-ised and 'real'. Work and learning then are no longer realised within actor-networks that are mediated by postal communications; by the necessity to wait for a reply to a letter sent through the post to a client or for data from a colleague, half the way around the world. They are mediated electronically, compressed in space–time, and always partially there as potential conduit.

Our argument then is that workplaces given the economic and symbolic work of such spaces are a key network through which this work is done. Hence the spectre, since even as it may not be apparent, globalising processes can be said to be actants in the workplace, the ghost that constantly haunts the work and the learning that is done there. But how is this achieved? To address this, we focus solely on the realisation of globalising processes through the compression of space–time made possible by communications technologies. This does not represent a form of technological determinism, as should be clear from the above. The uptakes of technology are not determined by that technology alone, as anyone using a computer or mobile phone well knows. New technologies are entwined within those already existing. Thus, as Farrell and Holkner (2004: 136) suggest,

> workspaces are hybrid. Then, not just because they are constructed and mediated by a range of communication technologies but also because, when established and new technologies are brought together in these ways, their interaction creates new discursive resources, discursive resources that make available new working identities, values and practices and sideline others.

They draw upon the example of collaboratively constructed databases in a multinational textile company to discuss the negotiations of self and presence that take place for those communicating in this manner. Thus, the inputting of information on deadlines in the mending shed is read next door in the weaving shed, in the company head office in another city, as well as by suppliers and clients elsewhere in the globe. There is surveillance here for all concerned in negotiating certain

norms for communicating in this situation. But there is also a realisation of globalising processes – space–time compression – through the connections made
possible and the particular learning that is possible with the connectivities, surveillance and self-surveillance at play 'behind the scenes'.

There is also a multimodality (Kress 2000) to the communication practices in
play, which multiply the workplace literacies of the workforce. Text and page,
icons and screens, all are in play in the realisation of work. The supervisor in the
mending shed still keeps her exercise book of information, in addition to contributing to the computerised database. People write notes for themselves as well
as read and write e-mails. Instead of the much hyped 'paperless office' therefore,
there is a proliferation of communications and texts. 'In the globally distributed,
ICT-enabled workspace, work practice has to a significant extent become textual
practice. [These] texts are the contexts in which we do our work, and...these
texts, like all texts, are contested sites' (Farrell 2005: 8). It is the multimodality
of these practices that in part help to ensure the continued connections, even
when some part of the technological network goes down (Holkner and Farrell
2005). It is through this semiotic work and the learning that occurs in and
through such work that globalising processes are realised. There is thus a very
real sense in which we can say that semiotic practices are a significant dimension
of globalising processes – and of course in foregrounding semiosis we are
reminded that meaning depends not only on what is present but also the hauntings of what is absent or not-present.

Alongside the complexity of relationships, there is a diversifying of literacy
practices in workplaces. Thus, the 'crisis' of literacy much talked about by governments, employers and others in relation to the perceived growing
requirements of the globalising knowledge economy is indeed tangible. However,
this is not necessarily in the ways in which it is usually framed. We witness not so
much a crisis of basic skills – a lack – but a crisis of possibilities, of unfulfilled and
perhaps unfulfillable and multiple potentialities. With the proliferation and
hybridisation of artefacts and genres of communication come many different possibilities for reading and writing the self and/with others, and the negotiations of
languages and cultures that this entails. What then is appropriate is multiplied,
not reducible to a single standard. When pharmaceutical companies bring
together scientific and business staff from different countries around the globe to
make decisions about the development of new medicines, there is a huge amount
of semiotic work being carried out. The spectral ghost of globalisation then has
many personalities and representations. Thus Farrell's earlier (2000) framing of
workplace literacy tutors as 'discourse technologists' itself has possibilities that go
beyond any simple inculcation into the workforce of a monolithic global corporate culture.

Such practices are increasingly common in the day-to-day performances of
work, either explicitly or implicitly. They both require and enable the multiplication of difference, but also impose certain constraints. The networks are not
completely open and they can be subject to resistance in the form of opposition,
play, irony, and nostalgia for a mythic past. They reveal the presence–absence of

otherness, even as they mediate differences through the introduction of certain standards. As with the harmonisation of railway gauges in the nineteenth century and its significance for nation building and trade, so in the twenty-first century, the standardisation of communications technologies is modelling a certain global imaginary – thus the centrality of the English language to this phase of globalisation and the explosion of English language learning associated with it.

To talk of globalisation processes as spectral actants is to point to their capacity, not only to compress space and time in order that new conduits for flow occur, but to bend space around themselves, to make elements dependent upon them, to construct alternative languages, and so to *reconfigure* time and space forcefully (Nespor 1994). Such reconfigurations are realised both materially and representationally. Thus, the collaboratively constructed electronic database is such a reconfiguration. Networks and actants *produce* 'space and time by mobilising and accumulating distant settings in central positions' (Nespor 1994: 10), rather than being located within them as past, present and future work is accumulated through a particular centralised and collective re-ordering. Realising globalisation entails the production, distribution and reception of information and knowledge in this way, often in complex patterns of communication and connectivity. However, within the workplace, the database acts materially as a reconfiguration of time and space; it acts to reconstitute activities. There can be a degree of creativity in this for those involved. However, organisations, whether commercial or non-commercial, *need* that information to be captured and harnessed to meet their corporate goals (Farrell 2005). There is thus a tension between, on the one hand, organisational control (in the compression and then re-ordering of space and time in particular ways, in the fashioning of elements and languages necessary for this, and so forth) and, on the other hand, the exercise of individual and group judgement. In workplaces this is not new per se but the challenges to globally distributed workplaces are greater. We are in the realm of control–decontrol, or, to put it another way, of (dis)locating and (dis)located practices.

We have argued that globalising processes are a ghost haunting work that now increasingly is articulated as entailing learning. This learning is itself often tacit and spectral rather than fully explicit. It is both present and absent, visible yet invisible, both explicit and implicit. How then do we pursue these spectres so that they may be researched, when our approaches to research also help to realise that which we enact? Here research becomes itself performative – as much part of the actor-network of globalisation, even while commenting upon it (Law 2004). Globalising processes are themselves in part realised as compressions of space–time made possible by electronic forms of communications technologies. They require the material and representational re-ordering of space and time. The question is over these compressions and re-orderings and their effects on learning and work.

The actor-networks within workspaces are systems of ordering through which organisations control and produce appropriate activity. Whilst systems of electronic communication quite radically compress and reorganise space and time, the institutional strategic plan, the meeting agenda and minutes, the office memo, are also, for example, enmeshed and intersect with these. They become re-worked and joined up within actor-networks, to harness action to organisational (and increasingly globalising) purposes – the production of the flexible and enterprising worker, the global extension of the networks of the institution, and the always newly creative product designed for markets that are themselves increasingly globally interconnected – all at the same time continuing to steer (or translate) networks at a distance. There are strategies of translation, attempts at ordering within workspaces – transformations and equivalences, devices, agents, and forms of organisation – that function to make globalising processes durable and mobile, and with the potency to act at a distance. The deployment of discourses of lifelong learning and flexibility are one such device. The provision of a desktop computer to workers, and the actor-networks that this actant is required to participate in, might be another. There are questions here then about what strategies regulate and delimit the space and what activities they require. What are the struggles to negotiate and overcome these limits? Where do these ordering processes break down so that elements 'make off on their own' (Law 2003: 5), and with what consequences?

Ghost-busting – globalising from below

Workspace and workplaces are contested. This contestation can occur at a variety of levels and from diverse sources, both internal and external to the organisation itself. It can take place at the local, regional, national and global level. It can come from workers within a particular workplace, worker organisations more generally and also from consumers, given, for example, the increased influence of ecological movements. Increasingly these contestations are themselves patterned by globalising processes. This is often positioned, although inadequately we would argue, as a form of globalisation from below. Globalisation haunts the ordering of opposition to trends in work and employment, even when that opposition is to globalising processes themselves.

Insofar as there are changes in the availability of work and in the types of work available, then there will be contestation. Contemporary globalising processes change the spaces, places, forms and content of work and employment. As such they disrupt existing patterns and interweave different ones. In this chapter to date we have focused primarily on the general trends associated with this. For some, this will have resulted in a focus on what we have termed globalisation from above, with a resulting de-politicisation of the processes at play. However, in relation to opposition, there is no doubting globalisation from below, particularly to economic globalisation. Whether it is the defence by Western trade unions of jobs being shifted to other parts of the globe, or environmentalist opposition to the pollution associated with new sites of industrialisation, or anti-globalisation protests at the meetings of the leading global economic powers, all these pose a contest to some or all aspects of the changes taking place to work and the workplace.

And all themselves attempt to be global in different ways and to a greater or lesser extent. We have only to return to the aspirations of the Communist Internationals of the nineteenth and twentieth centuries to witness the desire for solidarity among workers across workplaces and nations – workers of the world unite, you have nothing to lose but your chains! Trade unionists therefore aspire to organise globally in order to oppose some of the economic and workplace policies associated with globalisation even as the World Bank and International Monetary Fund attempt to impose global norms on national economies. Similarly, as the concept of the risk society (Beck 1992) attests, environmental degradation is not always clearly bounded by the local, regional or national. The best example of this is the global warming associated with the emissions from the production and consumption practices that are fostered through economic globalisation. These cannot be countered without at one level engaging with the complexities of global opposition. And anti-globalisation protesters come from many countries and move from country to country in order to make their voices heard, for example using mobile technologies that require satellites to order their protests.

The tension then is that, while many such groups oppose globalisation and its consequences, they actually engage in globalising practices in order to build and sustain their opposition. These forms of globalisation from below might therefore be better characterised as oppositional to particular aspects and outcomes of globalising processes rather than opposition to globalisation per se.

Associated with such practices is learning, if of a different kind to that we have focused on so far, learning embracing not simply the changing requirements of work – although many oppositional groups are also workspaces and places of their own – but also developing contextual understandings of the significance of those changes in relation to wider issues – of work, the environment, power. However, once again, they can often mirror the practices of the workplace we have associated with globalisation, as they rely on the same technologies of computer, mobile phone, the Internet, etc. that we have argued are the carriers of globalising processes. Here, as with an antibiotic to fight a virus, the spectre of globalisation which haunts the workplace is itself necessary for engaging in ghost-busting activities. Thus globalisation from below cannot do without globalisation from above, even as it opposes it. Similar arguments are also possible in relation to the anti-modernisation stance of some religious groups; they rely on aspects of the very globalising practices they oppose in order to organise their own opposition to globalisation. Thus the interconnectivities of globalisation from below rather than simply their binary opposite are but another aspect of globalising processes.

New spaces of learning

The globalised world of intersecting and networked flows reshapes the subjectivities and perceptions of learners – what is involved here is a cultural change about who is a learner and what learning is. As we have noted, contemporary discourses displace learners from educational sites of learning by constituting learning as 'flexible' and 'lifelong'. This is perhaps most clearly articulated, for example, in the notion of 'socially distributed knowledge' now foregrounded as a significant form of *contemporary* knowledge. Here once again, we witness binaries at play, in that the acquisition of this significance and the consequent power of this articulation resides to a very large extent in its being contrasted and opposed to 'culturally concentrated knowledge'. Spatially, disciplinary knowledge has been characterised as bounded and inflexible, and socially distributed knowledge, of which work-based knowledge is a leading example, as unbounded and flexible.

Earlier we spoke of the bringing to the fore of 'learning' as against 'education' in terms of a recognition that learning can plausibly be said to take place in a multiplicity and diversity of sites. This recognition in itself challenges the educational spaces and places of enclosure traditionally constituted by the book as disciplinary text, the pre-determined curriculum, the classroom and the practice of studying for a fixed period of time with fixed starting and end points. We can highlight all these developments as a *displacement* of the educational spaces of enclosure and it is this displacement which has contributed to the foregrounding of the workplace as a legitimate site of learning. Coupled with this, ICTs in enabling more flexible modes of organising and delivering learning, such as distance learning and e-learning, considered particularly appropriate to workplace learning, have hastened this development. Furthermore with flexible learning comes the 'flexible' learner, a worker who combines work and learning but is too busy to be absent from the workplace and located in an educational institution for long periods of time as classroom education would require.

At this point however we need to clarify our terms by making a distinction between workplace learning and work-based learning. The former, for example in the form of co-operative education programmes, has been around for some time whilst the latter is much more recent and is perhaps a more radical development. Work-based learning is articulated as not just a matter of studying in flexible mode with periods of classroom learning alternating with periods of work placement as in workplace learning. It is rather where the disciplinary curriculum and the defined space of learning is displaced to make way for a curriculum sourced in the socially distributed knowledge of the workplace, thus where work and the workplace become the site and source of learning. This development is perhaps the most significant of a number of recent developments that could be said to constitute a process where the 'student' as traditionally conceived is displaced by the 'learner', located in a variety of sites, and learning in a variety of (dis)located ways.

Earlier we mentioned the significance attributed to socially distributed knowledge and it is undoubtedly the case that it has found its moment within the folds of globalisation. With notions of the knowledge economy gaining purchase, the capacity of labour to process information and to generate knowledge is increasingly seen as an important source, through the potential for innovation, of productivity and of economic growth that benefits both business and the state in the globalised competitive environment of fast capitalism. Knowledge, flexibility and symbol processing skills are key to the globalisation of capital in its contemporary form of 'reflexive accumulation' (Lash and Urry 1994). Hence the contemporary highlighting in the domain of business of knowledge management and intellectual property accumulation and protection and the state's intervention in the formation of human capital by educational institutions at all levels.

Technological innovation has become the means of keeping ahead – and technological innovation requires the capture in electronic databases of both existing knowledge and the generation and deployment of new knowledge – a knowledge that is applied, specific, transient and commodifiable, oriented to the identification and solution of problems generated in the workplace – in other words, on the socially distributed knowledge of the workplace. Thus the emphasis on work-based learning as the mode of learning most appropriate to the demands of the knowledge economy.

This is a potent way of understanding the contemporary situation insomuch that it points to the critical entwining of the workplace, learning and globalising processes. Clearly without the exigencies generated by the latter the workplace would have continued to be articulated as a marginal source of knowledge and learning. Globalising processes are based on, and enhance, hybridity, relationality and connectivity, all of which it could be argued also characterise learning and knowledge in the workplace. However, as always a note of caution is necessary since there is an over-simplification in this argument given the complexities of notions such as socially distributed knowledge that tend to be ignored. First, to create a binary in knowledge of socially distributed versus culturally concentrated is ultimately unhelpful. It is not unreasonable to argue, for example, that socially distributed knowledge requires culturally concentrated knowledge and that this is ignored when a polarised distinction between these types of knowledge is made. Equally, not all learning in the workplace is socially distributed, for example research and development carried out by businesses might well be applied in orientation but it depends heavily on culturally concentrated science. Furthermore, and this is perhaps most germane to our purpose here, once learning and knowledge sourced in work becomes subject to validation in *educational* programmes the resulting need for a credentialling process itself raises subject(s) and discipline(s) issues. For example, in this situation, socially distributed knowledge has to be articulated as, and presented in, the form of culturally concentrated knowledge if it is to be credentialled.

Earlier we spoke of 'spaces of enclosure' and suggested that these were seen to be characterised by the tight boundary marking of culturally concentrated knowledge and the educational institutions wherein such knowledge was generated and disseminated. The binaries at work here would suggest that the socially distributed knowledge of the workplace thus has the opposite characteristics. However, we would prefer to argue that it is not so much that socially distributed knowledge is always unbounded, but rather it is more that whilst boundaries are still present they are different – locally specific, more complex, more contested and more fluid, yet nonetheless they do involve a different kind of regulation, subject, and discipline. To put it another way, dislocating always involves new and different forms of locating. This is why it is more helpful to talk of the (dis)located learner – a learner who is simultaneously dis-located *and* located.

It could be argued therefore that there has been a reworking of knowledge boundaries and a dislocation of learning that is both cause and effect of the new spaces of knowledge. This redefining of the boundaries happens at a number of levels and all have a significant influence in re-shaping the identities of both learners and learning. Thus for example it is now perhaps more useful to articulate a learner not as a foundational subject of consciousness but as a *hybrid* subject shaped by the networks and flows in which they are enfolded.

In other parts of this text we have foregrounded the postmodern condition and have argued that it is always discernible in globalising processes and as such is always manifested through a fundamental tension. This tension can also be characterised as a hybrid since it is generated by the interaction of elements of performativity and regulation with elements of openness, diversity and active biographical self-construction. Here, subjects can be thought of as hybrid insofar as they are at one and the same time both active and acted upon – and nowhere is this more evident than in the contemporary workplace in conditions of globalised capitalism. In these spaces, learning is both open and closed, the 'curriculum' is both explicit and hidden, both without discipline(s) and yet disciplining. The flexible learning of the flexible worker can itself be understood as a process of biographical self-construction (Edwards 1998) centred on the learning of flexibility, a process of surveillance through self-regulation that is simultaneously empowering and disempowering.

We have used the metaphor of space and the concept of socially distributed knowledge to explore the different positioning that now locates learning and learners in the contemporary workplace. We have noted that a new binary, that between culturally concentrated knowledge and socially distributed knowledge, has been created, and a locating of each of these in a different and polarised space – culturally concentrated knowledge in the 'unreal world' of the academy and socially distributed knowledge in the 'real world' of the workplace. As we have noted, this polarisation is itself problematic but undoubtedly it has been crucial in bringing the workplace to the fore as a significant space of learning. Once again this development is both a consequence and a contributor to globalising processes. The latter bring forth new and different learning arrangements through the ongoing negotiation and contestation that characterise the opening up of new domains of knowledge such as the workplace.

Yet it would be mistaken to argue from this that the consequent displacement creates an unbounded pedagogical space, a complete opening up of the spaces of enclosure. The space could be said to have been made roomier but it is not unbounded. The boundaries are perhaps more fluid and permeable, although even the post-Fordist workplace does not always possess all these characteristics – and within such spaces there is indeed discernible a greater emphasis on the relationality and flexibility of flows and networks. There is certainly prescription here even though it is located not so much in disciplines but in the demands of globalised capital and the kind of workplace that is structured from these demands. Boundaries are therefore present – all we can say is that they more readily have the potential for the articulation of a space amenable to the contingency that characterises the interactions and new relationships that have formed and are continuing to form in new sites and modes of learning.

Earlier we spoke of the spectre of globalisation and foregrounded the notion of hauntology in the sense both of something unsettling and of something that is simultaneously present and not-present. In articulating the learning sourced in the workplace as (dis)located, bounded yet unbounded, it is clear that such learning possesses the hauntological qualities that characterise globalising processes. It is unsettling in the sense that those who are learning in the workplace may not be happy about the articulation of what they do at work *as* learning and given the rise of knowledge management and credentialling may feel that they are not in any case fully in control of that learning. Furthermore, the learning sourced in the workplace is both present and not-present. It is often, for example, tacit and may for that reason elude the demand for articulation. Then again it could be argued that there is a 'curriculum' even though it is hidden – learning flexibly but perhaps more significantly learning flexibility.

Glimpse five
Globalisation, the academy and new knowledge

> Transdisciplinary approaches...involve border crossings across disciplines from text to context, and thus from texts to culture and society.
>
> (Kellner 1995: 28)

In this part of the text, we will look at the impact of globalisation on the university (or the academy), focusing in particular on the changing role of the idea of the university, what it stands for, and of the academics who work in that site. For the latter, the role traditionally has been one combining teaching or pedagogy with research or knowledge production, a combination or balance which has increasingly been disturbed. We are aware that knowledge production can be construed as involving more than academic research and, indeed, are mindful that in globalised conditions by no means everything considered 'knowledge' is produced through research of this kind or within the spaces of the academy.

What globalisation has contributed is to bring to the fore the significance of different forms of knowledge and the meaning-making practices that any knowledge form involves, and we shall say more about these different forms later. As we have suggested already, producing knowledge is now recognised as being something that not only academic researchers do but all, in different forms, are engaged in as learners. This is an argument which is at the heart of educational discourses of lifelong learning, although as we shall see later 'lifelong learning' has other possible significations. Globalisation then enhances culturalist or constructivist views of knowledge, even as the proliferation of knowledge, knowledge production, knowledge producers and knowledge transfer results in greater uncertainty as to the status of what is knowledge. In effect, this brings about a deconstruction of knowledge in its canonical forms. The contemporary significance and paradoxes of constructivism and deconstruction can be seen therefore as themselves symptoms of intensified globalisation.

This glimpse examines some of the paradoxes that are played out within contemporary knowledge production and the significance of what have been called 'new modes of knowledge production' (Gibbons *et al.* 1994). These can be seen as both a consequence and a realisation of globalisation. However, our discussion will be framed mainly in the context of the relationship with, and the effects of this on, knowledge production practices in the academy. In particular and again, we will look at the role of information and communication technologies (ICTs), computer-mediated communication (CMC) and their impact on the academy as a work site. We will argue that knowledge production in the academy is being reconfigured by globalising processes and the cultural practices within which new technologies and modes of communication are implicated in those processes.

Inevitably, and we do recognise this, there is a danger of a Western and therefore partial gaze being construed as generalisable. The role of the academy and the academic is neither universal nor uniform but rather varies according to context, funding and institutional structures. There is also a difference that needs to be borne in mind between the idea and ideology of the university and the actual practices of higher education. Accordingly, it is necessary to introduce a post-colonial dimension to the discussion to bring to the fore the contemporary location of knowledge production within the ambiguities and tensions of globalisation, while also recognising that all knowledge workers and producers, wherever they may be specifically located, are now in an important sense part of the global game. They are part of what Green (1998) refers to as the 'global academic', by which he means not just the jet-setting activities of specific individuals but the trend, with many different and complex aspects, towards the globalisation of knowledge within which the university is now only one of many players.

We believe it is important to emphasise that the relationships between knowledge production as research on the one hand and teaching and learning on the other are inevitably changing in globalising conditions. Prestige accrues to those institutions with the most symbolic capital as measured by research grants and outputs. As a consequence, teaching is considered to be less significant in reputational terms in many places. ICTs have also played a part in this trend as they have enabled not only an increase in the amount of information available, but also a blurring of the hitherto tightly defined boundaries between knowledge and information. With that comes a breakdown of bounded definitions of what constitutes knowledge and traditional hierarchies of worthwhile knowledge. The attempts to tighten national controls over curricula, particularly the school curriculum, only point to the significance of determining what is or is not worthwhile. At the same time, there has occurred a significant change in the way learning is construed. It is now seen as something that occurs not only in formally designated institutions of education but as a condition of being. Thus, many more than ever before – and, for some, all – are seen as being engaged in learning in a variety of forms and locations and throughout the life-course. We can also note that pedagogy, where ICTs create and enable a demand for flexible and accessible structures of knowledge, is no longer so readily seen as the authoritative transmission of canonical bodies of knowledge by research-based experts. Thus research and pedagogy are beginning to follow different imperatives even in the academy where the link between the two has always allegedly been closest. Equally, now that 'learning' rather than education is increasingly given priority, we note a separation of institutionalised pedagogy from learning. This both reflects and contributes to the perceived inappropriateness of notions of peda-gogy as transmission and acquisition, and more generally to wider processes throughout the educational domain that re-evaluate inputs in favour of outputs, and content in favour of competences or capabilities.

However, although these trends are clearly present, their significance and effects are a matter of debate and contestation. The only thing that does seem reasonably clear is that the debate is taking place in a context where notions of flexible learning, the virtual university and education for the 'real world' now have prominence, not only in educators' discourse but also in the policy-making domain. All this can be seen as a reflection of the challenge to institutionalised education, face-to-face pedagogy, the idea of the liberal university, and the rise of alternative expectations about what constitutes worthwhile knowledge and acceptable pedagogy (Kenway *et al.* 1993). These expectations can be argued to be an aspect of the reflexive questioning that is itself posed by intensified global-isation. Our task here then is to begin to elucidate some of the many implications for knowledge production, relating our discussion to the widespread dissemina-tion and use of new developments in ICTs and their accompanying computer-mediated communication. These developments, linked to the so-called 'knowledge economy' and 'information society' or 'information age' (Webster 1995), are central to understanding the possibilities now being opened up as well as the forms of closure that some argue are taking place.

We will argue that the dissemination and use of these technologies has con-tributed to challenging, in complex and contradictory ways, the academy's long-standing traditions of knowledge production. They have helped to facili-tate, on the one hand, an emphasis on *performativity* – the maximising of productivity and systemic efficiency (both within the academy and in the eco-nomic world which the academy is now supposed to service) – and, on the other hand, an emphasis on new types of learned outputs in multiple sites, from diverse sources and related to a plurality of aims. While on the face of it these seem to be completely incompatible and irreconcilable tendencies, we will argue that there is nonetheless a linkage. This is that outputs now function as *signifiers* within new contexts of the performative and in the sign economy within which knowledge production is now enfolded (Lash and Urry 1994; Usher and Edwards 2007).

The changes in the nature of educational research or knowledge production that we will focus on for purely strategic purposes here can, at one level, be attributed to the radical epistemological and methodological questioning, the generalised doubt about universalistic truth-claims manifested in postmodern perspectives and of which performativity is but one, albeit significant, aspect. Thus, we would not want to give the impression that performativity is the master concept that explains everything, nor that it has a single signification. However, in examining globalisation, it is impossible to ignore those processes that consti-tute performativity, particularly in terms of their significant impact upon education. Equally, however, we would want to argue that rather than seeking mono-causal explanations it is perhaps more productive to see educational research as currently subject to dual trends which have a common basis in the *performative* (and its accompanying performances) but which also, as we have just noted, have paradoxical effects. This can be expressed very simply at this stage in the following way. On the one hand, there is a pull towards closure and a locking into an economy of the same, based upon requirements to produce research that 'works'. On the other hand, there is also greater diversity and complexity in contemporary knowledge production – or what can be termed an economy of difference. Thus, we have argued that globalising processes are marked by heterogeneity and homogeneity; and these can also be identified in relation to knowledge production itself.

We will examine performance and performativity in relation to new modes of knowledge production and look at how these are played out (performed) in contemporary processes. We will look at the increased regulation of research in the academy in the name of accountability and excellence and its increased engagement with organisations outside the university, in particular the world of business, as part of an attempt to reconfigure practices around knowledge mobilisation and transfer. Many university systems are now subject to some form of research assessment through a performance measuring regime that discursively constructs knowledge production and researchers in complex and paradoxical ways. While this serves to construct a location within an economy of the same, for example through the prioritising of outputs rather than inputs and process, and by the differential weighting attached to different kinds of output with a corresponding downgrading of others, we argue that within this there is also another kind of performativity at work. This performativity is based on a notion of performing, where academics enactively inscribe themselves as 'active' researchers on a global stage as the means of accountability and the mark of excellence and are judged on this basis. In this situation, the significance accorded to inscribed performance also has the paradoxical effect of stimulating the diversity and hybridity that we have suggested is enfolded in globalisation.

In this part of the text, therefore, we will first take a glimpse at the way knowledge is being reconfigured in the context of globalising processes and the relationship particularly of this reconfiguration with the development and spread of ICTs. Here, knowledge production becomes not simply an issue of truth but also subject to other criteria. In particular, there is a concern here with processes of making meaning as well as the meanings made. We will explore what this implies for knowledge production as research and its relationship with pedagogy and learning. We will then consider what have been described as new modes of knowledge production, examining particularly the important work produced by Gibbons *et al.* (1994) in this context. Finally, we will argue that, although knowledge production has now become performative, this is not something that can be understood solely in terms of a narrow definition of performativity. We will examine the implications of this for the place of the university and the role of researchers in that space in relation to the globalising processes that bring to the fore the semiotic dimensions of the knowledge economy and information society.

Knowledge production in performative times

Lyotard (1984) in *The Postmodern Condition: A Report on Knowledge* posed the question of how the educational system, or the means for the production and transmission of a certain kind of knowledge, is affected by two contemporary globalising processes. One of these is the demands of performativity, the other is the impact of ICTs and their associated computer-mediated communication. He argues that these processes are changing fundamentally the hitherto dominant functions of knowledge, namely the production of new knowledge (research) and the transmission of established knowledge (pedagogy). He argues that the modernist educational project is being reconstructed in terms of what it can contribute to the best efficiency and effectiveness of the socio-economic order, its task that of producing the knowledge specifically needed by, and those with the skills indispensable to, the contemporary globalised system. As we have noted elsewhere, these have now become the knowledge and skills seen as necessary for staying ahead in the competitive world market in conditions of globalised market-driven capital. Here, performativity is located within wider discursive practices of economic globalisation, neo-liberal economics and national competitiveness. Education becomes re-configured as the means of attaining and maintaining the flexibility and generic skills that are considered necessary in the face of the technological and socio-economic change required by these conditions. It is 'restructured as part of the economy...no longer viewed as a universal welfare right so much as a form of investment in the development of skills that will enhance global competitiveness' (Peters 1996: 99). For many, this performativity associated with the knowledge economy has become the defining aspect of globalisation.

These skills can be seen also as the means by which people are created or shaped in ways, albeit complex and often contradictory, appropriate to the maintenance of the social order's internal cohesion in this globalised condition and the changes in modes of governance associated with it. Lyotard (1984) argues therefore that education's task is no longer that of the dissemination of a model of life legitimised by the grand narratives where knowledge is defined as that which is in the service of truth or of human emancipation. With performativity, the questions asked of knowledge are no longer 'is it true?' or 'does it contribute to human progress?', but 'what use is it?' and 'how will it enhance the performance of people and organisations?' This is not the same as classical utilitarianism, as there is a systems logic rather than the greatest good of the greatest number that is addressed through the notion of usefulness. In this situation, knowledge becomes commodified with the questions asked of it changing, and therefore it is perhaps hardly surprising that the nature of what constitutes knowledge and how it is to be produced become themselves subject to change and contestation.

Lyotard (1984) argues that with the dominance of performativity we are witnessing the creation of a market for competence in operational skills and applicable or instrumental knowledge. This has inevitable effects not only on the nature of knowledge but also on the nature of the student body and the curriculum on offer. He noted (and in this he is proving to be right, at least within Eurocentric university systems) that students in universities will no longer predominantly be the liberal elite seeking a liberal education – a training in civility and sensibility – or an education appropriate for entry to the traditional elite professions – a training in rationality. The increasing emphasis on employment-related training, particularly for the growing number of knowledge workers and the symbolic professions (Reich 1993), on new domains of knowledge linked to new technologies, on job retraining and on continuing education coupled with the general trend in the vocationalisation of the curriculum have all been seen, albeit perhaps often in a totalising and simplistic way, as particularly significant in producing the human capital necessary for optimising the performativity of the socio-economic order.

Furthermore, the increasing deployment of knowledge in all domains creates a situation where knowledge in its traditional canonical discipline-based sense is reconfigured by the demand for, and the constraints imposed by, computer-stored information. This itself stimulates the demand for new skills and new kinds of learning, while at the same time creating conditions where knowledge is more readily commodified and valued in economic or instrumental terms rather than for its social and cultural significance. To put it another way, it is valued for its exchange value in the market – 'knowledge is and will be produced in order to be sold, it is and will be consumed in order to be valorised in a new production; in both cases the goal is exchange' (Lyotard 1984: 4).

At the same time, the effect of ICTs is to accelerate the trend towards an individualisation of learning, although this is not the individuality of the traditional paradigm of liberal education. Moreover, whereas many would argue that this is a highly problematic trend in educational terms, there is no doubt that it takes place in an active way and with complex effects. Poster (1997: 214) argues that 'canons and authorities are seriously undermined by the electronic nature of texts…as texts become "hypertexts"…the reader becomes an author, disrupting the stability of experts or "authorities"'. Through the Internet, e-mail, PDAs, CD-ROMs and hypertext, possibilities are presented for individuals to access information, interact with it and with other learners, and thus learn more flexibly and without the need to attend institutional centres or designated spaces of learning. However, it also needs to be noted that with the increasing incidence of open, distributed, flexible and e-learning this type of individualisation is now also to be found within educational institutions. At the same time, subjects (in the sense of bodies of disciplinary and canonical knowledge) and their transmission seem less significant in relation to, on the one hand, curriculum developments such as work-based learning and, on the other, the development of new skills and capacities such as multidisciplinarity, multi-literacies and transcoding (Cope and Kalantzis 2000).

Even if one argues that, regardless of the mediating and transformative potential of new technology, students still have to be taught something, there remains the argument that disciplinary content per se is perhaps likely to become less significant than knowing how to use and work with ICTs. Lyotard (1984: 50) argues, for example, that the most significant development brought about by ICTs is not simply their use as efficient tools but that they demand the need for 'a refined ability to handle the language game of interrogation'. What he was pointing to was the need not just for an ability to gather discrete bits of information but for the skill of evaluating and making sense of these, for imaginatively arranging them in new ways, through connecting together information formerly seen as separate and unconnectable; in other words the skills and competences of multimodal symbolic analysis. More generally, this can be understood as a kind of trans-disciplinarity, itself an aspect of dedifferentiation, a breaking down of knowledge hierarchies and disciplinary boundaries and a bringing together of hitherto compartmentalised and separated knowledges, of which this text is itself an example. This dedifferentiation also marks a breakdown in the hierarchy and the distinction between knowledge and information, with a consequent (dis)location or decentring of knowledge. Here, knowledge becomes difficult to distinguish from information. What is hitherto regarded simply as information attains the status of knowledge, even if only because both are now located in an environment where epistemological boundary marking and policing is not so potent, thereby rendering problematic epistemological conceptions of what constitutes knowledge and, as we have said, what is worthwhile knowledge. Although we are in sympathy with this trend we would also want to argue that information in this sense is not the same thing as computer-stored data. Although it is undoubtedly the case that the mode of storage and dissemination has an impact on the way knowledge is reconfigured and redefined, it is over-simplistic in our view to assimilate all new forms of knowledge, and changes in the conception of what is knowledge, to the particular constraints and possibilities of computer-stored data. This is particularly apposite in considering the characteristics of new forms of knowledge and different ways of constructing and validating knowledge. Rather than perpetuating now somewhat sterile debates about whether information is 'really' knowledge, what is perhaps more significantly emphasised is that predictability, certainty and totalising explanation have become less the norm. Paralogy, or the acceptance not only of unpredictability, indeterminacy and the unexpected, but also of dissensus and conflict about what constitutes knowledge, has become less the mark of deviance and error but rather more readily seen as a positive value. And this itself can be seen as an aspect of a more general awareness and the beginnings of an acceptance that the globalised world is indeed chaotic, ambivalent and emergent (Urry 2003).

New modes of knowledge production and changes in conceptions of what constitutes knowledge are therefore the concrete enactments of decentring, a decentring that has implications for knowledge production/management and transmission/transfer, research and pedagogy. Counter-intuitive as it may seem, there is moreover a relationship between decentring and performativity, although the relationship is a complex one. Lyotard (1984) argues that there is a strong link between performativity and contemporary research to the extent that the latter has been transformed by the former. He argues that as knowledge production practices become more complex, so the more complex the proof demanded and the greater the complexity of the technology necessary to achieve this. Knowledge production in the scientific mode and technology thus become interrelated and inseparable, and with this two vital dimensions are introduced. One is that knowledge production, following the thrust of technology, becomes orientated to system efficiency and optimal performance rather than to truth and free enquiry – 'scientists, technicians and instruments are purchased not to find truth but to augment power' (Lyotard 1984: 46). It is power that now legitimates knowledge production. The other is that because technology requires money the production of knowledge becomes costly and increasingly dependent on external funding whether from public or private sources. This creates a pressing need for the academy to enter into relationships with business and industry generally, given that governments are no longer prepared to fully fund universities. Through these two dimensions there is established 'an equation between wealth, efficiency and truth' (Lyotard 1984: 45), with knowledge becoming seemingly orientated to performativity in its narrow sense. At the same time as the state, because of the impact and demands of globalising processes, expects universities to do more but with reduced resources and therefore partly withdraws in favour of control by the market, so greater responsibility is placed upon universities to support and enable national economic competitiveness in conditions of globalised capital. While there is remorseless pressure to keep costs down, universities are at the same time expected to be leaders in the innovation that it is assumed enhances the national economy and to make effective changes in such things as governance in line with the globalising processes affecting them (Kenway *et al.* 1993).

Of course, it could be said that Lyotard's argument tends to ignore actual on the ground complexities and the differences that exist within and across universities. In the first place, it is not at all clear what technology is being referred to. It is possible to construe him as meaning information technology, although if this is the case the effects of this technology are by no means as straightforward as he implies. In globalising processes, ICTs undoubtedly reinforce power, but they can also destabilise it. This is particularly the case with disciplinary power (Nicoll and Edwards 1997). Second, it is by no means the case that all contemporary knowledge production requires large inputs of technology and money, and educational research is probably a good example of this. However, Stronach and MacLure (1997) argue that performativity is nonetheless having an impact on educational research, even though technology in a material sense is not so significant. More generally, educational research is expected to enhance the performativity of the education system in ensuring national economic competitiveness by producing knowledge that can be used in evidence-informed policy development and in practice. However, the most significant aspect in all fields is that external funding, and the more the better, is now considered the hallmark of good research, although whether such funding is always critical to its success is another matter. It could be argued that this only shows that success is no longer something defined purely by the knowledge-producing academic community.

One possibility here is that external funding has greater significance for its sign value than for its substance. In other words, external funding is a sign that the university is no longer confined within its own walls but is becoming more flexible, reaching out to the world outside the ivory tower and adding value to that world. This, of course, may have a longer history and be more established in situations where the market is a more significant source of funding and also in post-colonial situations where education has played a longer and more significant role in nation building. It is important not to generalise too extensively, given that different models of skills formation and knowledge production precede the current period of globalisation and the spread of performativity.

Stronach and MacLure (1997) argue that the consequence of the linkage to external funding is that for educational research its spaces have been compressed and more obviously politically influenced in the sense that it is now less autonomous or less answerable to its own knowledge-producing communities. One way of understanding this is that educational research, in the face of demands for relevance, largely gives up on whatever pretence it may have had of being disinterested. On the one hand, this is for immediate policy pay-offs and direct instrumental contributions to funders taking the form of outputs that relate to the 'real world'. On the other hand, there are those measures that count in research assessment regimes and evaluations of research quality. In effect, there is now more research with 'commitment', although whether all academics would feel comfortable with this is another matter. In any event, what emerges from this on the ground is the intensification of research work through shorter contracts, job insecurity for research workers and greater control over the content and direction of research by state and quasi-state bodies and commercial organisations. Stronach and MacLure (1997) refer to this as Game 3 research, where mainstream research paradigms and cultures (Game 1 research) are now being played out in different milieux with their key methodologies still deployed but at the same time transformed, no longer signifying what they once did. Knowledge production is no longer, if indeed it ever was, a leisurely conversation confined exclusively to academic communities. The need for results, or outcomes that perform in the 'real world', is greater and more urgent, and without it there is often limited opportunity for any kind of conversation at all.

While performativity may well have led to a greater linkage between research and policy, it could be argued that it has also had the effect of contributing to a trend towards the separation of research from pedagogy and to a dilution of the connection between the two. Certainly, in universities in the Western world, the greater accountability of researchers and the construction of the 'active researcher' in terms of the amount of external research funding successfully netted has tended to create an elite group of researchers, usually located in elite institutions. This seems to be the dominant trend in those universities which see themselves as global world class institutions or brands, a trend which is itself an interesting aspect and an effect of globalisation. Their reputations are built, in very large part, upon research, this being valued more highly than the pedagogical function. Increasingly, they regard the training of minds and sensibilities as a peripheral activity or one that can be undertaken by universities lower in the hierarchy of research excellence.

However, it could also be argued that the increased incidence and changing nature of research assessment has led to a greater, rather than a diminished, emphasis on scholarship and research in a traditional sense. Yet this does not really negate the argument that the amount and source of external funding, now shared by many more, has become a significant factor in assessing research performance. The categories and criteria by which research performance is assessed lead still to a valorising of, for example, the single-authored book, the article in an academic journal and the refereed conference paper – traditional scholarly criteria and categories. However, the increased incidence and changing nature of research assessment has been accompanied by an increase in the number of universities and researchers who previously did not engage in scholarship and research in its traditional sense and who are now reconstituted as research 'active'.

These developments have perhaps also enabled a more vital synergy between research and pedagogy. In a sense, even more so now with types of knowledge production whose outcomes are seen as more relevant and responsive to the concerns of practice, user groups and stakeholders. Pedagogy, as we have already argued, is no longer seen simply as the authoritative transmission of canonical bodies of knowledge by research-based experts. Another effect, again to do with synergy, is that the disseminative power and speed of CMC has enabled research outputs to more swiftly inform curriculum and pedagogy, particularly in forms of distributed, blended and e-learning. But while pedagogy itself has undoubtedly changed, this is perhaps more for reasons to do with the changing emphases resulting from new kinds of students, new discourses about learners and the impact of new technologies than simply from an increase in the number of elite researchers who have neither the time nor the inclination to teach. The new factor in the equation is the proliferation and diversification of research texts that have been enabled by ICTs – 'networked text distribution upsets the gatekeeping hierarchies of written texts surrounding the printing and publishing industries in ways that disturb both the market and traditional modes of regulation of the text' (Peters 1996: 173). There has been also an expansion of traditionally paper-based academic and professional journals whose costs of production and distribution have been cut because of globalised technologies. Research is also now made available through terrestrial and satellite television, videos, CD-ROMs, etc. There is a proliferation and globalisation of research conferences made possible by cheaper travel and enabled by the ease of communication afforded by e-mail and mobile phones. Even physical presence at a single conference location is no longer required with the growth and sophistication of video-conferencing and the like. With the World Wide Web, there has been an explosion in developments that have made research available in a range of formats, for instance through restricted bulletin boards, conferences in formats following along the lines of traditional academic journals and through open access e-repositories. Academics and researchers have themselves developed their own home pages on the Web, from which interested surfers can download copies of articles and papers. All of these developments and many more can be seen as constitutive features of what we earlier termed the global academic.

Yet, despite these developments which can be seen as a freeing-up of knowledge production, an economy of difference, diversity and plurality, there is still a problem in the undoubted tendency to understand performativity in a very narrow way, simplistically casting it as the villain of the piece. In contrast, we would argue that the relationship between knowledge production and performativity is both complex and multidirectional. While the place of research is ambiguous and the space it occupies unclear, it is however possible, as we have suggested earlier, to discern two trends pulling in opposite directions. The demands of performativity not only valorise outputs but outputs of a particular kind. This valorisation means that knowledge production in the academy is pulled towards closure and pushed towards a locking-in to an economy of the same, where

> less and less is it curiosity driven and funded out of general budgets which higher education is free to spend as it like; more and more it is in the form of specific programs funded by external agencies for defined purposes.
>
> (Gibbons *et al.* 1994: 78)

But, equally, this situation means that there is also more of a possibility for a hybrid research that works between the spaces of established research cultures on the one hand and of newly emerging and performatively and performance-orientated research cultures on the other. This hybrid research can be characterised as a (dis)located research that is multi-located in both the closed and the open, the bounded and the unbounded, the traditional and the emerging – and very often is reflexively aware of this. At the back of this (dis)location is what Stronach and MacLure (1997) refer to as a contemporary 'un-ruliness' of knowledge. One aspect of this relates to the multiple sources of funding now available for research. As Gibbons *et al.* (1994: 79) point out, whereas the targeting of research through the use of market mechanisms leads to more 'mission-oriented research', the 'greater pluralism of research funds [contributes] to intellectual diversity, counteracting perhaps other prevailing trends'. Whilst we would not wish to be construed as saying that this diversity is solely an outcome of diverse sources of research funding, it is nonetheless a significant factor.

The unruliness that Stronach and MacLure (1997) write about can be understood as another way of referring to the decentredness of knowledge and the dedifferentiation mentioned earlier. This is the breakdown of fixed and bounded rules, the paralogy or dissensus about what constitutes knowledge and knowledge production manifested in the epistemological and methodological questioning or doubting which is a feature of globalisation and postmodernity. In this situation, we can begin to think of research as not only located in a hyper-real world (Baudrillard 1996) but as itself characterised by features that could be called hyper-real. It is here that we can begin to discern the connection between performativity and decentredness. In subverting the very notion of knowledge as something that has to be discipline based and validated by a scientific epistemology, and in undermining traditional ways of doing research, performativity demands both closed and open possibilities. As Gibbons *et al.* (1994) point out, knowledge can no longer be regarded as discrete and coherent, its production defined by clear rules and governed by settled routines. Instead, 'it has become a mixture of theory and practice, abstraction and aggregation, ideas and data. The boundaries between the intellectual world and its environment have become blurred...' (Gibbons *et al.* 1994: 81). As knowledge is decentred, the university itself is changing in parallel and related ways. As it begins to see itself in more managerial, corporatist and less consensual and collegial terms, the last itself being a particularly potent form of masculinist mythology, 'the knowledge which is its chief commodity has become diffuse, opaque, incoherent and centrifugal' (Gibbons *et al.* 1994: 83). As we have noted earlier, universities have become more consumer orientated, more dominated by a managerial discourse and a logic of accountability and excellence. Performativity therefore contributes simultaneously to both the strengthening *and* loosening of boundaries.

To return to Lyotard (1984) for a moment, it is worth reminding ourselves that he originally wrote his report in the late 1970s, at a time when computers did not have the speed, power and accessibility that they possess now, a time also before the World Wide Web had come into being and where the use of the Internet was still largely confined to the US military and a few large universities doing defence-related work. Lyotard's work does at one level seem remarkably prescient in relation to the link between performativity and new technologies, but at another level, as we have already seen, it is highly problematic. Lyotard (1984) did undoubtedly regard performativity as the villain of the contemporary moment and feared that its power, which he seemed to see in terms of a technological determinism, would produce a future of clearly dystopic dimensions. As Poster (1995: 92) argues, he saw information technology and CMC as 'complicit with new tendencies towards totalitarian control, not toward a decentralised, multiple "little narrativity" of postmodern culture'. Lyotard's answer to this dystopian threat was to throw open the databases and to encourage paralogy. As far as paralogy is concerned, what Lyotard failed to appreciate is that it is actually a *consequence*, albeit perhaps unintended, of performativity. Paralogy and performativity are linked to one another, therefore, rather than being polar opposites, in the same way that we might refer to *glocalisation* as an attractor in globalising processes rather than a continuum or opposition between the global and the local. Furthermore and related to this, Lyotard (1984) took a restricted view of technology, one which seems to relate it very strongly and exclusively to 'big science' and the demands of global capital. Whereas undoubtedly computer-mediated communication and the Internet can be seen as originating in the imperatives of military science, this has not limited their development. In other words, because of his restrictive view of technology, Lyotard did not anticipate the decentring which ICTs have facilitated and which are *intrinsic* to it. This perhaps explains why global capital has tried to control, for example, the Internet but has only been partially successful in so doing.

It could be argued therefore that performativity is paradoxical and has multiple significations. Once knowledge becomes a value-adding commodity rather than its pursuit being an end in itself, its production and transmission ceases to be the exclusive responsibility of researchers and teachers in the academy and becomes as it were up for grabs epistemologically and within multiple contexts of practice. Perhaps, therefore, it is more apt to read Lyotard's (1984) slant on technology as a metaphor for the knowledge-transformative potential of computers and to the opening up of new spaces where knowledge can be reconfigured in a more flexible, fluid and pragmatic way. Again, to quote Poster (1995: 92),

> the Internet seems to encourage the proliferation of stories, local narratives without any totalising gestures and it places senders and addressees in symmetrical relations; moreover these stories and their performance consolidate the 'social bond' of the Internet 'community'.

In any event, Lyotard did recognise that performativity accompanies a world of decentred knowledge even though he failed to recognise that it is a feature of this world, where with dedifferentiation the distinction between knowledge and information becomes problematic. Here, in a condition of endless production of information that ICTs and media technology enables and indeed fosters, there is an accessibility and connectivity more than has ever been the case hitherto for many more to much more. The point about performativity being a *feature* rather than simply an accompaniment of decentredness is that it is precisely in these conditions that performativity works best. Thus, what Lyotard (1984) misjudged is the nature of the relationship between performativity and decentredness. Rather than binary opposites as he understood them, they are more readily seen as interactive, with each the condition of possibility of the other.

This is what emerges from Stronach and MacLure (1997). As we have noted earlier, for them it is performativity that itself provides the conditions for hybrid research. This hybridity can take a number of forms. One such is the multi- and trans-disciplinary mixing that is present when research is located in specific contexts of application and geared to the production of transient practice-oriented, problem-solving knowledge. We shall have more to say later about this form of hybridity. The kind of hybridity that Stronach and MacLure (1997) refer to is somewhat different, although not unrelated. It involves a way of carrying out research that does not reject existing methodologies but rather injects an element of transgression in the spaces opened up by the new ways of carrying out research influenced by performativity. It recognises the conditions that make it necessary to perform research in this way, but rather than accept these passively hybridity seeks to 'play the game' while introducing a transgressive element. This is an interesting notion, but apart from examples from work by Stronach and MacLure (1997) there does not seem to be much of this hybrid research around. Perhaps, however, what they describe is best seen as another manifestation of the challenge to methodological realism, the hope for certainty through method and 'pretensions to naked unadorned truth' (Green 1998: 1) that have conventionally or epistemologically structured social research. Perhaps also it is a mark of the reflexivity which characterises much knowledge production even within the experimental sciences. The important point then is that hybrid research in whatever form resists closure and incorporation into an economy of the same. It is about working between the spaces, in an in-betweenness, a (dis)located research that simultaneously closes and opens spaces. This then is the tension which characterises contemporary knowledge production.

New modes of knowledge production

> The core of our thesis is that the parallel expansion in the number of potential knowledge producers on the supply side and the expansion of the requirement of specialised knowledge on the demand side are creating the conditions for the emergence of a new mode of knowledge production.
>
> (Gibbons *et al*. 1994: 13)

The perceived loss by universities of their status as primary producers of a particular kind of knowledge and, correspondingly, of their monopoly position as certifiers of valid knowledge production has significant implications for the latter. These developments are both cause and consequence of changes in modes of knowledge production and in their relative valorisation. This is an ambiguous situation, and questions such as 'what then is research?' and 'who is a researcher?' can be appropriately asked. For example, given the way that cyberspace has expanded through a logic that is both participatory and interactive, one of its effects has been to subvert the traditional conventions of authorship (Lankshear *et al*. 1996). As Peters (1996: 173) points out, 'the computer is restructuring our economy of writing, changing the cultural status of writing...altering both the relationship of the author to the text and of the author and the text to the reader'. In the process, there has been a weakening of the distinction between informal communication and scholarly publication, raising issues of quality and, ultimately, of legitimacy in the evaluation of that which is written. Academic conventions of peer review as a basis for establishing the validity and quality of research continue, but are not necessarily any longer the only and final word. This has made possible the repositioning of knowledge production as something not exclusively in the hands of university-based researchers. Here is another aspect of the tendency for the commodification of knowledge and the individualising of learning that ICTs have helped to bring about. However, as we have already noted, there is a countervailing trend as ICTs have also enabled a collaborative approach to learning, bringing together groups hitherto dispersed by physical and emotional distance.

Furthermore, in a move separate but also interlinked with performativity and with knowledge increasingly commodified, knowledge production has begun to move out of the ivory tower and into the marketplace – largely but not exclusively. For instance, as knowledge becomes a factor of production and becomes subject to commodification its market value increases, thereby requiring that access be restricted through patents and intellectual property law. It may thus be no accident that the notion of intellectual property rights has surfaced as an attempt to police the spread and use of certain forms of knowledge, even as knowledge transfer is encouraged as a key to systemic efficiency. In effect, the entrepreneurial benefits to universities and their commercial funders and/or partners of certain kinds of knowledge cuts across the power of computer-mediated communication to spread participation through open access. This itself has led to new forms of globalised hacking. Universities become part of a wider and globalised knowledge market, forced to compete with research and development companies, consultants and think-tanks. This involves, as Plant (1995) puts it, universities melting back into the circuits of culture from whence they came, although not 'imploding' as she also maintains. Despite the demands of performativity and the sheer explosion and disseminability of knowledge that characterises globalised conditions, universities are now less able to control the production and exchange of knowledge and access to it even whilst the assessment of that knowledge becomes an important way of maintaining control/standards, policed by audit bodies.

Different kinds of knowledge are being produced through the academy's forging of research partnerships with government, industry and other organisations and users, partnerships which have forced academics to question conventional discipline-sanctioned ways of doing research. Not surprisingly, the demands of performativity feature strongly in this situation, with the emphasis switching from enquiry to application, from ideas to outcomes, and away from the traditional academic virtues of discipline-based truth and the disinterested pursuit of knowledge. With these developments comes the need to think anew about what constitutes research and its relationship to pedagogy.

At this point, and as a means of looking at the impact of globalisation on knowledge production, we will focus on the distinctions in knowledge regimes first put forward by Gibbons *et al.* (1994). They distinguish between two modes of knowledge production, which they refer to as mode 1 and mode 2. The former produces culturally concentrated knowledge consisting of those intellectual products produced and consumed inside traditional research universities whereas the latter produces socially distributed knowledge that is problem-solving and task-specific, produced and consumed outside of traditional university settings. Although mode 2 is not exactly a new way of producing knowledge, according to Gibbons *et al.* (1994) it is becoming increasingly prevalent and has assumed a significant place alongside the traditional and hitherto dominant culturally concentrated knowledge of mode 1.

Globalisation and flexible capital accumulation seem to depend upon the ability to reconfigure knowledge, although new modes of knowledge production can also be seen as a consequence of globalisation and the reconfiguration of capital. At the same time, the capacity of so-called knowledge workers to process information and generate knowledge is seen increasingly as the source of productivity and of economic competitiveness, with notions of the knowledge economy gaining in popularity, if not in rigour. Lash and Urry (1994) have referred to contemporary socio-economic processes as a 'reflexive accumulation' where knowledge, flexibility and symbolic processing skills are key. In this economic environment, technological innovation becomes essential to keeping ahead. This requires the generation and deployment of new and specialised knowledge and also new structures and means of learning. Hence, the emphasis on lifelong learning and on learning flexibly. The demand for mode 2 type knowledge requires, and indeed depends upon, the sophisticated means of communication provided by ICTs. The information technology that has a global scope provides the means for the necessary access to knowledge production that itself is now global in its incidence. As Gibbons *et al.* (1994) argue, and as Lyotard (1984) foresaw, what is now needed is the bringing to bear of multi- and trans-disciplinary practices and perspectives to the solution of complex problems that involves a process 'being built around the clustering of innovations in information, computer and telecommunications technologies' (Gibbons *et al.* 1994: 125). Gibbons *et al.* (1994) refer to this as the new information technology paradigm, which they maintain is replacing one dominated by the technologies and organisations of mass production. This is a paradigm elaborated in debates about the existence, significance and causes of the shifts towards neo- and post-Fordism in the organisation of work to which ICTs are argued to be central.

The characteristics of mode 2 knowledge production have certain implications and raise several important issues in thinking about the role and place of universities in globalising processes. First, the global growth of higher education with consequent increases in the output of graduates has led to more people becoming familiar with and competent in knowledge production processes. Commitments to research-based professions and evidence-informed practice and policy become a possibility if not always an actuality. Here, although there remain important hierarchies in the production, reading and evaluation of research, it is no longer an activity reserved for a select group of academics. With the parallel growth of knowledge industries, many now work in ways which incorporate a research or inquiry dimension but where the worksite is no longer the university.

Second, there has been an expansion in the demand for specialised knowledge, a critical factor in determining any organisation's comparative advantage and competitiveness. Organisations have now become involved in a complex array of collaborative arrangements – collaborations that very often but not always involve universities. Furthermore, this demand is not purely commercial or located only in industry. It also originates in what Gibbons *et al.* (1994) describe as new markets for knowledge and expertise or 'hybrid fora', meeting points for a diverse range of actors. Examples of hybrid fora are public inquiries, government commissions and 'a whole spectrum of institutions, interest groups and individuals who need to know more about particular matters' (Gibbons *et al.* 1994: 12). As T. W. Luke (1996: 9) points out, 'specific problems of environmental protection, crime prevention, infrastructure re-engineering, or health monitoring for example, require trans-disciplinary teams with various heterogeneous methods to address a shared problem until it is mitigated or contained'.

Third, the task-focused context of application characteristic of mode 2 knowledge production means that it produces knowledge that is problem-solving in form and orientation, specific to the context of application (the next problem will be different because the context will be different), transient and eminently commodifiable. All of these are features that are argued to be absent in mode 1 knowledge.

Fourth, the nature of quality control is a characteristic which crucially distinguishes mode 1 from mode 2 knowledge production. Quality in mode 2 is not judged by purely technical or traditionally scientific criteria. Other questions also have to be asked, such as, for example, 'will the solution...be competitive in the market? will it be cost effective? will it be socially acceptable?' (Gibbons *et al.* 1994: 8). It is important to note here that, although these are criteria motivated by performativity, they also go beyond performativity construed in a narrow sense. It follows from this that mode 2 knowledge is not answerable to truth in the sense that disciplines define it, nor is it answerable to research paradigms and traditions in terms of the processes by which knowledge is produced and hence validated. Most importantly for our purposes, mode 2 knowledge production is output driven, not motivated simply by the spirit of curiosity and free enquiry and not seeking to discover the deep truths and underlying laws of the natural and social world. The focus is on application rather than contemplation, despite the pedagogies of reflection which are often to be found in the pedagogic practices of universities, where this itself is enacted as efficient technique.

The significance of mode 2 knowledge production for universities and university researchers cannot be underestimated. T. W. Luke (1996: 9) argues as follows:

> The long-term implications of Mode 2 knowledge production and consumption are only now being faced by many universities...whose key traditional source of legitimacy – their effectiveness at culturally concentrating homogeneous traditions of academic knowledge in hierarchical disciplinary canons at fixed intermural sites to teach the next generation the most valued wisdom from past generations filtered through the insights of the present generation – is being rapidly eroded by the apparent utility and flexibility of socially distributed knowledge.

He points out that there is a strongly held view that the culturally concentrated knowledge structures are mostly ill-adapted to the socially distributed knowledge requirements of individuals as lifelong learners and corporations as learning organisations.

Furthermore, mode 2 knowledge production poses particular problems for university researchers. The authority of mode 1 research in this environment means that the dominant mode of dissemination is the academic book, the scholarly refereed paper and the conference presentation. Mode 2 knowledge is disseminated or transferred much more informally, if at all, through such means as the summary report, the seminar and, increasingly, through online postings and other forms of electronically mediated communication. These developments pose problems of both a structural and a personal kind for researchers, given that for financial and managerial reasons universities have had to engage with mode 2 knowledge production. While mode 1 knowledge continues to be valued more highly than mode 2 in research assessment regimes, researchers producing mode 2 knowledge, although engaging in collaborative research, find their workload doubling by having to rewrite their mode 2 knowledge production into a mode 1 form. Of course where impact is of greater significance in such evaluations, the reverse may also be true. The important point to note is that what is involved here is not a matter simply of the most efficient and effective means of disseminating knowledge but of the very legitimacy of different kinds of knowledge production and the criteria by which knowledge is validated as worthwhile. It is research assessment in conditions of globalisation which brings these questions of legitimacy to the fore, questioning what is to count as research and how what is countable is to be demonstrated, enacted or performed.

The binary opposition which structures the argument and presents mode 2 knowledge production as a radical new departure, implicitly valorising it in relation to traditional and 'irrelevant' mode 1 knowledge production, is however both flawed and unhelpful. What perhaps is more helpful is to see modes 1 and 2 as always interlinked and interrelated, always existing in tension with, and yet necessary to, one another and changing in their relative valorisation through processes located in the larger socio-economic and cultural context. As Godin (1998: 478) puts it, 'there are probably not two modes of research but a single one – Mode 2 – with a varying degree of heterogeneity over time' – and, we would add, across space too. This now suggests another way of looking at the work of Gibbons *et al.* (1994). Godin (1998) argues that the model of new modes of knowledge production that they present is in effect a performative discourse. This means that in arguing for the reality of a new mode of knowledge production they are actually participating in its realisation. In other words, to put it simply, they are doing by saying, which may be the case for all texts, including this one. There is, therefore, a crucial sense in which *New Modes of Knowledge Production* is a key text of contemporary globalisation at a number of levels. First, and most obviously, it reports significant new trends in knowledge production, although the newness and uniqueness of these trends is, as we have seen, open to debate. Second, it brings to the fore certain dimensions of globalising processes in relation to knowledge production which we have noted as critical themes throughout this text, such as heterogeneity, hybridity, relationality, dispersal, the permeability of boundaries and what might be called the relational 'networkedness' of the contemporary. Third, it gives priority to the performative dimension of knowledge production. *New Modes of Knowledge Production* is both a celebration of performativity and an instance of the performative, itself a knowledge product which is also a performance. What it lacks, however, is a reflexivity about itself, an account of its own positioning as a text within the folds of globalisation.

Performativity and performance

Before closing this glimpse, we would like to pause reflexively for a moment to locate our own argument within this context. This is a context of knowledge production in the form of a writing of a very traditional kind (a mode 1 production?), yet a writing which can also be characterised as a performative performance, as it is both performative and a performance. Interestingly, as universities lose their position as the only site of valid knowledge production, the accountability of academics, and thus also of ourselves as academics, is heightened. Research assessment regimes are now not only a means for rewarding outputs but also an instrument of the performativity that the state in globalised conditions demands of universities. These regimes are a technology that responds to accountability and transparency (Strathern 2000), the need 'to tell and show people what you do'. As it is about showing, this public accountability is thus a semiotic process. Research has to be demonstrated in terms of the relevance of its quality outcomes and impact, whether this be in terms of research assessment regimes or in terms of collaborative projects with organisations in the 'real world'. In other words, performativity also implies and indeed requires *performance* for its realisation. It is the performance constituted by a process of enactive inscription that now provides the means to do this, itself a process of writing that *enacts* the identity of knowledge producers through their inscription in the documentation required by assessment regimes.

What we are arguing here therefore is that, leading as it does to pressures for accountability and demands for transparency, performativity both in a narrow sense and in the wider sense of performance has made research assessment a semiotic process. It has now become part of a sign economy where the commodity in which it trades, i.e. knowledge or *knowledges*, has a differential sign value with the significance and legitimacy of the sign value gained through a process of enactive inscription. Research assessment regimes then are not simply about stimulating and rewarding excellence as the public rhetoric proclaims. Knowledge is now a commodity tradable in the market and as a commodity in a consumer culture it has a sign value as well as a substantive value, with the former perhaps more significant than the latter. It could be argued, therefore, that the assessment process is now a matter of producing signs to be consumed by certain target audiences. These audiences are increasingly global in scope and to a large extent located outside the academic community. In a sense, it does not really matter whether it is mode 1 or mode 2 knowledge because their relative differential valorisation will be a matter of ebb and flow, always the site and stake of struggle. Even if mode 2 knowledge is given greater weight at any particular point in time, it will still be located in a process of enactive inscription. This sign production serves as a public and transparent demonstration of accountability, where accountability processes are now more and more taking over the hitherto dominant role of disciplinary/disciplining communities, although they are themselves not without disciplining features, albeit of a different kind. What we mean by this is that, while the process of enactive inscription means a greater degree of regulation, this is a different kind of regulation, one that works more through self-regulation than through external discipline. Performance is itself enfolded in power.

Those working in the academy are now involved in increasingly different and often new ways of producing knowledge at a time when definitions of research and knowledge are changing and are the subject of fierce debate. To take ourselves as an example – at the same time as we actively demonstrate the outcomes of our knowledge production (of which this book is a manifestation), we inscribe ourselves (literally), and through this are inscribed and identified as particular kinds of knowledge workers, demonstrating (or not) that we are in the business of producing relevant knowledge. While we are not arguing that what we are writing is false or is not about the real world, its truth in a disciplinary sense is not its main significance. This book as writing, as text, is rather an enactment within a practice of writing, both performative and a performance, but within a practice that now relates not only, or perhaps even mainly, to an academic community but is heavily implicated in the folds of globalisation.

Within these folds, the introduction of information technologies and CMC into the practices of knowledge production brings to the fore, and radicalises, the textuality of research texts, their status *as* inscriptions. Here, we are not referring simply to the computer as a handy tool for writing, significant though this is, but to the implications of the virtual or hyper-real for the very identity of the researcher. At the heart of the hitherto dominant modernist way of understanding knowledge production as representing the search for truth is the rational and humanistic researcher seeking to make original contributions to knowledge. This powerful narrative of how researchers should be governed and how they should govern themselves sees the identity of the researcher as forged by reason and the liberal values of the elite university. This narrative of knowledge production is enmeshed in the practices of academic communities who, even as they police research texts, also and at the same time establish boundaries for the identity of the researcher, boundaries grounded in the discipline, in both senses, of the particular community. But this identity formation is not explicit. Rather, the process is one in which the external real world is mirrored in a constructed internal real world of the researcher. When knowledge production is understood as the truthful representation of an external real world out there, so the researcher is represented as an authentic self, consciously governed by reason and liberal values. In other words, the real world out there is posited upon and itself posits a real world in here (Edwards 1997b) and vice versa. Thus the identity of the knowledge producer is centred, unified and authentic – mirroring the nature of the world which it comes to know through producing knowledge.

With globalisation rendering modernist notions of a centred world problematic and with knowledge itself decentred and commodified, there is a reconfiguring of researcher identity. In an increasingly hyper-real world of simulacra (or copies without originals), a narrative of authenticity no longer has the same legitimating power and the policing of boundaries is no longer so potent.

The possibilities of simulation enabled by ICTs in the production of texts means that researchers can produce multiple texts, so questions of authenticity, and indeed originality, become difficult to resolve. With the proliferation of texts, their differential production schedules and with the possibility for continual reworking, authenticity, origins and originality become problematic. Knowledge not only appears in a variety of forms and formats but there is also a need to foreground the intertextuality and significatory effects in practices of writing. 'Copy', 'cut' and 'paste' are not simply procedures in the literal construction of (plagiarised) texts but also a metaphor for the identity of the researcher in a hyper-real world of hyper(-real) texts.

Of course, the identity of researchers has always been shaped in one way or another. It is not a matter of modernist narratives of identity being overthrown for a situation where there is no regulation and no identity formation. Knowledge production and knowledge producers are always subject to some form of regulation and shaping of identity. We have argued that performativity is now a key element in the contemporary moment and that this involves performance. It is this which we suggest is becoming influential in regulating and shaping subjectivity and identity. At the same time, however, it is also necessary to add that this is a troubled regulation, subject to breaks, discontinuities and countervailing pressures. As we have seen, performativity can take many and seemingly contradictory forms. So too, performance as a power-knowledge formation can be in the service of regulation, even whilst it also enables a loosening of the constraints of the boundary marking of traditional disciplines.

However, the important point here is the foregrounding of performance, a foregrounding that accords with the contemporary significance of semiotic processes and notions of the hyper-real. In the so-called knowledge economy, based on the transforming by human capital of symbolic resources, the cultural and the symbolic are paramount. Performance is now widely recognised as a tool of assessment and the dominant social model of evaluation. We would argue that there are two aspects of globalisation that are significant in this context. First, communication in terms of new forms of mediation located within a consumer culture where communication is so closely implicated with an economy of signs. Second, there is the reconfiguration of knowledge where, again within a consumer culture, knowledge is commodified. In such a culture, commodities signify, they communicate values. For the academy, it is the intersection, constituted by globalisation, of signifying communication and knowledge commodification that now opens up a space wherein knowledge production takes place, and performativity with its many significations is located in that space of performance.

We have argued that with globalising trends and their manifold effects comes a contemporary unruliness of knowledge, a dissensus about what constitutes worthwhile or legitimate knowledge, a questioning of epistemological and methodological paradigms and academic values and cultures, and a growth of different forms of knowledge. The performative both reflects and contributes to this condition. The production of knowledge outside the academy linked to the self-surveillance of the researcher through processes of enactive inscription, the co-presence of closure and openness, conformity and transgression – all the contemporary trends subsumable under the performative – make it necessary to think anew about what constitutes knowledge, knowledge production and the knowledge producer in the (dis)locations of intensifying globalisation. These tendencies raise questions about the very identities and auto/biographies of knowledge producers and pedagogic workers more generally.

Glimpse six
Mobility, connectivity and learning

In this glimpse we explore more fully the significance of information and communication technologies (ICTs) and computer-mediated communication (CMC), the Internet and the World Wide Web (WWW) in relation to globalising processes, developments which we take to be both cause and effect of these processes. We argue that the development of ICTs has been both an instrument and a motor of change, and as such an essential if often problematic component of globalisation. In this glimpse we focus particularly on the relationship between immediacy, ICTs and globalisation and the impact of this relationship on knowledge, learning and pedagogy.

Cyberspace is a term that began life as a metaphor and has now become common usage for everything that is 'out there' in the virtual world of electronic communication. It signifies the network of sites that can be accessed over the Internet and the information available on that network, in principle accessible from almost anywhere on the globe. The term is often used simply to refer to objects and identities that exist largely within the computing network itself, so that a website, for example, is said metaphorically to 'exist in cyberspace'. In this sense, events taking place on the Internet are not therefore happening in the time and place where the participants or the servers are physically located, but 'in cyberspace'. Cyberspace therefore is a reality that can be nowhere localised even whilst its presence is everywhere.

Cyberspace figures as a cultural imaginary, an immensity, a non-physical terrain created by computer systems through which one can surf for networked information, a reservoir of data, always in the making, limitless in capacity, unbounded and with no final closure. This is a space potentially of perpetual interactions, yet, and subject to technological resources and limitations, a space relatively easy to move around in and within which to communicate. Being in cyberspace means being online, so it also signifies *connecting*, being in that virtual world in which Internet users live when they are online. It also signifies perhaps, once online, being part of a network that can be formed when computers and users get together. Like physical space, cyberspace contains objects such as files, mail messages, graphics, icons, moving images, etc., different modes of transportation and delivery, and different venues for expression.

Unlike other forms of space, exploring, and getting around in, cyberspace does not require any physical movement beyond pressing keys on a keyboard, using a joystick or moving a mouse. Once connected, a variety of activities become possible and it is these that constitute the network of relationships that *are* cyberspace. These activities encompass communicating, working and playing, all of which assume a significant part in many people's lives with more and more people defining and experiencing cyberspace as real. In an important sense then, cyberspace connotes *connectivity* and *relationality*, a networked world of relationality through connectivity, the enabling of a deepening and extending of relationality through the almost infinite connectivity that characterises globalising processes. As we have noted in previous glimpses, globalisation has led to an increasingly connected world where borders and boundaries of all kinds become less rigid and less predictable and where human interaction on an unprecedented scale across many borders, both physical and virtual, is shaping a different and interactive human/non-human environment.

ICTs, and here we include the mobile technologies of phones, PDAs and laptops in our framing, are significantly contributing to this refashioning of the social order. In other work, we have characterised the contemporary scene as a society of signs (Usher and Edwards 2007), a social order where image and text interplay and where an increasing range of electronic technologies play a significant part in multiplying a plethora of signs. We argued that symbolic exchanges mediate the social relations and materiality of the world through the production, circulation and reception of signs that often are detached from referents and yet have value or meaning in their own right. Here information, like images, does not have a definite connection with a fixed subject or a concrete referent but rather flows promiscuously, mirroring the infinitely expanding and 'promiscuous' Internet, stimulated undoubtedly by the doubling in the amount of information on its sites every five years.

This world of extended flows and global connections – of connectivity – contributes to an enveloping of the lifeworld. Correspondingly, as interconnection approaches growing extension, the experience of presence for many is reconfigured, with the lifeworld becoming both more technologically and semiotically textured. ICTs connect but also distance and, with social relations becoming electronically mediated, the need for the face-to-face presence of other humans seems to become less significant. The more virtual communication becomes widespread, the more humans become an 'absence' who are nonetheless still 'present', given that those online are still a very real 'presence' to one another. This is the notion of absence–presence to which we have already referred.

Whilst ICTs have led to new modes of communication and with that of learning, the question still remains as to whether the Internet provides a means for the better realising of learning for all. The promise that ICTs will lead to endless and low-cost connectivity making learning available any time, any place and for anyone has been invoked by the more fervid proponents of e-learning. Education, they claim, has been transformed in the process of taking up ICTs with the latter both expanding and transforming the learning process. Clearly, these claims must be treated with an appropriate degree of scepticism. There is still a long way to go before that promise can be fulfilled. At the same time it would be mistaken to go too far in the other direction and argue that ICTs are simply a more efficient tool. This assumes that the relationship between people and technology is one where the former manipulates the latter to achieve pre-given ends and does so from pre-given capabilities and subjectivity. This too is problematic. If ICTs are articulated merely as a more efficient tool, the socio-cultural effects that impact upon their implementation and realisation are thereby displaced: '...as long as we remain within an instrumental framework we cannot question it, define its limits or look to new media in relation to how it might generate new culture' (Poster 2001: 16). And, as Burbules (2000: 346) argues,

> in other spaces or places the characteristics of the environment are to some extent independent of the means used to represent them; but with the Internet these two levels are utterly intertwined. Paths of movement are also connections of meaning-making.

Even while they themselves are shaped by socio-cultural influences, technologies do have transformative power. The message is transformed by the technological mediation through which it is delivered and, in the case of ICTs, through which it is generated. Computer-mediated communication is in many significant respects materially reshaping the social order and culture, both through the practices it enables and the ways in which these are signified through changing metaphors of the social, not the least of which is the metaphor of the network itself. ICTs dematerialise communication, transforming the subject position of those so engaged, in the process configuring a new set of relationships between people and machines, and between machines and non-matter. With this ever-changing potential, ICTs therefore have a powerful effect on the reconfiguring of the relationship of technology to culture and computer-mediated communication does not simply provide better and quicker access to information but equally has the potential for developing new kinds of capabilities.

With electronic communication, where for the first time in the history of the world one person can now reach another person or a million with equal facility, ICTs increasingly shape many significant dimensions of life and practices. This is why understanding ICTs as just signifying more efficient and more widespread information storage and retrieval is very limited. By enabling new ways of communicating, they enable new forms of knowledge production and dissemination, as well as the fostering of new associations and connections among people. Here communication is an interactive creative process and as interaction has increased so too have come opportunities for new learning. All of this has an undoubtedly transformative potential and is already having an impact upon the what and how of people's learning, what it means for learning and for the means of learning and, perhaps most significantly, what is *meant* by learning.

Knowledge as the body without organs

It is argued that computerisation and electronic communication are significant dimensions of the knowledge complex that powers the contemporary globalised economy (Burbules 2000). With this has come an increasing commodification of knowledge, with its production, distribution and manipulation itself becoming a significant economic and cultural activity. Its capacity for commodification gives it a marketable value, with knowledge becoming 'intellectual property' that can be managed, guarded, and bought and sold. In this knowledge-based globalised economy where the emphasis is on the advantages in innovation that knowledge creation and management can bring, businesses have become dependent on ICTs to play out their strategic core activities in a global space in real time. Many would argue that the very basis of globalisation is innovation and, with the growth in the discourse of the knowledge economy, knowledge has been seen as essential to innovation.

The Internet signifies a radical change in the way knowledge is coded and valorised. For example, there is the dilution of institutional control over knowledge with knowledge now understood as being sourced in a multiplicity of sites. With ICTs, knowledge becomes globally transportable to the extent where it is now possible to talk of a multiplicity of transnational global knowledge webs. ICTs have enabled different kinds of knowledge to flourish as well as providing tools for new approaches to learning and knowing that go beyond the use of e-mail or the surfing of websites to include search engines such as Google, list servs, transportable databases, threaded discussions, chat rooms, and increasingly video-conferencing. With the Internet bringing to the fore abundant and accessible information, knowledge has increasingly come to be coded *as* information and vice versa. Due to the speed of dissemination, this very proliferation of information flows and their accessibility challenge long accepted definitions of what properly constitutes knowledge to the point where some would argue that there are no permanent structures of knowledge any more.

This ties in with something we have noted in earlier glimpses that what constitutes knowledge is now not solely bound and thus defined by disciplinary canons sourced in and policed by the university and academic communities. Whilst disciplinary knowledge itself is found in abundance on the Internet, so too all other kinds of knowledge flourish in its virtual spaces. Any individual or group with access to the Internet and with some computer literacy practices can develop their own knowledge and engage in its (virtual) publication, with someone, somewhere, accessing it and finding it useful. Here it is undoubtedly the case that the Internet is not only extending but also changing the *quality* of social interactions. By decentralising the apparatus of cultural production, by placing cultural acts in the hands of its participants, where people can create their own website and place their cultural products online, all web pages become 'publications' to be accessed. This trend is propelled by the very economy of the Internet, an economy where more is no more costly than less. Thus the 'value' of the Internet increases with every increase in its users and with every increase in its content. This is a built-in dynamic for exponential growth, for more and more connectivity. Virtuality therefore expands the possibilities for connectivity rather than reducing it, even as it reconfigures its forms.

There is also a removal of a time constraint, which results in an immediacy in communicating. This furthers knowledge creation and dissemination to escape closure even whilst knowledge itself becomes more ephemeral. Here it is worth noting that openness and ephemerality are characteristics which education often finds difficult to accept, given the traditional embodiment of knowledge in printed texts characterised by a seeming solidity, permanence, continuity and closure. Further, as fixity is subverted, whoever author-ises knowledge no longer necessarily has the same author-ity. Authorship, and thereby authority, is transferred from the writer to the reader in a process of decentring where readers can more readily shape meaning or manoeuvre it in whatever sequence or way they choose. What is happening here is that the source of author-ity is changing, since now it is what the online reader makes of knowledge that has a much more significant role in meaning-making. This trend is accelerated when online texts take the form of hypertexts, refashioned in the act of reading, where, as reading itself becomes subject to the logic of the screen rendering the reader an author, the stability and power of experts or authorities is subverted. As a consequence, canons and authorities are not so readily accepted or formed.

In effect therefore, and to deploy a Deleuzian term, knowledge assumes the form of a 'body without organs', decentred, multiple and less hierarchical. With permanent structures of knowledge subverted and knowledge sourced from a multiplicity of sites and deployed for a multiplicity of purposes, what is authoritative becomes less and less easy to recognise. Knowledge, we would argue, is created and re-created through connecting, the making and remaking of networked connections. This is witnessed in phenomena such as Wikipedia, wherein the monitoring of a mass of peers provides the basis for knowledge construction rather than it being transmitted by authorities subject to more restricted peer review.

Hypertext accelerates this process of making connections since it does not just break down the boundedness of disciplinary knowledge and disciplinary definitions of what constitute knowledge. Burbules (1997: 17) puts it this way:

> The conventions of writing...assume a fundamentally linear and hierarchical organisation of information with passage following passage in a sequence governed by (a) the relative importance, formalised in the discipline of the outline and (b) the narrative structure of argument formalised in the discipline of the syllogism.

This is the literacy of extended linear prose and the reading of books. The outline and the syllogism have defined the space of writing and in the West at least have been the predominant mode of communicating 'knowledgeably' since the advent of the scrolled parchment. Hypertext however marks a radical difference – a difference in keeping with the rhizomaticity of the Internet – nomadic, multiple and decentred networks in a constant state of flow and movement, continuously try-ing to avoid/evade being bounded or enclosed. Movements and flow are multidirectional, enabling a multiplicity of entwinements. As Deleuze and Guattari (1988: 21) put it,

> unlike trees or their roots, the rhizome connects any point to any other point, and its traits are not necessarily linked to traits of the same nature; it brings into play very different regimes of signs, and even non-sign states.

The point here then is that hypertext, hyperlinks and the logic of the screen (Kress *et al.* 2001; Snyder 2002) are not simply navigational conveniences but products as well as tools, real avenues of and for learning. The form of writing appropriate to hypertext is, argues Burbules, the bricolage and the juxtaposition and with these new expressive possibilities are opened up. These new forms of writing not only stimulate a different pragmatics of reading, they are also a differ-ent way of communicating 'knowledgeably' and hence have significant implications for pedagogy. It is perhaps therefore not surprising when the possi-bilities for reading and writing in different forms are multiplying that literacy has become such a touchstone of controversy in education.

Indeed it could be argued that the cyberspace is one enormous hypertext, with any one site potentially linked to all others – to some extent, potentially the all-encompassing library, particularly now that Google aims to put online every book ever published. Moreover, hypertext stimulates the formation of networks in the sense that there is a live link directly to other work. This associative link-ing enables relationships among people in addition to relationships between ideas and knowledge. Networks can be formed based on exchange of informa-tion, hobbies, games, interests, culture, or political leanings. The formation of these electronic affiliations or neo-tribes (Maffesoli 1996) links people in ways that would otherwise be impossible. And the significance here is that exchanges of information, games, etc. have traditionally not been considered 'knowl-edgable' activities involving learning but now it is recognised that learning is ever present there, even if it is only as a ghost haunting these networkings.

Through the space–time compression that ICTs make possible, networks with a global extension now have the *potential* to connect people everywhere and any time, with a seeming either absence of time and place when connected, or the development of alternative places and times, as can be found in sites such as *Second Life*. While this worldwide reality is virtual, it is nonetheless a virtuality that is no less *material*, a virtual that is realised through the bringing together of human and non-human actants. For those online, the separation and distance of geographical place has been replaced by existence in seemingly the same virtual space. The space of distance becomes rendered as one space, in effect no-space, and temporally endless as the immediacy of being online seems to undermine time as a constraint on communication. Place and time therefore no longer sig-nify the firm boundaries of the possible that they once were, with rhizomatic practices taking precedence over linearity. To put it another way, boundaries have become more permeable, porous and traversable with greater ease. In cyberspace there are networks with fewer borders, limits, or even rules.

The Internet, an ever-expanding continual, ongoing process, with its immediacy, accessibility and increasing ubiquity, is the most significant manifestation of ICTs. Whilst the argument of technophiles that the Internet will inevitably and fundamentally transform the social order and culture must be treated with appropriate caution, there is no doubt that the changes wrought by ICTs have had and continue to have an effect on communication patterns, relationships, knowledge creation and distribution, and learning. There is a sense in which to speak of the electronic landscape binding people together with instant connectivity is neither entirely metaphorical nor hyperbolic.

The Internet is above all a decentralised communication system. The possibilities of worldwide communication that would have been mind-boggling not so long ago are nowadays a commonplace. Indeed it is difficult if not impossible to conceive of ever returning to a situation where this mode of communicating did not exist. Who now apart from junk-mailers communicates by letter post? Even e-mail is considered old-fashioned and slow by young people, for whom texting and SMS-ing are the preferred forms of communication. For some, even the use of landline telephones is diminishing as a dominant communication medium. The Internet and the WWW have begun to revolutionise the way we communicate, not only with other individuals but with the world as well. Some would argue that it is almost impossible to imagine life without the WWW, without e-mail, without Google, without access to breaking news, no up-to-the-minute weather reports, no online shopping, no chatting with friends or with those with whom we share interests and hobbies, even though for many there is still no access to the Internet, let alone to all these other services. Not all can manage the expense involved in logging on to the Internet through an ISP and not all have bandwidth access.

With its interactivity and one-to-many broadcast capabilities, the Internet does have unique features that set it apart from other communication media. As we have noted, ICTs have helped shape a new set of expectations about knowledge that subvert certain educational traditions of reading, writing and linear print. People can communicate with and associate online, with others based on interest rather than geography. That interest may take many forms, not least the sometimes mundane aspects of chatting with friends or organising one's social life. Most important for our purposes, ideas and knowledge can be widely disseminated directly from individuals, no longer needing to be filtered through organisations and institutions. This is made possible by the decentralised and non-hierarchical structure of cyberspace – ruled by no one and relatively open to all – once again a body without organs – that in turn has produced new structures of interaction.

All this of course has affected learning. Learners are increasingly able to make their own decisions as to the best method for progressing their learning. They become aware that any learning is likely to have a number of, rather than a single, outcome(s). They become more open to an 'emulsified and combinatory intellect' (Cole 2005). ICTs enable learning that not only consumes knowledge, for example through copying text and browsing the Web, but also creates it, for example uploading material to share and collaborate, and programming, and thus, over time, 'the focus of activities moves from purely consumption (of other people's material) to the production and publishing of material, and finally to shared creation of new connections and knowledge' (Hartnell-Young 2003: 1).

A fast world

Over the last fifteen years or so the social order has increasingly been coded as one of 'fast capitalism' and 'fast culture'. In the early 1990s, writers of popular management texts coined the term 'new' or 'fast capitalism'. They argued that fast anticipatory action and quick responses were needed for 'just in time' or speedy ways of managing and doing things in the 'new work order' consequent on the growth of a hyper-competitive global market for goods and services. As we saw in an earlier glimpse, this was to some extent sourced in the perceived need to harness the information or knowledge embedded in the work process itself (Lash and Urry 1994), and for the new 'knowledge worker' demanded by this form of capitalism to be flexible enough to engage in a continual process of up-skilling and re-skilling; to engage in lifelong (l)earning.

In effect, the identity of the worker in the workplaces of fast capitalism has been fashioned, or more precisely refashioned, with knowledge and innovation, as we have noted earlier, now seen by many as critical to business success. In re-signifying knowledge in this way, fast capitalism has also re-signified learning as lifelong, reflecting the need for knowledge workers to keep up with the pace and intensity of a change characterised as never ending. Lifelong learning has become a key feature in the discourse and practices of economic rationalism where the needs and interests of the economy, of markets, and globalised capital are to the fore. This has been linked to the notions of a 'knowledge society' and a 'knowledge economy', social forms characterised by a ubiquity of lifelong learning, even though it is still not entirely clear what such a society or indeed what such learning might look like. Nonetheless, in this context, lifelong learning has come to be articulated as essential to the development of fast capitalism and the knowledge economy, in the process, as we have already indicated, raising critical questions as to what kind of pedagogy is most appropriate.

One of the most significant characteristics of fast capitalism is its de-territorialising thrust that both mirrors and reinforces the society of signs mentioned earlier. As Deleuze and Guattari (1988) argue, capitalism in its sole concern to maximise profits must subvert all territorial groupings, such as the church, the family, the group, indeed any social arrangement. What is discernible here is a movement from fixed and relatively closed structures – traditions, institutions, work practices, place and nation states – to relatively more fluid ones – the relative porosity and traversability of boundaries we mentioned earlier. Signs, it is argued, begin to flow freely and promiscuously with no clear connection to a subject or a concrete referent. As the society of signs takes hold, the lifeworld becomes semiotically textured, with social life becoming more *virtual* – a trend that is of course accelerated with the growing impact of ICTs.

As we have noted in many places throughout this text, there is considerable agreement that ICTs and computer-mediated communication have the effect of compressing space and time. This, in turn, has significantly both contributed to and resulted from the exponential growth of globalising processes and fast capitalism. Furthermore, and alongside this, there has occurred a culturalisation of work and civil society with a growth in importance of culture and lifestyle practices in the aestheticisation of life and the cultivation of identity. The culture industries spread out from the realm of production to the realm of culture and commodify the latter. The boundaries between high culture, popular culture, the market and everyday life become blurred or at least less fixed (Lash 1990; Featherstone 1991). In effect, everything becomes 'culture' with a culturalisation of the material world of goods and products that goes alongside a materialisation of the world of culture. With the proliferation and accelerated circulation of signs, there is a hyper-commodification and mediatisation of culture. Thus, as fast capitalism intensifies and grows ever more competitive, culture is turned into commodity signs and itself becomes fast. Images and information, signifiers as cultural artefacts, become pre-eminent hallmarks of economic growth and innovation. Signifying practices, the production and re-production of meaning through communicative media, whether via the word/symbolic, the visual/iconic or via contiguity/indexicality, have now become central to fast capitalism and fast culture, critical to the process of generating and reproducing value in the global economic system.

Here then we can begin to foreground the significance of speed and its correlate, immediacy, that is very apparent in the space–time compression of ICTs. We can ask, therefore, what then is the relationship of globalising processes to speed? What impact does this have on immediacy and connectivity and from this on learning and pedagogy? If, for example, learning is now more mobile, what does this do to more contemplative traditional notions of learning, based upon long and slow immersion in books and other printed texts?

There is an abundance of statements that the speed of technological change is transforming the social order and that in a technologically driven global culture no aspect of life is left unchanged. It is almost a truism to say that we now live in a world where it is possible to travel virtually from one end to another in a matter of seconds. Time has become not only individualised but also highly accelerated. The vastly increased speed of communication has been identified as being of key significance in the interactions that people, particularly young people of the so-called Net generation, have with each other. Thus, as we have indicated, for some students even e-mail is already a slow, old-fashioned technology. All of this highlights the impact of speed and the way it is altering consciousness and subjectivity.

There is a doubled aspect to speed here. First, there are the ways in which aspects of change are coded as speeding up or fast, including of course changes in the contemporary forms of capitalism and culture. Second, there are the effects of speed on hitherto settled and bounded meaning-making practices as meaning-making itself becomes increasingly on the move. What then does this imply for the bodies of knowledge that are often positioned as 'that which must be learnt'?

As we have seen, there are various discourses of globalisation currently in the ascendant that are fast overtaking the globe, in the process creating a fast globe. These are reflected and enacted in a whole ensemble of specific practices. All are linked to what can be referred to as a doubled movement of the 'will-to-speed' and of governmentality. The will-to-speed, or dromology (Virilio 1986), is realised in the destruction or compression of space. Here the principle of the 'desire to get somewhere', of mobility in its many forms and very often for its own sake, reduces the space of the world to a virtual no-thing, in the process precipitating the epoch of globalisation. What Virilio refers to as 'dromocratic power' releases this will-to-speed, where the 'violence' of speed precipitates the implosion of space. Speed becomes a higher realm of ordering to which people become subordinated. Virilio argues that in particular the speed of technology is continually accelerating and, as it does so, it produces the paradoxical effect of slowing the movement of people to a standstill. It is this inertia that brings about the contraction of the sense of expansiveness of space and place. As the technologically textured spaces people inhabit increasingly enlarge, with the instantaneous access to those spaces increasingly enabled by changes in communication and transportation, so correspondingly their experience and the signification of place disintegrates.

As for governmentality, the proliferating discourses of risk, competition, self-monitoring, efficiency, effectiveness and excellence clearly signify the ways in which technologies based on speed work to order the world into which people are 'thrown'. The increased possibilities for surveillance and regulation are the downside of globalising processes sourced in speed. Each element, the will to speed and governmentality, feeds on the other. The 'strata' of the disciplinary society or the society of control, now significantly augmented by the activities of the national security state, actively produces this violence in a variety of forms, for example the factory, the prison, the school, as a governmental technology for the ordering of populations (in Virilio's terms, 'populations at speed'). We are 'lost in space' through the will-to-speed.

What we would like to highlight here, however, is that this technologically induced speed makes possible the *immediacy* of the Internet, with the consequence that the world is itself re-signified as an electronic space, a space of infinite and fast flows. As we have noted, ICTs have made increased interconnectivity possible on a global scale, bringing about a state of *hyper-connectivity*. Here, hyper-connectivity signifies not only connections in a quantitative sense of the Internet, but also refers to a situation where it is impossible to envisage the world and one's place in it as not being *always already* connected or, to put it another way, as being fashioned and existing through connections and through connecting. This is the thrown-ness referred to earlier. In other words, we are thrown into an already connected world and we cannot now imagine living in a world without that connectivity – and as a result the latter becomes more and more apparent.

This notion of hyper-connectivity blurs any distinction between the connected and the not-connected, or between the abstract and the virtual, the concrete and the face-to-face. The structure of this *always already connected* space is that of the network, here signifying both the complex patterning of interactions and positionings that now takes place on a global scale, and to cyberspace itself which makes this complex network possible and is itself an effect of that patterning. This condition of hyper-connectivity shapes the contemporary world, both physically and in terms of subjectivities. As forms of connectivity become ever more significant, it is therefore no accident that individualistic accounts of learning are being displaced by relational understandings, such as are found in conceptualisations of learning drawing upon activity theory, situated learning theory, complexity theory or actor-network theory.

With speed collapsing time and space constraints, transforming the 'what' and 'how' of communication, the impact of the Internet is not just a matter of changes in styles of communication, but, more importantly, it also creates new relationships among people, and new possible meanings for their relationship with knowledge and learning. Consequently it has effects in relation to power and control, and thus of the relative balance between meaning-making and meaning-taking, with important implications for pedagogy and learning.

Pedagogy and learning

> As technologies like computers, telephones, televisions, and new multimedia devices converge computer-mediated culture will continue to provide an encompassing environment in which people work, play, relate, learn, and internet. Becoming computer-literate in this broad sense thus requires expanding notions of literacy and learning how to create, communicate, and interact in novel cybercultures.
>
> (Kellner 2000: 8)

The condition of thrown-ness or hyper-connectivity highlights what it means to be in a globalised world, where the distinction between the real and the virtual is not the same as that between the material and immaterial. We have suggested that, although still a distinction with some potency, the distinction between the real and virtual when exploring the significance of ICTs is nonetheless not very useful in framing the practices in which learners are actants. In principle what hyper-connectivity means for learning is that potentially it can be just-in-time, just-when-needed, and always-there. On the face of it, this represents the ideal conditions for the realisation of the dream of lifelong learning for all.

However, behind this aspiration, issues to do with both access and meaning loom large. Both the cost of access for many and, as we noted, the practices needed to make full and productive use of the Internet's potential for learning are far from resolved. These issues continue to militate against the *actuality* of learning that potentially is made possible. And even if access issues could be resolved, learning of this kind and in this way would not sit too easily with institutionalised education.

The problem lies in the very fact that education is *institutional* whereas learning can be, and increasingly is, located outside of formal institutions of education. Potentially, the further development of hyper-connectivity could mean many more people identifying themselves as learners, and moreover as learners who do not need to go to an institution of learning in order to learn. There is a foregrounding here of what individuals and networks of learners consider worth learning, not what an institution tells them they *ought* to learn. Behind this in turn is a contestation over what is to count as learning and what constitutes 'worthwhile' knowledge and legitimate ways of knowing. Is learning outside of educational institutions 'really' learning? Is it worthwhile learning? Is learning through the Internet at best only the pursuit of hobbies and interests, at worst the accumulation of trivia?

It could be argued that one of the reasons why the Internet and its associated technologies have inspired such unprecedented adoption is because they can more quickly and easily increase the learner's capacity to make connections, particularly connections to *content, context and community* – all of which can result in more extended and powerful learning experiences. With the Internet making information more readily available than ever before, learners can make rapid connections to virtually any content. With this comes the need for learners to be able to sift through and select from the mass of data made available – to become critical consumers of what is abundantly available. Even more powerful connections can be made using ICTs to connect learners to the context of what they are learning. With ICTs even learning discipline-based knowledge can place curricular content in a richer context that enhances the extent to which content can be understood as relevant and applicable. But most important, perhaps, is the way ICTs can enable connections to community to be created that bring people together as learners. Tools such as e-mail, list-servs, threaded discussions and synchronous chat rooms make possible the collaborative potential of learning.

It is certainly the case that, in educational settings, we have witnessed the development in an exponential way of greater connectivity and networking with faster networks leading to newer services and from thence to new uses (Garrison and Anderson 2003). Electronic networking has penetrated into all academic disciplines and formal bodies of knowledge, in the process expanding the space of learning environments. From this it has been argued that

> the true power of...Internet technologies...may lie not only in distance and asynchronous learning, but also in their ability to foster hybrid models of interactive learning involving in-class, online, faculty-driven, student-driven, synchronous, and asynchronous options...we are most inspired by the potential of the Internet to bring diverse educators and students together, helping us connect with learning and learners from around the world.
>
> (Milliron and Miles 2000)

Some go so far as to argue that this virtualisation is creating a global learning space, the 'global matrices of minds'. Others would question these developments, arguing that since mutual relations of presence are necessary in producing and using worthwhile knowledge, such relations are not possible online. This is an aspect of the wider questioning concerning the possible replacement in meaningful communication of face-to-face interaction by electronic connectivity. The argument here is that even if there really are networks in virtual spaces these are so ephemeral and anonymous that they always limit the Internet's potential as an educational and maybe a learning space; 'no longer are individuals "commanding presences" for each other; they have become disposable experiences' (Borgmann 1992: 102). It may therefore be unsurprising that issues of social presence have become significant among those concerned with the development of e-learning (Garrison and Anderson 2003).

Nonetheless the impact of the Internet and the WWW has provided fertile ground for changes in what learning means. Here, signifiers of space and boundaries have proved particularly potent. For example, as we noted earlier, it is argued that education's 'spaces of enclosure' of the book, the classroom and the curriculum have always worked to en-close meaning and experience such that learning becomes the extraction of a singular canonical understanding and teaching the exercise of authority in terms of correct interpretation and accuracy. Knowledge is understood as expressed through denotative meaning, 'out there' waiting to be found. In cyberspace, however, these spaces of enclosure are called into question since with a more readerly environment knowledge no longer simply involves the consumption of fixed and definitive meanings. The logic of the screen enables an assembling of pages and sites in non-linear ways, and the interplay of image and text, giving rein to the serendipity of the library shelf but with scrolling replacing strolling. Knowledge can be fashioned through increasingly diverse truth-telling practices.

As we have hinted earlier, rather than being a matter of absorption of the knowledge produced by disciplinary experts it becomes something that can be created by individuals or groups. Mirroring the rhizomatic features of cyberspace, meanings become less bounded and hierarchical, more readily negotiable by users. If people do not simply assimilate accepted understandings but actively participate or collaborate in their creation, they are consequently more likely to understand their own identity to be that of a 'learner' and more likely to be in a position to determine their own learning and paths of learning. It may not be surprising therefore that with this multiplicity comes a corresponding crisis narrative around educational standards, a narrative that seeks to stabilise certain practices and meanings as more educationally worthwhile than others.

A significant aspect here also is changes in the means or paths of learning. Here, it is plausible to talk of a 'Net generation' of those who were born during or after the 1980s and who have spent thousands of hours logged on to the Internet in their formative years. There is an immersion in a globalised popular culture, expressed through the consumption of globally potent signs and images. This has not only stimulated learning online but has also meant new learner identities which subvert a classroom model of pedagogy. They appear to share a number of characteristics:

- The hours spent online appear to have affected not so much what but *how* they think.
- They have a highly developed level of visual literacy and are able to weave together texts, images and audio.
- They are oriented to fast- and multi-tasking.
- They make no distinction between physical and virtual reality and can move quickly between these worlds.
- As learners, the Net generation clearly perceive the open space of the Internet and the WWW, of Google and Wikipedia, as their information universe and they prefer these as a way of researching.
- They have hypertext minds in the sense that they can leap around, piecing together information from multiple sources. They are not into careful investigation, placing more value on speed than on accuracy.
- They thrive on interactivity, e.g. online SMS and messaging. They tend to have poor listening skills but they do like to learn with others.

Here it is worth reminding ourselves that, as we saw in an earlier glimpse, this culture is one where a fragmented sense of time leading to reduced attention span and an impatience with sustained enquiry is very likely to be prevalent. What is invariably construed by an older generation as impatience is something the Net generation consider immediacy – in cyberspace responses have to be fast; anything that is not immediate has little value.

What is significant in all this for our purposes is, first, the critical importance of online resources in providing the *content* of learning; second, the use of online tools as a prime *means* of learning; and third, the enabling possibilities opened up by speed in communicating and interacting – itself the condition of possibility for the content and means of learning. Of course all these developments pose significant questions for institutional education at all levels. All the modernist signifiers of centre, margin, hierarchy and linearity, proximity and familiarity can be turned on their heads, with a consequent questioning of modernist systems and frameworks of education. Most important perhaps is the subverting of the notion that learning in order to be authentic and worthwhile must be something that has to be slow, in depth and drawn out over an extended period of time.

Now the signifiers are more those connoting multi-linearity, nodes, links and networks. Cyberspace can be deployed to undermine rhetorically and performatively the apparent stability and coherence of all aspects of the educational project of modernity, even as audit, standards and standardisation are increasingly invoked in an attempt to halt the cultural tide that the very processes of globalisation supported elsewhere have unleashed. This challenging provides resources for justifying changes in what constitutes knowledge, the way it is produced (research), organised (curriculum), presented and disseminated (the book), delivered (pedagogy), justified (face-to-face participation) and the time of learning (the course) as well as the spaces of learning (the classroom).

At the same time, cyberspace's new forms of textuality, intertextuality and hypertextuality are producing a re-signification of the subject, in the sense both of the person and the curriculum. Learning can now be more readily signified in terms of multiplicity, of multiple paths, nonlinear forms, moving from the fixed institution-based space of education to the more open and unbounded terrain of learning. Here learning has the potential to become, and to be understood as, mobile and more immediate. In the virtual classroom (that need not necessarily be at a distance), the focus moves along a continuum from teacher as the central authority transmitting knowledge through the written text and responsible for validating input and encouraging consensus, to the learner pursuing a multiplicity of contextually defined goals in a variety of associational ways. And perhaps it is the dangers of these developments to governmentality and the social order that have resulted in the ever greater emphasis on specified outcome, accountability and audit, as the potential for learning to undermine education becomes ever more apparent.

With these developments the emphasis shifts potentially to a pedagogy that is more self-directed (learner-centred) and purpose-driven (interest- or problem-based), and which therefore can encompass a multiplicity and variety of changing goals and purposes. With this comes the potential for a re-coding of the teacher–student relationship. On the Internet each can be an expert, given the abundance and availability of information in the sites and networks of that space. The phenomenal growth of Wikipedia is perhaps the best example of this logic. The argument is therefore that the skills of accessing, evaluating and using the knowledge found in cyberspace are what is most needed. With these developments have come calls for an emphasis on new literacies – multi-literacies, silicon literacies, IT literacies and the like – all of which involve image as well as text, and the emergence of what Kress (2000) refers to as a 'logic of the screen' that is displacing the 'logic of the page', where the focus is on the multimodality of meaning-making and meaning-taking practices. As we noted in an earlier glimpse, there are greater possibilities for the development of meta-level awareness and reflexivity. As Kellner puts it:

> computer literacy involves learning how to use computers, access information and educational material, use e-mail and list-serves, and construct websites. Computer literacy comprises the accessing and processing of diverse sorts of information proliferating in the so-called 'information society'. It encompasses learning to find sources of information ranging from traditional sites like libraries and print media to new Internet websites and search engines. Computer-information literacy involves learning where information is found, how to access it, and how to organize, interpret, and evaluate the information that one seeks.
>
> (Kellner 2000: 8)

Knowledge comes to you, rather than you going to it

With the Internet becoming an important form of communication and having significant implications for pedagogy and learning, questions of access assume a greater significance. Connectivity depends on speed as increasingly we expect to be connected speedily. One of the reasons why the Internet has impacted on learning is because it has the characteristic of immediacy – we can find content immediately and the tools we need to find what we want to learn are very often immediately to hand. And underlying immediacy is the ease of speedy connection and if we don't have this – as indeed those without bandwidth access are unlikely to have – then the Internet's potency for learning largely disappears.

This issue of ensuring immediacy is usually cast as one of ensuring that everyone has access to the Internet. From the standpoint of widening educational participation through electronic connectivity this is important but it is not the whole story. The downside of hyper-connectivity is that for many who seek to use the Internet it is very often a bewildering maze. Navigating this maze thus becomes critical and implies, as we have noted, a clear need for some kind of Internet semiotics and literacies as well as the skills to make use of content when found. Access therefore is more than just having the ability to use a computer to access the Internet and to able to access the Internet speedily. It is also about learning and developing the necessary semiotic practices – and this in a context where even print literacy is still not as widespread as would be desirable.

At the moment then, whilst it is undoubtedly the case that both the Internet and electronic communication generally are here to stay, the potential impact on learning and pedagogy could be limited by, first, the speed at which bandwidth becomes the norm and, second, the speed at which the necessary skills and practices become disseminated. As far as the former is concerned, immediacy and the impact this has on learning is lost unless there is a much greater access to bandwidth facilities. With the latter, it is only those who have the necessary skills, and those located within the necessary practices, that will be in a position to take full advantage of the Internet for learning and as learners.

To bring this glimpse to a close and drawing on the conceptual resources provided by Deleuze and Guattari (1988), we would argue that learning can be considered both as strata and as rhizomatic. As the former, it is a vital component in contemporary governmentality and the globalised market form that capitalism now takes. To that extent, the mobility and multiplicity of learning that we have foregrounded is likely to be limited. But if as we have argued earlier the Internet is more rhizomatic than stratified, connecting people in all sorts of unexpected and immediate ways, then learning becomes more like lines of flight that cannot be totally fixed and regulated by totalising strata, where learning assumes one dominant and definitive meaning.

Of course, learning has always been subject to stratifying, to a coding that attempts to fix it in place definitively as one thing and one thing alone. But in cyberspace learning can stretch and be stretched, connect and be connected, across time and space in unexpected and multiple ways, in rhizomatic ways, very often making both intended and unintended senses. As well as the learning allowed and valued by socio-cultural and educational strata, learning is much more likely to come about through the connections that people make rhizomatically in cyberspace.

Glimpse seven

Pedagogies of (dis)location – (dis)locating pedagogies

> Globalisation in this [post-colonial] guise has had dramatic effects, effectively dislocating and dis-locating (in any number of senses of those words) the story of modernity as it used so often to be told.
>
> (Massey 1999: 28)

We have explored now the notion of globalisation and suggested some of the uncertain reframings which appear to be possible both as a response, a contribution and, indeed, as part of it. Following this, we have suggested that many attempts to reframe pedagogy in the current period remain contained within modernist assumptions which construct globalisation as an extended form of internationalisation and tend to produce forms of relocation where people are still 'kept in their place', even whilst there is a diversification of places within which they/we can be kept. The pedagogic zoo may have become more exotic in some senses, but those within it are still kept apart. An obvious question to which we need to respond, therefore, is that of the significance of globalisation as we have framed it for pedagogy.

The first, important, point is that we do not wish to put forward a single notion of pedagogy for globalised times – *the* pedagogical response to globalisation or *the* globalised pedagogy. This is reflected in the title of this glimpse in which we talk of *pedagogies*. The second point is that given the increased importance given to space and the increased use of spatial metaphors to help to understand both pedagogical and other cultural practices, we ourselves wish to pursue a particular metaphor, that of (dis)location. This emerges from the attempt to occupy a space of movement, a non-space in a closed and bounded sense, a space of meeting and engagement with the de-territorialising and re-territorialising practices of the contemporary period. We attempt to go beyond the binary of location/dislocation that is to the fore in many influential conceptions of pedagogy and politics in certain parts of the globe. The ground upon which we stand therefore is a diaspora space, one which 'often invokes the imagery of the trauma of separation and dislocation...But diasporas are also potentially the sites of hope and new beginnings' (Brah 1996: 193). Here, it is necessary to remind ourselves of the reflexive point that, in positing pedagogies of (dis)location as a way of examining practices in, and developing practices for, globalisation, we ourselves and this text are subject to the self same (dis)location.

This glimpse therefore attempts to sketch out a general framework for pedagogies in the spaces opened by what has gone before. It will do this through a separate examination of the two structuring notions that we have brought together – dislocation and location. We will then outline more fully our notion of pedagogies of (dis)location and briefly attempt to illustrate its potential interpretative and practical power for those who wish to engage in, and with, globalisation, including challenging its various dimensions. At this stage, the analysis will be largely conceptual, although reference will be drawn to specific practices where appropriate.

Dislocation and dispersal

In glimpses two and three, we made mention of the feelings of dislocation which are held to be part of the disruptions of relatively stable patterns experienced by many in different parts of the globe in contemporary times. This suggests that dislocation is a psychological experience, but one, as Massey (1994) points out, associated with very real forms of an economic, social, political and cultural disturbance. As Massey also notes, the sense that dislocation is only a current phenomenon is misplaced and may reflect more the experiences of certain groups who were previously unaffected by these practices. Here, dislocation may have well not been given so strong a voice since it only affected the less powerful, although Bhabha (1994), among other post-colonial writers, argues that formerly colonial subjects experienced a form of dislocation associated with a profound splitting of identity, a splitting that also acted back on the colonialist, engendering both a dislocated and a dislocating identity. What might be said then is that the experience of dislocation has intensified and spread because of the compressions of space–time and the ambivalence produced by and through globalisation.

Dislocation can be seen in ongoing acts of dispersal associated with the increasing spread of capitalist relations around the globe and the integration of local into global markets. Whereas the early processes of modernisation and industrialisation brought people together in large-scale industries in a particular part of the globe, for example Western Europe and North America, the speed of communication and transportation now enable large manufacturing and service industries to be dispersed around the globe, exploiting the low production costs and workforce skills most appropriate to the types of business involved. These produce new patterns of urbanisation, as has been witnessed spectacularly in recent years in China. However, at the same time, the processes of urbanisation associated with industrialisation and mass production – the need for a secure and readily available supply of labour – are being challenged by developments in flexible specialisation. There has been an increasing use of distancing strategies in the organisation of workplaces. Employers have relocated outside the previously dominant urban areas and, in many countries, home-working has increased. This dispersal of working populations and the restructuring of employment opportunities accompanies contemporary experiences of dislocation. We are witnessing a wide range of dislocations as part of global dispersal and compression of space–time.

Inevitably such processes are uneven, as are what they engender and the differing ways in which they are experienced. For example, China is undergoing a massive process of industrialisation in which the migration from the rural to urban areas between 1984 and 1994 has been estimated at 90 million people (BBC2, *The Giant Awakes*, 12 March 1994). However, that process of industrialisation is dependent on the technological advances and global integration of the economy and these have a different impact elsewhere, for example where deindustrialisation and the growth of service industries has been to the fore. The flows of capital are not necessarily matched by flows of people as many countries harden immigration rules, a hardening that itself points towards the increased impetus for migration.

In certain parts of the globe, geographical distances between paid work, unpaid work and leisure are increased for many by communication and transport possibilities that reduce the need for the concentration of populations into a few urban conglomerations. Thus, while physical distances increase, technologies enable people, goods and services to be brought together. At its most extreme, this now allows the possibility of some not having to go to a workplace at all. They may live some distance from their employers, but technology – for example faxes, modems, broadband – enables them to have all their activities, including learning, located in the space of their own homes. People are able to work increasingly 'at a distance', but nonetheless to be in constant contact and therefore available to their employers and of course subject to their surveillance (Rosen and Baroudi 1992).

Processes of dispersal and dislocation can be seen also in the deployment of new information and communications technologies in education and training, particularly in forms of distributed, flexible and e-learning. As the relationship between learning and face-to-face interaction is broken, so the necessity for people to attend specific places of and for learning at specific times is undermined. Here the *place* of the learner – their learning setting – rather than that of the provider is brought to the fore. Geographical dispersal and the compression of space–time mean that learners and providers no longer need to be in the same place, let alone the same country, but are increasingly available to each other on a global scale through the various forms of media. As we mentioned earlier, Evans and Nation (1992: 181) suggest that 'distance education and open learning have been key dispersal agents' in the movement towards a post-industrial society.

However, it is necessary to position these relations in relation to globalising trends. The very distances covered bring places together and compress space–time, thereby dislocating traditional pedagogic practices and assumptions. The extent of this process is dependent in part on the media through which the learning is made available. The sending of printed materials through the post brings about a specific spatial–temporal relationship between places, one which is transformed through, for instance, the use of computer networking. The dispersal of work, employment and leisure is supportable through dispersed forms of learning, that enable learning to take place in settings closer to other aspects of the learner's life. As workplaces become dispersed, so too do the opportunities to learn, a situation which ironically may result in *relocation* more than dislocation as possibilities increase for people to be 'kept in their place' geographically, even as that space traversed as it is by the effects of globalisation becomes ever more diasporan.

All of the above offer different forms of dislocation for those involved, the effects of which may be diverse. For instance, Bernstein (1996: 76) suggests that the current phase of capitalism has created a 'disembedding of identities and so...the possibility of new identity constructions'. These he terms decentred, retrospective and prospective. Decentred identities are constructed from market or therapeutic resources. Retrospective identities are constructed from grand narratives of culture and religion. Prospective identities involve a re-centring of identity around gender, race and region as a way of providing a new base for connection and collectivity. For Bernstein (1996: 80), the 'dislocation between the organising principle of identity formation, internal and external to education, may well be an important condition for critical reassessment of educational institutions and the principle and focus of their discourses'. While we agree with this sentiment, we also feel, however, that the typology offered by Bernstein maps the terrain too tidily. Nonetheless it does indicate that any suggestion that dislocation is solely a negative phenomenon is too simplistic, investing it with an inherent meaning, just at the point when we wish to argue for the slipperiness of signifiers. Dislocation is in our view a far more complex and mixed experience than is often suggested. Indeed, as Bernstein (1996) argues, it can also offer positive opportunities, with the disruptions associated with dislocation also offering different openings and possibilities.

In his influential study, Laclau (1990) used the term 'dislocation' specifically to characterise contemporary social formations with a plurality of centres that engender a condition of de-centredness where no fixed essential identities can be produced. In this condition, new and multiple identities emerge from a multiplicity of centres and locations. The openings engendered by dislocation allow for the possibilities of politics and for diverse actors to work together politically for progressive change, which is no longer gained through the emancipation of the working class as the universal representative of humanity but through the range of dislocated struggles conducted by diverse social actors.

In many ways, Laclau's (1990) position is consistent with our own and dislocation in this sense could be characterised as the diaspora space of globalisation. However, significantly, Laclau does not analyse dislocation spatially. Indeed, as Massey (1993) argues, Laclau (1990) works within a traditional distinction of space and time, wherein the temporal frames politics against an inert background of space. Ironically, he positions the spatial metaphor of dislocation within the temporal. Thus, Laclau (1990: 41) argues that 'dislocation is the very form of temporality. And temporality must be conceived as the exact opposite of space – the "spatialisation" of an event consists of eliminating its temporality'. The space of politics and possibilities and the politics and possibilities of space are thereby rendered silent. A history is made on, rather than in and through, space; and, as Massey (1993: 149) argues, there are strong gender assumptions in such positions – 'where time is dynamism, dislocation, and History, and space is stasis, space is coded female and denigrated'. This points to the significance of the spatial to and for feminism, and with that maybe a particular range of openings engendered through contemporary globalising processes. It is certainly the case that the notion of location is central(!) to much feminist writing, a point that will become apparent as we turn to the discussion of differing conceptions of location.

Location and identity

Like other concepts, location opens a space within which and about which its nature is discussed and contested. The politics of location have been critical to certain strands of feminist thinking, but implicitly have a wider and longer history/geography than that. This can be formulated in a number of different ways. For instance, it can be constructed as the place where one stands, a bounded space from which to defend one's territory/assert one's interests. Location here is the place of identity and security, indeed the very spaces from which many feel dislocated by contemporary globalising processes.

Politically and pedagogically, location is about the exercise of power, but not necessarily dominant power. It can be seen in forms of national curricula and indeed in the very notion of a *national* curriculum in which the nation is invested with certain unitary and universal interests separate or distinct from those of others. This may be noticeable particularly in curricula which invest the nation with ethnic or religious rather than civic or economic significance, but, even within the latter, aspects of the curriculum can be located in a narrow sense, as feminist and post-colonial critiques of many history curricula demonstrate. Here, location and identity can be deployed within and against the play of dislocation and difference, which is surfaced in postmodern renditions of globalisation. Rutherford (1990) argues that conservative forces use notions of identity to set up firm boundaries between self and other, and in its neo-liberal economic form construct otherness as the exotic to be consumed. Identity is secured through location and locating practices.

This bounded sense of location can be seen also in certain forms of religious fundamentalism and the forms of learning associated with them (Turner 1994). The very universality of the claims of certain religious organisations result from, and in, the establishing of a firm boundary between the believer and the non-believer. Necessarily, people are located on either side of that boundary, although still able to cross it and be 'converted' or 'saved'.

Even in certain radical challenges to exercises of power, this bounded sense of location can play a role. Here, being firm about the ground upon which one stands provides the foundations from which to challenge exercises of power. Thus, although radicalism usually is associated with mobility – the 'movement', etc. – it is largely a temporal conception of the latter that is at play. The spatial is the inert location of bounded identity wherein one stands and across which one moves. It is the arena of self and social certainty from which struggle is organised. Here, locations can become essentialised and in a sense an unproblematic space, as a support against the challenges of the outside – 'the grounds on which struggles are defined are permanent, fixed and universal' (Pile 1997: 28). Certain forms of radical feminist separatism and aspects of feminist standpoint epistemology can be seen in this way, as can certain notions of (usually male) working-class solidarity. Location is a defensible and defended space.

This essentialising can be seen in certain pedagogies of experience and voice as authentic expressions of identity that in some spaces are constructed as a radical form of politics. Here, identity is located within the person as a representative of a particular group, wherein the experience of the latter signifies a certain type of authority from which to speak. One is located as a member of a particular group. However, as Giroux (1993: 73) comments,

> the emphasis on the personal as the fundamental aspect of the political often results in highlighting the personal through a form of 'confessional' politics that all but forgets how the political is constituted in social and cultural forms outside of one's own experience.

To locate identity within an authentic experience expressed through voice can result in a denial of the conditions of possibility for particular experiences and the expression of those experiences (Fenwick 2001). Thus, there is a need, for instance, to make a 'distinction between "Muslim woman" as a discursive category of "representation" and Muslim women as embodied, situated, historical subjects with varying and diverse personal or collective biographies and social orientations' (Brah 1996: 131). Social orientations are important not only for pedagogies of experience within social movements, but for experiential learning more generally. For, as Brah (1996: 116) argues, 'experience does not transparently reflect a pre-given reality, but rather is itself a cultural construction', a point which echoes Hall (1990: 224) that identity is not 'grounded in archaeology, but in the *re-telling* of the past'. The latter points to the constituted auto/biographical but not determined nature of identity, to identification as an ongoing practice rather than to identity as a thing.

A politics of location then has been a central component in the politics of identity, wherein interests are sometimes held to rest inherently in the category of person one is – white, black, female, male, working class, gay, heterosexual, etc. Problems arise as the number of identities proliferate and as groups cohere around different dimensions of identity. It has become increasingly problematic to exclude others in the assertion of a particular identity, a situation which has led to the politics of location as a bounded space being made problematic. Here, location has to embrace difference and diversity rather than identity and unity. This has not been without controversy, as for some the undermining of location and identity is itself a political strategy aimed at denying the possibilities for effective oppositional politics. As Hartsock asks (quoted in Aronowitz and

Giroux 1991: 79), 'why is it, exactly at the moment when so many of us who have been silenced begin to demand the right to name ourselves...that just then the concept of subjecthood becomes "problematic"?' However, part of that questioning has come from within the 'silenced' groups and has resulted in the development of a notion of location more resonant with diaspora space and globalisation generally.

The work of Mohanty (1992) has been particularly influential in this respect, as there is the attempt here to locate the politics of location reflexively, in other words to map experience spatially and temporally. This involves moving from assumptions of shared locations – and practices to reinforce them, for example consciousness-raising groups – to examining the diverse locations of subjects. Here, while bounded senses of location can provide safe spaces, they can also deny differences:

> While the sameness of experience, oppression, culture, etc. may be adequate to construct this space, the moment we 'get ready to clean the house' this very sameness in community is exposed as having been built on a debilitating ossification of difference.
>
> (Mohanty 1992: 85)

The locating of experience results in a politics of engagement rather than transcendence, a re-territorialisation through struggle, a place on the map and a remaking of territory, maps and mapping.

Mohanty's (1992) argument is important in opening up the notion of location as 'a space that is fragmented, multi-dimensional, contradictory, and provisional' (Blunt and Rose 1994: 7), one that is made actively rather than being an inert background. Here, location is constituted, not found, uncovered or pre-existing the practices that take place within it. Within the political arena then, 'location is both the ground which defines struggle and a highly contested terrain, which cannot provide any secure grounding for struggle' (Pile 1997: 28). Pedagogically, this means that each location has to be examined for its possible conditions of existence. This process will itself contribute to the territorialisation of space–time in particular ways, the desire to find out in part resulting in particular forms of finding and findings. The provisionality of this means that 'location is simultaneously about unity and difference, about definitions of who occupies the same or similar place and who does not' (Pile 1997: 28). In similar ways, pedagogy can be seen to be about what is included and excluded, who participates in what and who does not, and the ways in which these mappings are inscribed and ascribed in the production of pedagogies and in pedagogical performances. This brings to the fore the political and ethical judgements upon which certain inclusions and exclusions are made and their legitimacy in particular situations.

The insertion of difference into the notion of location begins to make problematic the very notion of location itself, with location remapped as a space no longer of firm boundaries and identity but one of a shifting ground of relations and encounters within which the multidimensionality of identities, both individual and collective, come into play. It could be said also to be a condition for, and a part of, the actual experience of dislocation we discussed in the previous section. Here, '*cultural diversity* is the refusal of "fixity of meaning"' (Brah 1996: 91, emphasis in original). For Massey (1994: 168), as social relations exist in and across space,

> a 'place' is formed out of the particular set of social relations which interact at a particular location. And the singularity on any individual place is formed in part out of the specificity of the interactions which occur at that location...and in part out of the fact that the meeting of those social relations at that location...will in turn produce new social affects.

This is the diaspora space to which we have referred previously.

To some extent, we agree with Giroux (1993: 77) that educators need to develop a pedagogy of place. However, we do not see this as restricted to critical pedagogues or those explicitly engaged in radical identity politics. Nor is it simply place, but rather space–time. In a sense, identity politics involves specific pedagogies, but also all pedagogies either explicitly or implicitly are productive of subjectivity in its many and various forms (Chappell *et al.* 2003). It is for these reasons that we feel spatial metaphors for politics and pedagogy signify at least potentially the workings of globalisation. The globalised and postmodern diaspora space

> marks the intersectionality of contemporary conditions of transmigrancy of people, capital, commodities and culture. It addresses the realm where economic, cultural and political effects of crossing/transgressing different 'borders' are experienced, where contemporary forms of transcultural identities are constituted; and where belonging and otherness is appropriated and contested...Here, politics of location, of being situated and positioned, derive from a simultaneity of diasporisation and rootedness.
>
> (Brah 1996: 242)

Reflexively, 'occupying' this uncertain and in-between space

> displaces the histories that constitute it, and sets up new structures of authority, new political initiatives, which are inadequately understood through received wisdom...This process of cultural hybridity gives rise to something different, something new and unrecognisable, a new area of negotiation of meaning and representation.
>
> (Bhabha 1990: 211)

For us, this is signified through the notion of pedagogies of (dis)location. Here, location is precisely the point of dislocation and dispersal, where the two are enfolded within each other, complex, diasporan and hybrid. In a sense then, we are using the notion of (dis)location to deconstruct the binary of location/dislocation, the former with an emphasis on place, the latter on movement. We

wish to map different possibilities. It is to this notion of (dis)location that we now turn.

(Dis)location – the difference that difference can make

Such a turning is not without its ironies and difficulties, however, marked as it is by a boundary between the sections within this glimpse. This textual device provides a particular spatialisation of the narrative, a territory within the text to explore the notions of de- and re-territorialisation within globalisation and pedagogies. However, this location is itself insecure and uncertain – intellectually tentative despite its range – but also one wherein the flows from the previous discussion of dislocation and location wash through, over and around what we try to argue herein. (Dis)location signifies the moveable and relational spaces of diaspora and hybridity. It is not a singular or single space but one in a constant process of reconfiguring, and multiple in the sense that it inscribes a notion of power, difference, engagement and negotiation rather than transcendence. We accept also that others will adopt different positions within and about this (dis)located space.

Before proceeding further, we need to emphasise that we will not at this point be discussing concrete pedagogical practices of (dis)location in detail. We will touch upon some aspects of this later, but our main concern now is to map the outlines of a theoretical or conceptual terrain. It is important to bear in mind also that this framework has two distinct possibilities. First, it can be used to analyse contemporary practices, as to some extent we have already done. Second, the implications of the analysis can be used to develop pedagogical practices more resonant with the diaspora space of globalisation. In this sense, pedagogic imagination and action are interrelated.

At one level, the notion of pedagogies of (dis)location is a metadiscourse that brings to the fore the positioning of learners in relation to the possible positions available in a range of practices that are neither homogeneous nor static. Here, we are drawing on the paradox that to open a space is to deny the other spaces that make that opening possible, the spaces so opened depending on the spaces that are thereby closed by the opening (Derrida 1981). We recognise that the spatialising of pedagogy provides 'a field of metaphors wherein multiple and dynamic possibilities for meaning may be generated' (Stronach and MacLure 1997: 28). The dynamics of (dis)location both refuses a privileging of particular locations and voices and accepts the inherent power–knowledge dynamics of all pedagogic situations. Thus, pedagogies of (dis)location signify ambivalent pedagogies or pedagogies of ambivalence in the uncertain reconfigurations taking place under intensifying globalising processes. As we have already indicated, these (dis)locations can be conceptualised in a variety of ways, for instance the spatial–temporal, geographical, crossed by class, gender, ethnicity, religion, age, etc. For us, the (dis)locations and practices of (dis)locating are already discursive, a position which is itself a reflexive response to the crisis of narratives that we suggested was associated with globalisation earlier. Following Foucault

(1980), the questions and possibilities for meaning-making raised by processes of globalisation are reflected in and reinforced by the workings of power–knowledge in discursively positioning subjectivities.

This positioning is also a (dis)location of multiple and conflicting identities, with an ensemble of diverse discourses through which identity is narrated (Usher *et al.* 1997). Here, 'identities have multiple layers, each layer in complex relationship to the others' (New London Group 1995: 12). Leitch (1996: 137) argues that 'the multiple subject positions constituting subjectivity casts the self as neither unified nor fixed, but as a layered site of conflict and contradiction, where submission as well as resistance to socio-historical representations are negotiated'.

In the context of globalisation, individuals need to rethink the relationship between identity and difference. This rethinking would involve a (dis)location or positionality in which the global and the local are always co-implicated and in which inherent in adopting a location is the recognition that there is a dislocating of other possibilities. As Rose (1996) argues, there is the need to counterpoise a spatialisation of being to the emphasis that has traditionally been given to the narrativisation of being. Within the diaspora space of globalisation, 'diasporic identities are at once local and global. They are networks of transnational identifications encompassing "imagined" and "encountered" communities' (Brah 1996: 196). There are conditions of possibility and constraint that are brought into being which produce an inside and an outside of location, a particular (dis)location.

As a location is simultaneously a dislocation from other positions, pedagogy therefore becomes a process of constant engagement, negotiation and (en)counter, in which the latter signifies the relatedness of a position and the diverse modes of investment in it. Encounters can be countered, a useful notion, although one that should not be read as a binary of power and struggle but rather of attempts to work beyond that in the complex spaces of engagement. Here, what is central is not the fixed position (a state of being) but the active and open state of becoming that is an integral feature of the process of positioning, what Frith (1996: 110) refers to as 'the experience of the movement between positions'. Rather than being kept in their place, there is an emphasis on the ambiguity of the constant playing out of (dis)location. This requires, as we will go on to explore in more detail in the next glimpse, the ability to map different locations and translate between them, to shift and move and negotiate uncertainties and ambivalence, an aspect of which is the very uncertainty of identity and location. For many, of course, this is too dislocating and the attempt to re-inscribe a binary and security takes hold.

Here there is an endlessness to the processes of teaching and learning (Elam 1994), of which the increasing calls for lifelong learning are a signifier (Edwards 1997a). Globalisation and the spatialisation of pedagogies provide an impetus for lifelong learning and pedagogies of spatialisation. Thus, even as education and training become more central in response to processes of globalisation, they become reconfigured as lifelong learning. This in itself introduces new texts and new ways of meaning-making which, in particular, challenge traditional conceptions of the role, values and purposes of education. With new settings and wider groups of practitioners entering the terrain of pedagogical work, education itself becomes more a diasporan than a disciplinary space, with the associated concerns for loss of standards and authority.

It is perhaps also worth remembering that pedagogy mostly has tended to be discursively constructed by means of fixed conceptions of time and space, most obviously embodied in the timetable. This has been the case not only with didactic forms but also with experiential and critical-emancipatory forms. The very notion of a 'course' that takes place at a fixed time with predefined starting and end points, and within fixed designated spaces, is significant. Its inscription in timetables can in some ways be said to be critical to establishing certain spaces as specifically pedagogical, one wherein teaching and learning takes place. It provides the basis for the institutionalising of learning within specific organisations and frameworks – schools, colleges, universities, etc. – locations which have in the past become the privileged sites from which have emerged specific forms of educational discourse. This in itself has been disrupted and (dis)located in contemporary times as learning brings to the fore different learning settings – for example, the workplace and the home – different pedagogical practices and different practitioners. The very notion of a course then that takes place at a fixed time with predefined starting and end points and within fixed designated spaces is significantly and increasingly problematic, as space is restructured and time is transformed under the impact of globalising processes and where all social practices become potentially inscribable as learning.

Pedagogies of (dis)location is a notion that occupies different spaces and indeed needs itself to be (dis)located, about which there will no doubt be diverse views. We attempt to traverse the different terrains of (dis)location to explore, for example, the significance of national curricula, the growing use of information and communications technology in education and training, the international growth of competence-based assessment in vocational education and training, the development of inter- and cross-disciplinary study, the interest in core skills and generic capabilities. In the process of examining these as aspects of globalisation – the spatialising of pedagogies – we also start to develop practices which are part of the cartographic repertoire necessary for (dis)locating such pedagogies – pedagogies of spatialisation. These are discussions to be (en)countered reflexively by ourselves but also by readers.

Even as (dis)location may become a different point of authority to pedagogies in conditions of globalisation, processes of (dis)location also impact upon the hitherto bounded field of education. There is a dedifferentiating of borders and opening up of possibilities as well as new constraints. Here, people are seen more aptly as de-territorialised learners rather than firmly located students (Edwards 1996). Lifelong learning and (dis)location can be said to transform the possibilities for educational configurations and, with that, what it means to be a student. For the student, there is a clear location, role and identity. If we are a student, we are part of something, we belong within an institution. That sense of belonging is important in establishing both a boundary and sense of identity. Belonging provides a certain status that is important to ourselves and for negotiating boundaries with others. This is dependent partly on the value given to education and training and different forms of these within a culture. Nonetheless, being a student provides a boundary against which other demands can be defended. It is a serious role, which although capable of being a threat to our sense of self and our relations with others nonetheless provides the grounds for affirming a particular identity. This has been important, particularly for adults whose participation in formal education and training is dependent partially upon their ability to organise their learning, to defend a space for learning, around other demands (Morrison 1992).

This notion of the student is very much linked to the certain conception of education and training in which canons of knowledge, skills and understanding are transmitted to the participants. It is a serious and disciplined process of development and deepening, in which the relative stability of the educational institution is reflected in the relative stability of the canon and its ordering, and with that a certain stability in the identity of the student. In many ways, this conception of education and training continues and extends the monastic tradition of initiation, order and stability, replacing the religious elite and vocation with the secular elite of the modern nation state, also often with a strong sense of vocation. Locations here are bounded, strong and spatialised in particular ways, structured within a binary of inside/outside, where the role of one is to keep each discrete and separate. It is a view of education and training which for many is disappearing slowly in the contemporary period with the emergence of lifelong learning as a central goal. With it goes the relative stability of education and training institutions, the canon and the boundedness of student identity.

As the range of opportunities for learning have grown and diversified in many parts of the globe, and as those opportunities become subject to globalisation in practice and analysis thereof, so the very notion of what constitutes an education and/or training is reconstituted. Indeed, we are attempting such a reconstitution here as part of our own (en)counter with globalisation. In many areas, learning opportunities increasingly are packaged, commodified, consumable, their sources more diverse and open. In the process, the notion of a canon to be imparted itself is undermined with modularisation, new delivery mechanisms and consumer choice given greater play. With these come new forms of knowledge-making and identities (Nespor 1994). The sense of trust invested in educational institutions to impart the canon to students is undermined as more individuals are given greater opportunity to negotiate their own ways flexibly through the range of learning opportunities available to them, invest their own meanings within the learning process and negotiate the relationship between learning and other activities. Indeed, there are significant migrations of learners across local, national and institutional boundaries, with much learning undertaken through the de-territorialising practices of distributed and e-learning. As a result, the bounded sense of identity associated with being a student is challenged. The focus shifts from being a member of an institution to being an individualised, flexible and lifelong learner engaging in learning practices. The choices available and the conditions under which they are exercised thereby create situations of less certainty and a more unstable sense of identity (Shah 1994). Lest it be thought otherwise, we are not suggesting this to be true for all and everywhere. What we are highlighting is the significance of the changing discourses traversing the terrain of pedagogy, which at least in part can be mapped within and by the (dis)locating practices of globalisation.

At another level, by framing actual pedagogical practices in a different way, pedagogies of (dis)location offer a greater possibility of becoming reflexive about the range of (dis)locations available and possible in specific contexts. Much pedagogical work involves attempting to locate learners in specific ways and disciplining them through the practices of observation, normalisation and examination (Foucault 1979). Pedagogies of (dis)location draw forth a reflexive awareness of this and, in doing so, provide possibilities for a reframing of practices. For instance, drawing on Pecheux (1982), we can examine the ways in which (dis)location is manifested through a range of positions available to both learners and teachers. First, there is identification through which people consent to or identify with the locations available to them. Second, there is counter-identification, through which prevailing meanings are disrupted but not displaced. Third, there is dis-identification, of working on and against prevailing practices. Dis-identification is 'a critique that disrupts and rearranges "the pre-constructed categories on which the formation of subjects depend". The subject does not claim to speak from any group identity; rather she explores by critique the entire system that constitutes identity' (Natter and Jones 1997: 148). This resonates with the notion of a move from conceptions of identity as fixed and bounded to practices of identification within diaspora space. It also offers opportunities to develop hybrid understandings beyond simplistic and problematic binaries of dominance and resistance. In a sense, we are ourselves adopting a stance of dis-identification in relation to dominant views of globalisation and pedagogy, a stance which is not a privileged standpoint but part of an ongoing engagement.

The significance of Pecheux's (1982) ideas is that, rather than constituting a direct relationship between location and identity, (dis)location brings to the fore the ways in which identity always involves practices of identification – active subjects invested with, and investing, desire as well as reason. This provides the possibility for what Brah (1996: 93) terms a politics of identification rather than a politics of identity. Similarly, we would suggest that there are possibilities for pedagogies of identification rather than pedagogies of identity, although these also entail possibilities for counter-identification and dis-identification. The latter possibilities demonstrate the indeterminacy of learning and the inadequacies of transmission notions of teaching. They also indicate the ways in which questions of identification become both more important and more problematic in the contemporary phase of globalisation. In a sense, the pedagogies associated with the formal sectors of education and training become less authoritative at the very point at which there are attempts to inscribe them with revitalised authority.

Within the complex matrices of pedagogic practices, all three processes of identification might be at work at both a group and an individual level as part of the active processes of (dis)location. Learners and practitioners are involved either explicitly or implicitly in (en)countering the ambivalence of the multiple locations – material and discursive – available to them. Here, rather than having any singular intent – truth, knowledge, culture – (dis)location manifests itself as a dimension of globalisation, multiple, ambivalent and unending. This is despite attempts to relocate within boundaries of, for instance, national culture, fundamentalist religion and even emancipatory movements, in order to guard against such uncertainties. The pedagogical achievement of such closures merely points to the power of practices of location, even as the dislocations which make it possible are silenced. This gives rise to a politicisation of the curriculum precisely because the practices of enclosure and exclusion become more explicit by being denaturalised.

Initiatives, such as national curricula, might in this situation be said to resurrect nostalgically a more stable past of unified/universal knowledge and culture. Schools become theme parks or heritage sites, even as learners themselves engage in a wider and more diverse range of learning practices, including those offered by information and communications technologies, becoming as Green and Bigum (1993) suggest 'aliens in the classroom'. This is not to deny the powerful effects of classrooms, curricula and teaching, but rather to (dis)locate them – to map them on a terrain of openings and enclosures as a space traversed by other pedagogic practices, even as the possibility for an educational classroom is constituted by the capacity to exclude both bodies and bodies of knowledge. Further, there have always been aliens in classrooms in the sense of those who deviate from the norms. Information and communications technologies merely give different impetuses to the forms of alien, and perhaps alienated, performance available (Lankshear and Knobel 2003).

(Dis)location may be institutional and it can be used to examine the relationship of teachers and learners to knowledge. A further dimension of pedagogies of (dis)location is that they highlight the neglected performative and embodied aspects of such work. One aspect is the staging of the pedagogical event or pedagogy as performance. In formal settings where teachers and learners are physically present, the positioning of each in specific ways is an expression of power and authority, enabling specific possibilities for knowledge, discourse and practices while excluding others. C. Luke (1996: 286), writing about the university lecture, points out that 'authority and power are semiotically framed by the privilege of position at the raised lectern, the amplified voice, the lights focused on the speaker'. Even within less formal arrangements and settings, the positions of teacher and learner are not divested of these dimensions of performance, power and authority. These are manifested in different ways rather than being absent. McWilliam (1996a) discusses the embodied pleasure of pedagogic work and the necessity of mobilising desire to learn in response to the loss of authority invested in and deference to education and educators. The ways in which teachers and learners are located bodily is a central part of the pedagogical performance. Sitting, standing, the clothes one wears, one's tone of voice, lighting, make-up, etc. are all part of pedagogic style and performances. In this situation, the notion of learning styles takes on a wider and deeper meaning. One is required to learn and teach with style and look stylish. Indeed, the construction of the teacher and

which seeks to make the human being central, does so only at the cost of sacrificing everything about human beings that makes us recognisably human – our embodiment, our concrete humanity – and in so doing reduces us to inhumanly abstract, ghostly subjects.

(Falzon 1998: 26)

Thus, although experience is introduced into learner-centred approaches as a way of challenging the mind–body binary, where education is concerned with a cultivation of the mind and training with a skilling of the body, it becomes in fact subject to that binary. In other words, the embodied aspects of experience are lost and, through the processes of reflection embodied in these practices, become 'mind-ful'. The learning from experience of experiential learning and other forms of learner-centred practice therefore continues to produce despite itself the disembodiment associated with traditional disciplinary forms of pedagogy. Experience itself remains disembodied, as do the related pedagogical practices. The abstract individualism and technology of learner-centredness thus results in pedagogic approaches that disembody the subject, denying the corporeal and desire and, with that, particular forms of experience in teaching and learning.

Here, we are using the subject in two senses – the subject as embodied in the teacher and the learner, and the subject as that which is taught and learnt. In relation to the latter sense, disembedded might be more appropriate than disembodied, as knowledge and skill increasingly 'float' around the globe to 'meet the needs' of different individuals in different locations. Thus, even as experience is inserted into the learning process, it is abstracted and individualised, becoming a mind-ful cultivation of the self. In a sense then, learner-centredness becomes a pathologising and maybe even a pathological pedagogy.

Learner-centredness constitutes a certain form of active subjectivity, but one which is subsumed within certain binaries – mind–body, reason–emotion, male–female. In her work, McWilliam (1996a) attempts to reclaim the embodied pleasure of pedagogic work and the desires and ambivalence associated with that. She argues for the need to reclaim 'eroticism' and 'seduction' as dimensions of pedagogic work. These are notions going beyond the boundaries of discourses of learner-centredness. A re-reading such as this is informed by, and emerges from, strands of feminism and psychoanalysis, particularly those which focus on the lived body as a means of getting beyond the mind–body dualism, and the historical development and configurations of the relationship between the rational male and desiring female. Here, disembodiment involves both the assertion and the repression of desire in the female and acts as a dimension of the exercise of rational masculinist culture and power.

Ironically, perhaps, this process of disembodiment is also one actively pursued by certain strands of feminism and the demand for 'safe spaces' in which to learn away from the desiring embodied male – a pedagogy which itself denies the desires and pleasures of teaching and learning. In a sense, this alerts us to the dangers as well as possibilities of eroticising pedagogies and embodying pedagogic practices.

Embodied pedagogies require us to examine the postures and positions adopted in relation to certain bodies of knowledge in mobilising the desire, rather than motivation, to learn. Here the learner is constituted as an active lived body rather than an active developing mind, a lived body in which experience, emotions, actions and gestures cannot be taken to have universal global meanings but are (dis)located. This is a point illustrated by anthropological evidence of the different ways in which emotions are experienced and expressed in different cultures (Heelas 1986). Pedagogy therefore needs to be considered as *performance* and as *performative*. Mobilising desire becomes particularly important in the current period in which what constitutes legitimate learning is put in question. If practitioners can no longer rely on a natural thirst for what is on offer and the authority of institutions cannot be assured, then McWilliam (1996a) suggests we can induce a desire for learning through 'seduction'. In a sense then, an embodied pedagogy might be seen to be part of adjusting to a lack of social deference which now characterises many, but by no means all, learning settings. Hence the need to market education alongside other cultural and leisure services and industries. The contemporary world is one, therefore, in which there is a much more explicit problem of pedagogy, a situation that is illustrated reflexively by this text.

Learner-centredness would appear to position teachers as no-bodies in the pedagogical performance, thereby making it particularly applicable to forms of flexible, distributed and e-learning and the 'absence–presence' of the tutor (McWilliam and Palmer 1996). In some senses, this gives a legitimacy to the calls for a re-disciplining of bodies in the reasserting of teacher-centred, discipline-orientated and back-to-basics approaches. In other words, the desire for the embodiment of the teacher and learner comes from different directions with different configurations in response to the perceived failure of learner-centredness. Tensions and ambiguities exist here between the pursuit of embodiment to re-establish moral authority and social order, to release the pleasures of consumer sovereignty and to engender the desires for and in emancipatory practices. Some of these work within the mind–body dualism rather than seeking to overcome it, but each entails a form of embodiment. Issues then arise around the forms of authority for the teacher in their teaching.

Even as it positions subjects as disembodied, learner-centredness of course involves certain embodied practices, such as open body postures and formal equality between teachers and learners. Yet the desire and pleasure of these are denied/repressed and cannot be explored within the discourses of learner-centredness themselves. They also arise from and are part of particular locations. These are technologies of the self and of the relationship to the self, by means of which 'one locates oneself in relation to a culture's normative principles, and forms oneself into a moral subject' (Falzon 1998: 65). The self-ascriptions are of developing autonomy and empowerment as part of the liberal tradition of abstract individualism that denies the exercise of power – productive and at the same time constraining – embodied in acts of pedagogy. In the case of learner-centredness, this is a politics of individualism, of the individual with needs and the needy individual. Learners are schooled to perform in specific ways, but, as with all pedagogic approaches, in the process some transgress, subvert, resist or adopt apathetic or 'failing' strategies in relation to this approach. They are not simply positioned, but identify, counter-identify and dis-identify.

What of the bodies of knowledge and skill that are taught and learnt? One dimension of learner-centredness emphasises the experience of learners, experience as a resource and experiential approaches to learning (Fenwick 2001). This has been seen rightly as a welcome counterbalance to the formal structures of knowledge of the disciplines and is suggestive of the different knowledges to be found within the social order. However, in the light of the above, there are a couple of issues which arise. First, insofar as learner-centredness becomes paradigmatic of good practice, it starts to assert a uniformity in the production of knowledge similar to that previously asserted for the disciplines. Second, learner-centredness involves knowledge being produced through a process which leaps from experience to abstract reflection, wherein the body is merely a conduit for learning processes. Learner-centredness entails a form of active subjectivity but without reference to the forms of embodiment involved.

Learner-centredness is partly an attempt to reframe the pedagogic relationships among knowledge, teachers and learners. Yet its focus on learners results in bodies of knowledge being disembedded from the practices that give rise to them, enabling them to be mobilised across cultural, local and national boundaries. In a sense, although it espouses itself as challenging the universal dimensions of disciplinary knowledge, it can be argued that it provides a more effective pedagogic technology through which to spread certain messages. Here, rather than a pedagogy of (colonial) imposition, there is the imposition of a pedagogy of (post-colonial, ambiguous) engagement and enfolding. Rather than the cultivation of an educated person, there is the cultivation of the self as an individualised reflexive project. The disciplinary is displaced by the pastoral technologies of the self – of a more active subject in the processes of self-constitution. Here, the body becomes the adorned stage upon which is played out the multiple identities of the decentred self and lifestyle practices. The lived body is lived through the mediated mind. Mind and time are active, while body and space are inert.

It is, therefore, not only physical location which results in and from disembodiment, but also specific pedagogic practices. To see ICTs as removing the body therefore is misplaced(!) and overly simple. It is necessary rather to examine different forms of embodiment in different pedagogical practices, including those associated with the dispersal of teachers and learners. Indeed, it might well be the moves towards such dispersal that give increased significance to questions of embodiment and place, as what it means to live and learn become reconfigured for some. Thus, it is necessary to understand 'how new forms of pedagogy are being experienced or "lived out" when they demand the absence, removal, or semi-disappearance of the fleshy bodies of teachers and students from the university seminar room or staff room' (McWilliam and Palmer 1996: 164). Evans and Green (1995) refer to the 'telepedagogy' of distance learning. Teaching and learning are choreographed on the basis of the different forms of interaction and the styles of those involved. Here also, the location of the exchange may involve more clearly a range of (dis)locations as learners try to establish a space for learning in a context in which their other practices are often impacting upon them more directly, where, for example, time and space to study often has to be explicitly negotiated with other members of a household.

Changing locations of knowledge

Another aspect of the performative in pedagogy is to do with the notion of the performativity of knowledge in conditions of postmodernity (Lyotard 1984). As we have seen, the argument here is that in postmodernity the acquisition of knowledge is valued not for its own sake nor as a training in rationality but for its usefulness or efficacy. This performativity has tended to be seen in terms of the commodification of knowledge in market conditions and in relation to policies of heightening competitiveness in the global economy. However, it need not be seen purely in this narrow way, but rather as a conception that allows knowledge, and hence pedagogy, to be located in different and interrelated social practices, for example lifestyle, confessional, vocational and critical (Usher *et al.* 1997). Briefly, the argument is that the performativity of knowledge can take different forms because of its location in different social practices. This means that its efficacy may vary. For instance, it can enhance self-knowledge and lifestyle through personal development opportunities made available through the consumer market (Field 1994). In critical practices, it can be a pedagogy of performance which moves beyond a Western form of rationality and its preoccupation with the written word (the book) to embrace diverse forms of cultural learning across the globe. The general point is that, other than its efficacy for realising different socially constructed aims, knowledge no longer has a single canonical referent. Given this, pedagogy as the dissemination of knowledge can have both one and many locations – or, to put it another way, pedagogy, like knowledge, is itself (dis)located.

It is becoming clear therefore that any re-conceptualising of pedagogy must go hand-in-hand with a re-conceptualising of knowledge. As we have noted, canons of knowledge and traditional forms of pedagogy have become problematic. However, the most dominant pedagogical form is still one that privileges the transmission and mastery of a body of knowledge. This is a form where authority plays a central part – the authoritative educator ('the one who knows'), authoritative knowledge and the acceptance by the student of authoritative methods. As we have suggested, this is embodied in the image of the stern teacher exerting discipline over a class. The questions are: what happens when this emphasis on authority is rendered problematic, when knowledge, pedagogy and the teacher are no longer seen as necessarily authoritative in the specific conditions of globalisation – overwhelmed as they are by the abundance of signs and signifying practices to which their learners are also subject? These questions assume a vital significance in conditions of globalisation because it is precisely in these conditions, characterised by disorganised schooling, epistemological uncertainty and electronic textuality, that authority is subverted (Morgan and McWilliam 1995).

Thus, for instance, the sense of crisis over loss of discipline due to 'trendy' teaching in schools, the growth of modularisation in universities and, indeed, the characterisation of many contemporary education and training arenas as in a state of crisis – institutional and professional identity crises.

McWilliam's (1996a and b) explorations of the possibilities for seduction in learning are one way forward, although problematic given the dangers as well as pleasures associated with seductive practices. The reassertion of more traditional forms of discipline is another. Each is positioned in relation to one of the central paradoxes of education:

> (I)t's quite an achievement the way teachers manage to make learning unpleasant, depressing, grey, unerotic! We need to understand how that serves the needs of society. Imagine what would happen if people got into as big a frenzy about learning as they do about sex. Crowds shoving and pushing at school doors! It would be a complete social disaster. You have to make learning so rebarbative if you want to restrict the number of people who have access to knowledge.
>
> (Foucault, quoted in McWilliam and Jones 1996: 128)

Imagine! Yet in the era of lifelong learning there is a need for education and training to be more desired, and at the same time there are the continuing powerful effects of discipline and competence. We are witnessing changes both in the nature of the goods being delivered and in the mode of delivery, whether this is on a face-to-face basis, over distance, or online. Pedagogies of (dis)location both respond and add to this loss of authority. The argument we are putting forward for such pedagogies helps to provide an explanatory framework for what is occurring and indicates ways of working which may not re-establish traditional notions of authority – the loss of which might be argued to be largely mythical – but might result in more creative flexible pedagogic practices, some of which we have indicated throughout this text.

It may be thought that the notion of pedagogy that we are outlining may contribute further to the individualising processes often held to be at work in processes of globalisation and flexible accumulation. It could be argued that this undermines the possibilities for collective learning and endeavour as difference and the particular are asserted over shared circumstances, interests and universal messages. This is indeed possible. However, it is not necessary, although it does reframe such endeavours away from a base in a universal shared ontological condition – the working class, women, etc. – to senses of (en)counter based in 'groundless solidarity'. This can be understood as shifting coalitions 'brought together on the basis of shared ethical commitments but [which] make no claim to inclusiveness' and which are continually destabilised by 'the difference contained within and without' (Elam 1994: 109). In other words, these groupings are (dis)located and (dis)locating in the senses outlined above. Globalising processes therefore offer new possibilities for collective endeavour, even as older forms are undermined and made problematic. These coalitions or meeting places may be more contingent or, as Maffesoli (1996) suggests, 'neo-tribal'. They may be constituted also in a diverse range of ways within the global–local nexus, but that does not mean that they are without power or effect/affect.

In diaspora space, the boundaries defining and confining acceptable learning break down alongside the breakdown in the legitimacy of canons of knowledge. Furthermore, as we have seen, learning is occurring increasingly in a multiplicity of sites and outside educational and training institutions. In this context, learners cannot any longer be 'kept in their place' in quite the same ways as they have been. (Dis)locating pedagogical practices have a somewhat kaleidoscopic impact, where meaning-making, the mapping of meaning and the translations of meaning between and within different discursive locations result in a changing of the subject in the many senses of that term. The practices of (dis)location are neither easy nor straightforward, but they provide the basis for pedagogical forms which recognise meaning-making and the mediation of meaning as central to learning. In order to identify and to recognise how we are identified, we need to be reflexively aware of the forms of counter- and dis-identification that make this possible. This in itself undermines strongly centred notions of identification and constitutes the possibility of diasporic identities, (dis)located and at once global and local. It is for such reasons that we find the notion of (dis)location both resonant with our view of globalisation and capable of spatialising as well as narrating pedagogic practices as part of globalisation.

At which point, we reach another closure – of sentence, paragraph, glimpse, file. Having de- and re-territorialised questions of pedagogy, we move on to a more specific mapping of the significance of the argument to date for pedagogic practices.

Glimpse eight

(Dis)locating practices –
mapping and translating

> A conceptual shift, 'tectonic' in its implications, has taken place. We ground things, now, on a moving earth. There is no longer any place of overview (mountaintop) from which to map human ways of life, no Archimedian point from which to represent the world. Mountains are in constant motion. So are islands: for one cannot occupy, unambiguously, a bounded cultural world from which to journey out and analyse other cultures. Human ways of life increasingly influence, dominate, parody, translate, and subvert one another. Cultural analysis is always enmeshed in global movements of difference and power.
>
> (Clifford 1986: 22)

Clifford evokes well what we have termed the (dis)location associated with globalisation. It is a sense that can be found in many texts even though it is not new of course, for as we have indicated throughout, such ideas have a history, geography and politics of their own. However, there is clearly a more generalised sense of the shifting sands and lack of boundedness that influences and to an important degree shapes contemporary dispositions.

We have outlined a perspective on pedagogies of (dis)location that we have suggested is consistent with the conception of globalising processes with which we are working. We now move on to discuss what we wish to argue are two of the central practices that need to be developed through pedagogies as a response to, condition for, and as part of globalisation. These are the practices of *mapping* and *translating*. Both of these have been referred to earlier, and are to be found in the literature of feminism, post-colonialism and cultural geography. Both separately and together, these concepts have proved and are proving to be very rich metaphorical resources through which to explore the issues and implications of globalising processes. They are also to be found commonly with network metaphors of learning. This has mostly been at the level of social theory but, for us, mapping and translating are also central pedagogic practices in, for, and as a response to, globalising conditions. They are not practices of reflection, contemplation or abstraction from the world, but practices through which to (en)counter globalising processes.

A number of preliminary points are needed before we develop our argument further. First, it is necessary to highlight the double-edged nature of (dis)locating practices. We will suggest that mapping and translating are practices of (dis)location and also themselves impel a movement to (dis)locate practices; thus they are both a part of (dis)location and have the effect of (dis)locating. They are performative practices that (dis)order the world in various ways. And indeed, reflexively, these practices have themselves to be subject to the practices they promote. Mapping and translating are not decontextualised and therefore have themselves to be mapped and translated. The situated nature of these practices – or their own (dis)location – means that we do not think of these practices as either abstract or universal, as appears to be the case in much of the discussion in education and training regarding key skills, generic outcomes, core competences, transferable skills, etc. As practices subject to (dis)location, they will themselves be different and be productive of different meanings, situated and contextualised. Thus, even as we introduce them here in a particular way, they and we are subject to the same globalising processes we have already outlined. Mapping and translating are metaphorical (although no less 'real' for that) and signify in different ways with different degrees of power in the spatialisations and interpretations emerging from them. This is most notable in relation to questions of scale (Collinge 2005), for example local, regional, national, supranational, etc. Mapping and translating are simultaneously scale and scalable.

The other point that needs to be made is that they are active and ongoing practices. They are therefore integral to the practices of lifelong learning within globalisation. Thus, the use of the '-ing' form. Producing maps and translations is not the main point, although they can be temporary and powerful points of rest and order. Our concern is more with the active and powerful processes through which maps and translations can be made – what makes them possible to hold together precisely as maps and translations – the different forms that they can take and who makes and authorises them. There are, therefore, limits to what we offer below, limits that can be explored through the notion of (dis)location itself – the simultaneous play of locating and dislocating, of absence–presence and the margin which makes the centre possible.

This glimpse will be in a number of parts that will outline what we understand by mapping and translating, each of which we consider to be a condition for the other. We will then discuss these practices in relation to a central, but often overlooked, question: what makes a pedagogical context? There is often a taken-for-grantedness about this, but we wish to argue that it is only through often implicit mappings and translations that boundaries are established for specifically pedagogical work and work as specifically pedagogy. Mapping and translating in a sense then are 'infrastructural' (Derrida 2002), drawing 'attention to the coincidence of bounding and unbounding processes' (Collinge 2005: 2004). They are part of deconstructive educational practices, which seek to open the very closures that make the openings possible, and vice versa, in pedagogical work. Inferences for other pedagogies will be drawn en route and we anticipate readers will themselves make other mappings and translatings.

Mapping and translating

In the spatialisation that we have suggested is taking place in the contemporary period, the concept of mapping works as a central metaphorical resource, one which has been drawn upon particularly by those writers concerned to disrupt the pre-existing workings and positionings of power.

Historically, the production of maps has been tied closely to the practices of colonisation and the formation of territories subject to certain forms of economic, political and social control (Blunt and Rose 1994). These were powerful processes whereby particular spaces were made into places. In more recent years, different forms of maps and mapping have developed, creating new senses and understandings of territory but also increasingly attempting to de-territorialise, to map in ways which do not reproduce established dominant exercises of power. Feminist geographers have been particularly to the fore in these attempts (Massey 2005). This is not to say that such mappings have not been powerful in themselves of course, as any alternative mapping still entails some form of territorialisation.

What forms of mapping are possible and productive with the forms of de-territorialisation that we have suggested are part of globalisation? In his attempt to respond to the 'bewilderment' which he argues to be part of the postmodern spaces that are associated with late capitalism, Jameson (1991) argues for the need for cognitive mapping. Yet, such a project has different trajectories and possibilities. On the one hand, Jameson (1984: 44) suggests 'the incapacity of our minds, at least at present, to map the great global multinational and decentred communicational network in which we find ourselves caught as individual subjects'. A response to this is, in a sense, to provide maps that retreat from bewilderment by establishing manageable boundaries and borders which 'locate the individual and collective subject in relation to vast sets of structures and class realities so as to enable action and struggle' (Leitch 1996: 123). Here, cognitive mapping becomes an active political strategy that involves a particular set of dislocations quelling bewilderment and establishing a place on which to stand and struggle. However, it is also subject to failure as the very practice of mapping resurfaces the very boundaries and limitations which make the mapping possible.

In contrast to this position, Jameson (1984: 54) argues that postmodernism 'will have as its vocation the invention and projection of a global cognitive mapping', something which it might be suggested we are attempting in relation to pedagogies within this text. However, a certain caution is also necessary here, as it might be thought that such a mapping would involve the production of a totalising vision and a universal map for all. However, for us, this mapping might be global as a practice but its strategies, destinations and outcomes will be different, as each practice of mapping is itself (dis)located. Thus, as Leitch (1996: 147) suggests, such a mapping calls for 'critically linking our bewildered selves, however incompletely, to networks of global forces operating through local habitations'. This is a reflexive open and ongoing practice which keeps the dynamic of bewilderment and mastery in play rather than one being overwhelmed by the other. It is also a set of practices that are not merely cognitive, as desire, imagination and

materiality are also at play in the mapping in which we engage. The very denial
of these aspects in more cognitive understandings of pedagogy merely points to,
for instance, the intense desire to deny desire in educational spaces. This does
not deny the importance of the cognitive and of reason in pedagogy, but reflexively maps it into realms which are normally held to be outside the domain of
education and the associated practices that discipline desire to prevent possible
eruptions into pedagogic spaces.

In a sense, Jameson's (1984) argument illustrates the diversity of mapping
practices that can emerge as part of globalisation and the differing possibilities
present within the nexus of realised and realisable (en)counters. It also highlights the possibilities for locating oneself and others pedagogically/politically,
where location is a 'space that is fragmented, multidimensional, contradictory
and provisional' (Blunt and Rose 1994: 7). Here, mapping is less a representation and more a form of 'wayfinding' (Pile and Thrift 1995a), and thus the
significance given to metaphors of movement we discussed earlier. This points
to the powerful role of mapping in the politics of (dis)location. For example,
Moshenberg (1997: 89) says of the role of adult education and training in the
reconstruction of post-apartheid South Africa that 'map-making is a textual and
contractual construction and negotiation of land and people'. In a country
within which eviction and forced removal was a norm, the need for grounding
has a clear political message. However, this does not stop the need for wayfinding, as mapping 'directly addresses the politics of representation as they are
bound into the politics of location' (Blunt and Rose 1994: 8). The mapping
practices and who is involved in them provide the possibilities for different
kinds of maps, which brings to the fore the politics of such practices. As Pile
(1997: 30) suggests,

> we occupy many places on many maps, with different scales, with different
> cartographies, and it is because we both occupy highly circumscribed places
> on maps drawn through power cartographies and also exceed these confine-
> ments, that it is possible to imagine new places, new histories...

For instance, Coulby and Jones (1996) suggest some of the many ways in which
European education systems can be differentiated, or in our terms mapped: by
age; attainment; attendance; behaviour; contact; curricula; disability/special
educational need; gender; language; location; nationality; 'race'; religion; wealth.
As they (Coulby and Jones 1996: 179) comment, 'this list is not meant to be
exhaustive, nor are the categories mutually exclusive of one another. What is
clear, is that the range of possible differentiation is large and that much of it is
maintained at the expense of those within certain parts of it.' Mapping is not a
simple practice, as the question of scale makes clear. Indeed it may be precisely
because of the scale associated with globalising processes that bewilderment is a
key response, given the complex interrelationships through which those
processes are realised. It may therefore not be surprising that scaling theory has
emerged as an attempt to provide a way of mapping the mapping in trying to find

the relationships between practices in relation to, for instance, the local, regional, national, supranational and global (Collinge 2005).

Pile and Thrift (1995a) draw upon the distinction highlighted by Deleuze and Guattari (1988) between mapping and tracing. Where tracing attempts to 'read off' a true representation from the real, mapping

> is entirely orientated towards an experimentation in contact with the real...The map is open and connectable in all of its dimensions; it is detachable, reversible, susceptible to constant modification. It can be torn, reversed, adapted to any kind of mounting, reworked by an individual group or social formation.
>
> (Deleuze and Guattari 1988: 12)

Within this conception of mapping, rather than representation and closure, there is the possibility for maps to be subject to 'continual renaming and remapping in order to prevent...closure around one dominant cartography of meaning and power' (Pile and Thrift 1995a: 5). Meaning is *made* rather than found through mapping, and (dis)locating rather than locating as a way of making sense. Of course, this does not mean that closures will or should not be attempted and that locations should not be founded, even if their possibilities for success are reduced by the conditions of globalisation and the reflexivity of mapping practices wherein their conditions of possibility are more exposed. What it opens up to scrutiny are the possibilities for exploring the ethics and politics upon which such closures are founded.

We have suggested that mapping one's own (dis)location and that of others is a central set of pedagogic practices. However, such mapping also entails the capacity to engage with the other, that which is neither oneself nor one's location. To be able to map one's (dis)location, therefore, entails mapping the locations of others and other locations. Locating and mapping are therefore relational practices. Insofar as the relational and networking qualities of these practices is highlighted, the criteria by which they might be established as 'standard', the ground upon which one stands, itself becomes problematic: Educational standards require the other in order to be founded as a standard and there is much work involved in these processes. Thus, as the New London Group (1995: 9) argue in relation to what they term a pedagogy of multiliteracies for globalisation,

> local diversity and global connectedness not only mean that there can be no standard; they mean that the most important skill students need to learn is to negotiate dialect differences, register differences, code switching, inter languages and hybrid cross-cultural discourses.

Although we prefer to think of these as practices rather than skills that are concerned with more than literacy, this is nonetheless suggestive of the forms of translating necessary for mapping. Rather than resting within the enclosed space of one's 'mother tongue', there is a movement between tongues, a move-ment of many different sorts that one can see intensified in globalising processes. Here, as Kristeva says (quoted in Jokinen and Veijola 1997: 44), 'the state of translation is the common condition of all thinking beings'. This requires individuals to 'constantly remake their systems of representation and communication, in productive interaction with the challenges of multiple forms of difference' (Kress 1996: 196). Thus translating, like mapping, becomes a key metaphorical resource for pedagogy, as it is for social theory more generally (Latour 2005). Translating is not a one-to-one process, where the meaning of one term is immediately rendered in another. In the movement, there is also transformation, a space for misunderstanding as well as for greater understand-ing. Thus the cosmopolitanism that some aspire to within globalisation has to be marked by difference and *differance*, by ongoing translations rather than the mapping of all onto a single globe.

As we have suggested, globalisation challenges traditional continuities and bounded senses of identity through an increased and intensified engagement with the other. As Morley and Robins (1995: 108) argue, 'globalisation, as it dissolves the barriers of distance, makes the encounter of colonial centre and colonised periphery immediate and intense'. This is neither comfortable nor comforting, raising as it does 'the deep, the profoundly perturbed and perturb-ing question of our relationship to others – other cultures, other states, other histories, other experiences, traditions, peoples and destinies' (Said 1989: 216). It calls for what Bhabha (1989) has referred to as a practice of cultural translation. Here, 'the responsibility of Translation means learning to listen to Others and learning to speak to rather than for or about Others' (Morley and Robins 1995: 115).

Within a range of areas, therefore, the practices of translating are being brought to the fore as necessary for engaging with and being part of globalising processes within which one's (en)counters are diversified and intensified. Here, it is possible to be (dis)located within the spaces 'in-between' (Bhabha 1994) rather than seeking to translate others into one's own terms or 'go native' oneself, although these remain powerful and seductive practices. Such a space of (dis)location is one of ambivalence, uncertainty and questioning rather than one of certainty and mastery, of a 'superfluity of folds and wrinkles' (Bhabha 1994: 227). Here, as we have indicated, 'in the attempt to mediate between different cultures, languages and societies, there is always the threat of mis-translation, confusion and fear' (Bhabha 1989: 35), as cultural translation 'is inevitably enmeshed in conditions of power – professional, national, international' (Asad 1986: 163) – in particular, the power of Western languages and culture. However, it may not be possible to escape such practices and feelings as translating cannot itself be transparent. It is both a practice for, and an expression of, the ambiva-lence associated with globalising processes (Smart 1999).

> There is a sense in which no culture is fully translatable; translation is not
> a transparent transfer of meaning; it is always an interpretation and, as

such, operates as a mode of resignification. But the act of translation-as-a-resignifying practice is the very condition of communicative practice between individuals and collectivities.

(Brah 1996: 246)

Similarly, Chambers (1994: 4) suggests that 'to translate is always to transform'. As with mapping, therefore, translating is a set of practices that are provisional, risky and ongoing. Perhaps nowhere is this better illustrated, but also in some ways most submerged, than in the exponential growth of internationalism in education and the spread of the use of the English language. Contact between others and otherness is not simply erased in the linguistic and cultural translations that this is bringing about, but is actually highlighted and reconfigured, quite simply by the very making of those connections.

Mapping and translating different practices in different settings are not in themselves innovative politically, although pedagogically they have only been explored at the margins. However, issues to do with boundaries, networks and referral are central to pedagogical practices. This is not as straightforward as it may appear, for, as we have suggested above, mapping also inherently involves interpretation given that any practice will have many meanings to it. Practices have to be located in specific discourses to be given meaning, since it is through discourse that meanings are constituted, organised and articulated. For us then, mapping and translating are discursive practices and so the ongoing mapping of practice therefore entails an ongoing mapping and translating of meaning. Mapping and locating the discursively constituted meanings in and of practice and thus being able to translate between them thereby itself becomes a form of reflexive learning, which does not stop when one ends one's engagement with formal educational institutions.

Discourses produce specific ways of speaking, signing, writing. These tend to be constituted as universal ways of doing things when they need to be more readily seen as having specific locations which themselves can be mapped. Different locations bring forth only certain possibilities for certain forms of discourse. For instance, universities provide the possibilities for certain forms of academic discourse, which are then assessed and certificated. Guidance interviews governed by bureaucratic procedures and specified action plans govern what the client can say and how and when. These examples bring out both the locatedness of discourse and the always inherent issues of power. Who is speaking? Where are they speaking from? What effects are they trying to produce?

Discourses are...about what can be said, and thought, but also about who can speak, when, where and with what authority. Discourses embody meaning and social relationships, they constitute both subjectivity and power relations...Thus, discourses construct certain possibilities for thought. They order and combine words in particular ways and exclude or displace other combinations.

(Ball 1990: 17)

Securing meaning is therefore powerful, if always incomplete, as it validates certain discourses as legitimate over others. Here then, discourses are powerful in excluding, in attempting to make only certain meanings possible – thus discourses are themselves (dis)located and (dis)locating.

A discursive approach is therefore one which involves an examination of the exercises of power at work in the micro-practices of daily life. For instance, practitioners may find that their own discourse is legitimate in the workplace, but does not translate immediately into the academic discourse that is constituted as legitimate in universities. Similarly, users may have to translate their own discourses into the practitioner discourses of, for instance, 'learning needs', 'career interests', 'behavioural problems' and 'character traits' to find themselves legitimised within the practices of education. In other words, there is always a powerful struggle to establish certain meanings as legitimate within the differing locations of education and, with that, processes of identification, counter-identification and dis-identification (Pecheux 1982) on the part of all concerned. Mapping and translating meaning is dislocating, contested and unstable even as attempts to locate, secure and stabilise meaning remain powerful.

Our approach therefore results in, and from, the refusal to seek a universal explanation of pedagogical practices or a single way of doing and understanding things but rather in (dis)locating practices, in locating them and their conditions of possibility and in highlighting what they exclude. It entails recognising practices as ongoing processes of meaning-making and meaning-taking. Learning involves being able to negotiate one's own position within the range of different discursive possibilities. Even those areas which are often constructed as primal and therefore as having universal meaning and significance, such as the emotions or experience, need to be recognised as rather having particular meanings according to the culture and context in which they are articulated. The mappings and translatings are historical, geographical, cultural and psychological.

(Dis)locating learning contexts

We have pointed to the significance of boundaries and bounding in mapping and translating when considering questions of globalisation and pedagogy. Questions of positions and positionings arise when the possibilities in the practices of mapping and translating are considered. This points to the wider debates about how we understand the nature of context, in particular learning context, and what is the relationship between learning and context. Is globalisation the context? What do we mean by that? As we have indicated already, there are no straightforward answers to such questions.

Furthermore, these are not new questions. In their edited collection, Chaiklin and Lave (1996) suggest that all social practices are contextualised and all involve learning, but how those practices are conceptualised is more contentious. Questions of context are brought into stark relief by the developments promoted through a discourse of globalisation. A great deal of attention is being given to those domains outside educational institutions and other structured learning opportunities wherein people are held to learn. The workplace, the home and the community are all held to be domains of learning, within which there are specific sites. What is being articulated here is that learning contexts are distributed across the social order and embedded in social practices. This is particularly the case and has become perhaps most apparent in the development of distributed, blended and online learning through the use of information and communication technologies (ICTs) and the use of the Internet as a site and resource for learning with its associated network metaphors. All of life and living itself starts to look like a learning context.

Yet insofar as we expand our concept of learning to embrace apparently all domains of life, we might be said to start to lose the conceptual basis for talking specifically of a learning context. What is specific to a learning context which is not to be found in other contexts? What characterises a specifically learning context? Who names these contexts as learning contexts? The latter is important insofar as the discourses of educators and researchers are not necessarily shared by those who are engaging in practices within the domains now identified as contexts of learning. Thus, for instance, doing family history may be considered a leisure activity by those who are engaging in it, when for many educators this would be considered a form of learning. The meaning and therefore significance of social practices can therefore vary. And what scale do we take up to interpret such activities? The genealogist may spend days searching local records and graveyards, but also consult national databases, as well as draw upon the Internet to map the movements of family members around the globe. They are clearly involved in mapping and translating, but are they also learning? And, if so, what is their learning context and how would we describe it? It is here that detailed ethnographies – far more detailed than what is often taken to be ethnography – need to be elaborated, if we are to explore these issues in other than a gestural form.

Insofar as people do not identify themselves as learning in different domains, they may not draw upon the resources and relationships available to them for learning in other domains. A question is therefore raised about the extent to which globalisation haunts the practices of lifelong learning, extending learning into a constant disposition of mapping and translating, rather than these being restricted to certain institutionalised pedagogic spaces. And are such hauntings the concern specifically of educational researchers? Thus even as we map the possibility for life to be a learning context, we also pose the problem of the ways in which this reduces all social practices to learning as a single scale of meaning.

But how do we understand a globalised learning context, when the learning is not bounded by a specific set of institutional relationships and structures? Pedagogic approaches may seek to position and bound the learning and the learner, but there is also the sense in which there is a desire for learning to be mobile, to be for many different purposes, to be (dis)locating. In this sense, a context may be considered a bounded container within which the learning takes place or a more networked and relational set of practices wherein a learning context is an effect of specific practices of contextualisation. In the former, there is a sense in which there is closure to contain or structure the learning, which once acquired may, in principle, be poured from one domain container to another. A learning context is therefore a bounded space, the spaces of enclosure to which we referred earlier. Here

> In all commonsense uses of the term, context refers to an empty slot, a container, into which other things are placed. It is the 'con' that contains the 'text', the bowl that contains the soup. As such, it shapes the contours of its contents: it has its effects only at the borders of the phenomenon under analysis...A static sense of context delivers a stable world.
>
> (McDermott, quoted in Lave 1996: 22–3)

The relational framings find expression in theories of learning that emphasise practice and activity and draw upon network concepts rather than those of context. Here, rather than a *thing*, context becomes an outcome of activity or is itself a set of practices – *contextualising* rather than context (Nespor 2003). Practices and learning are not bounded by context but emerge relationally and are poly-contextual, that is have the potential to be mobilised in a range of domains and sites based upon participation in multiple communities of practice (Tuomi-Grohn *et al.* 2003). Mapping and translating therefore also entail contextualising and scaling in order that a specifically pedagogical space emerges.

In trying to address the question of what constitutes a learning context in the con-text of globalising processes (description), we are also therefore required to address the question of how we frame that description (conceptual) and vice versa. The two are interrelated. Yet in much of the discussion of learning and certainly in those policies that promote learning in different domains, there is little attempt to clarify such issues. In a range of domains, concepts of communities of practice, networks and activity systems have come to the fore to help frame our understanding of pedagogy in extended and complex contexts of learning. How such framings constitute a learning context and their implications for learning and teaching across domains therefore represents a major focus for consideration for those interested in both pedagogical research and practice. Our contention is that (dis)locating practices of mapping and translating, which recognise that this is not about resolution and rooting, but rather about realisation and routing, are helpful in this situation. They point to the contextualising that frames a space as a specifically pedagogical place or node.

If contexts are not inherently bounded, but are bounded through the forms of interconnectedness that make certain relations and erase others, then the ways in which we understand learning between contexts is also opened up for exploration. There has been much debate over the years about the gap between learning in different contexts and how to overcome it. To a great extent, this is formulated as an issue of transfer, from course to course, school to school, college to university, college to work, work to college, etc. Here people move from one container-like context of enclosure to another and the extent to which they do or can transfer their learning from one context to another is a crucial educational issue. The discourses of core skills, transferable skills, transferability of skills and skills of transfer have been much in play. Much of the discourse of transfer draws, often implicitly, upon classic work in cognitive psychology. The extent to which skills can be simply adapted to new context or involve higher order cognitive processing has been referred to as 'low road transfer' and 'high road transfer'. The former relates to situations in which there is sufficient commonality of context for intuitive transfer to be possible. The latter refers to where the contexts differ sufficiently for more deliberative processes – for example generalisation, drawing of analogies – to be necessary for transfer. The extent to which these practices entail the transfer of existing learning and new learning has been the subject of much debate.

However, in the views of learning upon which we are drawing, with the questioning of container-like conceptualisations of context, there is also increased recognition of the complexity of transfer and indeed a problematising of the very concept of transfer (Hatano and Greeno 1999; Volet 1999). In practice-based theories, it is sometimes suggested that, as learning is situated/contextualised, there is a requirement for disembedding/decontextualisation and of re-situating/re-contextualising for learning across and between practices. Eraut (2004: 256) offers one such conceptualisation of learning from one context to another. It entails the interrelated stages of:

- extracting potentially relevant knowledge from the context(s) of its acquisition and its previous use;
- understanding the new situation – a process that depends on informal social learning;
- recognising what knowledge and skills are relevant;
- transforming these to fit the new situation;
- integrating them with other knowledge and skills in order to think/act/communicate in the new situation.

However, this can be read as another example of high road transfer framed within an understanding of context as container, where the individual has to do the cognitive work of transformation. Relationality is gained through the learners' practices alone, when polycontextualisation can have many aspects based on, for instance, artefacts, affinity groups, storylines, emotions. So, for instance, the use of computers for games in the home and learning packages in the workplace affords certain social practices, which have similarities but differ in meaning. Similarly, multimedia and music students may do similar practices in their homes to those they do in their educational institutions, that is write computer programs, play or write music/songs, but conceive their home activities as leisure rather than as learning. Polycontextualisation relies on creating spaces for the relationships between such practices to be articulated more closely rather than relying on an individual's cognitive ability alone. In other words, relating learning polycontextually involves relational practices and relies to a certain extent on the affordances of different contextualising practices and forms of relationality. It involves grafting and following the intersubjective, interactant and intertextual/discursive traces in practices. Or to put it another way, it involves mapping and translating.

In a move away from the cognitive concept of transfer, a discourse of boundary zones, boundary-crossing and border-crossing has emerged, with associated notions of boundary objects (see Tuomi-Grohn and Engestrom 2003). This is to make explicit the practices and artefacts through which learning is mediated, but also to highlight that objects may be part of many contexts, given that the latter are not containers. Rather than focus on transfer of an existing skills set, the practices themselves, while identifiable as the same at some level, take on a different significance when networked into a different set of practices. They have been translated. So, for instance, a literacy event around the use of the computer in the home and workplace may be similar in terms of describing what someone is doing, for example writing an email, but not the same due to the symbolic and material practices within which that usage is mediated. Conventionally there is a tendency to focus on what occurs in one context to the exclusion of others. However, when we start to question this, what becomes interesting are the relational polycontextual practices, wherein people either do, or are invited to, map and translate different aspects of their practices from different situations or domains. These are not closed contexts but networked (dis)located practices, which give rise to alternative framings and metaphors, specifically those that focus on the boundary as a zone rather than a wall between contexts. In some senses, certain notions of simulations and authentic learning attempt to do this relational work within specific situations.

Here the notion of a boundary object is useful in helping to conceptualise learning as relational and polycontextual. The notion of boundary objects was developed in actor-network theory (ANT) (Star 1989), but has also been taken up by Wenger (1998) in his conceptualisation of communities of practice. We need to be cautious when assessing the various uptakes and the meaning associated with them. In ANT, 'like the blackboard, a boundary object "sits in the middle" of a group of actors with divergent viewpoints' (Star 1989: 46). Boundary objects circulate through networks playing different roles in different situations. Thus our use of the example above of the computer. Boundary objects are not merely material; they can be 'stuff and things, tools, artefacts and techniques, and ideas, stories and memories' (Bowker and Star 1999: 298). They are that which carries the intersubjective, interactant and intertextual/discursive traces to which we have already referred. They provide not only possibilities for translating across contexts, but also for scaling. They are objects which are not contained or containable by context, but are mobile and networked between differing situations, dependent on the various affordances at play. These can be based upon pedagogic performances which seek to map certain connections rather than deny them or simply because they are the tokens through which people map and translate their own practices from one situation to another. They do not pre-exist practices, but rely on those practices to make them into boundary objects.

What we are suggesting therefore is that discourses of lifelong learning both reflect and help to frame a practice-based understanding of globalising processes, polycontextuality and relationality, but also that such a notion of learning can be better understood through being situated within such discourses. This leads many of us into unfamiliar territory and introduces different and troubling conceptualisations, such as those of (dis)location, mapping, translating, scaling and contextualising where the very discourse of learning and the transfer of learning become redundant.

Reflexive difficulties of (dis)locating practices

The above suggests some possibilities more generally for pedagogies within globalisation. Yet, it is not without its own reflexive difficulties and paradoxes. For instance, we have posited the view that practices are traversed by many discursive mappings, each of which has a legitimacy of its own according to its location. This suggests that all discourses have a specific (dis)location that certain possibilities give rise to them and in turn they give rise to certain possibilities. Yet, this is also true for the discourse of discourses we have outlined. What is its (dis)location? What are the conditions for its own emergence? What effects does it have? These are all legitimate questions.

A further issue is that, in taking the discursive approach and re-conceptualising learning as embedded in discursive practices of meaning-making and meaning-taking, different possibilities start to emerge. This raises the issue of whether within academic discourse a discursive approach becomes the only way of mapping and translating the practices of learning. Do we simply drop psychological and sociological knowledge of and about learning? While we have suggested that mapping and translating meanings is central to learning and that this can be approached through a (dis)locating of practice within discourses, we recognise that it is also necessary to locate discourses of discourse in this process and to reflexively translate our own mappings with those of others, including those which make our own possible.

These issues might be thought to undermine our arguments for pedagogic strategies in relation to globalising processes. However, for us, they indicate something which has been a central theme of the issues discussed within this text: that there is no place upon which to stand which is bounded and uncomplex. There is no final frontier – no 'end' that is not itself endless. Thus we have not found a 'resolution' to the 'problem' of globalisation, but merely taken another step in the travelling through which meanings can be made. This points to the endlessness of learning that we referred to earlier and it is to a final glimpse at the journeying of this text that we now turn.

Glimpse nine
Endless learning

(Dis)located mappings

In an earlier glimpse, we discussed the argument put forward by Lankshear *et al.* (1996) that modernist educational practices constitute spaces of enclosure. One of these spaces is the book, so as we come to the final part of this particular text we ourselves are very conscious of en-closing, of bringing things to a close. However, unlike Lankshear *et al.* (1996), we have suggested that every closure involves an opening and vice versa. A text, although bounded, is also itself an opening and as such subject to multiple readings. Thus, the extent to which it is (en)closed must always be open to question. This final glimpse then is less a conclusion than another point of departure – both for us, and for readers of this text. In this sense, it continues the intention we articulated at the beginning – to offer glimpses of the subject of this text rather than to present a complete (closed) account that concludes with a summary or overview.

However, there is inevitably a tension in this procedure. We have located ourselves as working within the spaces of globalisation and as such (dis)located, enfolded in the particular sets of (en)counters that we ourselves have experienced, including (en)counters with each other. This narrative then cannot be an attempt at an overview, if only because some kind of perspective and positionality is inevitable, with diverse ways of engaging with the issues we have raised. The text does not, therefore, involve a definitive writing of globalisation and pedagogy since the complex and paradoxical processes surrounding such inscriptions are not themselves subject to a complete closure. Indeed, as we have indicated briefly in the auto/biographical accounts in the first glimpse, we have lived and are continuing to live many of the processes and practices about which we write. Here, we fully expect to be criticised for our failure to take a definite and singular stance or position, something which we have found to be a response to some of our earlier work.

This is particularly the case as we look at those writings on globalisation that seek to mark a new progressive and cosmopolitan terrain, or perhaps less quaintly a de-parochialisation (Appadurai 2001; Lingard 2006). Like us, some of this work draws upon aspects of post-colonial theory and the recognition of mobility and translation as key aspects of globalising processes. Unlike us, some of that work uses notion of difference to formulate a prescriptive stance about how things should be. Thus we find calls for the 'envisioning of a transcultural and cosmopolitan teacher' (Luke 2006: 135), at a time when much teaching is still marked by a parochialism which is not merely the result of policy but also of the practices of those working in pedagogical settings. Thus, while we find much in common with some of the analysis of globalising processes in such work, we are more sanguine about prognosticating for the future. Thus it is that while some might argue that globalisation brings everyone into greater contact with difference, this does not require a *pedagogy* of difference per se, since indifference to others rather than an engagement with the exoticism of the other may actually result in a greater tolerance of otherness.

It is precisely this sense of closure in some of the arguments for a global cosmopolitanism and a universal recognition of difference that is often implicit in taking an explicit stance that seems to us to be problematic. For us, our (dis)location signifies being open to possibilities, transgressing rather than boundary setting, locating ourselves within the diaspora spaces of the present and imaginings of the future – moving and meeting rather than standing.

At the same time, even our argument regarding (dis)location may be taken as offering, despite our intention, a fixed position, itself a totalising perspective on the nature of globalisation and its implications for pedagogy. This is the case particularly in relation to our notion of pedagogies of (dis)location as a conceptual resource for framing pedagogical practices. As a framework of analysis, this is less problematic perhaps than the pedagogical practices for (dis)location – locating, mapping, translating – that we have suggested. The former as a conceptual resource is a means of thinking differently, while the latter is suggestive of specific practices and may appear therefore as a pedagogical 'solution' to the challenges posed by globalising processes and, for this reason, could be open to the criticism that we made earlier of the argument such as that articulated by Bloomer (1997).

When any location is simultaneously a dislocation from other positions, pedagogy becomes a process of constant (en)counter and engagement. What is central is not the fixed position (a state of being) but the active and open state of becoming in a process of positioning and repositioning. Rather than being 'kept in their place', which we have suggested is also the case in the pedagogies of relocation associated with critical-emancipatory education, there is an emphasis on the ambivalence of the constant playing out of (dis)location. This also requires the capacity to map different locations and to translate between them, to shift, move and negotiate the uncertainties and ambivalence of the contemporary condition, an aspect of which is the very uncertainty and ambivalence of identity and location. This is why we foreground an endlessness to the processes of teaching and learning of which the increasing contemporary calls for lifelong learning are a signifier. This in itself introduces new texts and new ways of meaning-making which challenge traditional conceptions of the role, values and purposes of education. With new settings and wider groups of practitioners entering the terrain of pedagogical work, education itself becomes a diasporan rather than a disciplinary space. The very notion of a 'course' that takes place at a fixed time with predefined starting and end points and located in fixed designated spaces becomes increasingly problematic as space is restructured and time transformed within the intensifying processes of globalisation.

Thus, even as we suggest that (dis)location may be central to pedagogy in conditions of globalisation, processes of (dis)location also impact upon the hitherto bounded field of education, dedifferentiating the borders where it would be more appropriate to speak of de-territorialised learners rather than firmly located students. Learners and educators become involved in negotiating the ambivalence of the multiple locations – material and discursive – available to them. Rather than having any singular intent – truth, knowledge, culture – (dis)location manifests itself as a dimension of globalisation – multiple, ambivalent and unending. This is despite attempts to relocate within boundaries of, for instance, national culture, competent performance, fundamentalist religion and revolutionary movements in order to guard against such uncertainties. While such closures may constitute a pedagogical achievement, such achievements merely point to the power of locating practices, even as the dislocations which make them possible are silenced.

Any re-conceptualisation of pedagogy must go hand-in-hand with a re-conceptualisation of knowledge. We have argued throughout this text that canons of knowledge and traditional forms of pedagogy have become problematic in current conditions. Knowledge, and hence pedagogy, can itself be (dis)located, embedded and cross-hatched in different social practices. The contemporary emphasis on the performativity of knowledge often tends to be seen exclusively in terms of vocational practices and labour market positioning, but this need not always be the case. Performativity is a key feature of globalising processes but it is simplistic to think of it as having only a single definitive signification. Thus performativity can also signify *efficacy* and as such the performativity of knowledge can take different forms, according to its location in different social practices, of which the vocational is but one. It can also, for instance, function to enhance self-knowledge and lifestyle through the taking up of opportunities for personal development or, in critical practices, be a pedagogy of performance that moves beyond a Western form of rationality and its preoccupation with the written word. The general point here is that knowledge is now more to do with its efficacy for realising different socially constructed aims, and accordingly cannot and does not any longer have a single canonical referent. Given this, pedagogy in the sense of ways of disseminating knowledge can have both one and many locations – or, to put it another way, like knowledge, pedagogy is itself (dis)located. Pedagogies of (dis)location thus both respond, and add, to this loss of authority. They provide an explanatory framework for understanding what is occurring in globalised times and indicate ways of working which do not re-establish traditional notions of 'authority' in education – the loss of which may anyhow be argued to be largely mythical – but which could result in more creative, flexible pedagogic practices.

We have noted earlier that, in the diaspora space of globalisation, the boundaries defining and confining acceptable learning break down alongside, and linked to, the breakdown in the legitimacy of canons of knowledge. Furthermore, as we have also seen, learning is now increasingly understood as taking place in a multiplicity of sites. In this context, learners cannot any longer be 'kept in their place' in quite the same ways as they have been. In (dis)locating pedagogical meaning-making, the mapping of meaning and the translations of meaning between and within different discursive locations results in a changing of the subject in the many senses of that signifier. The practices of (dis)location are neither easy nor straightforward, but they do provide the basis for pedagogical forms which recognise meaning-making and the mediation of meaning as the central feature of learning. In order to identify, and to recognise how we are identified, we need to be reflexively aware of the forms of counter- and dis-identification that make this possible. But this in itself undermines strongly centred notions of identification whilst constituting the possibility of diasporic identities, (dis)located and simultaneously global and local.

The above is suggestive of a reconfiguration located in relation to contemporary globalising trends and processes of both the discourses and the practices of pedagogy. It is a reconfiguration that is itself part of a process of positioning located in particular institutional and discursive practices – national settings, the university, the academic terrain, a body of literature, the scholarly work – with only certain possibilities (and corresponding closures) for the framing of debates. As such, the effects of globalisation and the practices of, and possibilities for, pedagogies of (dis)location will look different to others, even as we hope they provide possibilities for negotiation and hybrid formulations (of which this text is already an illustration) rather than polarised rejection.

However, we find in our own text many of the paradoxes, complexities and play of binaries that we have critiqued in others – in this sense, we have exemplified the postmodern condition of having to critique that which we cannot do without. This perhaps in itself is unsurprising but, once again, it contributes to our reticence to close this text with a conclusion in a traditional sense. The processes at play here both at the level of the text and at the level of the culture in which it is located reflexively require a more conditional and modest approach to knowledge production and a working through of what that implies in terms of a condition of endless learning. This is the case as much for academics such as ourselves as for anyone else. At the same time, we recognise that no matter how modest or qualified we desire to be we cannot alter the fact that what we have presented will be read as an 'authoritative' text. Reading and meaning-making is after all a matter of positionality and relationality and, although multiple readings of this text are possible, it is not unlikely that it will be read as an endorsement of globalising processes. This is perhaps unavoidable, and certainly we have to recognise the 'performativity' of our text. No matter how critical and qualified we try to be, no matter how much we emphasise that we offer glimpses rather than a whole and complete story, we are ourselves located within (but also at the same time dislocated from) and related to a powerful contemporary discourse which constitutes globalisation and its associated processes as a domain of thought and action. This is simply something that has to be recognised and problematised. What it points to once again is the need for a critical reflexivity, an awareness of the space that one occupies and the power of spatial metaphors.

These metaphors, now so prevalent in contemporary discussions of pedagogy, have been argued to be consequent upon, contributory to, and part of, a globalising of imagination and processes. We also believe that notions of diaspora space and (dis)location have the potential to offer a means of negotiating the seeming paradox of the hybrid universal and particular, the global and local, and the endlessness of positioning and repositioning – and, hence, of learning – which this implies. The mapping of pedagogies of (dis)location brings to the fore the very locatedness of subjects, in both senses of persons and bodies of knowledge, thereby offering a framework for re-conceptualising pedagogy in contemporary conditions. In this sense, this survey is then itself a pedagogy of breaking boundaries and crossing borders with which readers may identify, counter-identify or dis-identify. As for us, given that there is no final frontier, we can but continue with our own endless learning.

Auto/biographical openings and closures

As this text is brought to a close, so too our own auto/biographies, or at least one 'chapter', also, albeit temporarily, comes to a close. At this point, it is customary to ask: what have you learnt? The notion of an author(s) who not only writes but learns, indeed who learns while writing, is an attractive one, particularly in the context of our emphasis on that endlessness of learning which both contributes to, and emerges from, globalising processes. Yet, given our emphasis is also on movement and migration, it might be better perhaps to rephrase the question and ask instead – how far have we travelled on our journey?

However, this too is unsatisfactory. The 'journey' is of course the archetypal modernist metaphor of change and development, and much used as a way of framing an understanding of learning (Edwards *et al.* 2004). However, it is also problematic because it is associated with a linear narrative where a life is articulated as a story of teleological progress, for example in the notion of *bildung*. Even though it could be argued that the mere finishing and subsequent publishing is the indicator of success in this context, when we reflect on the story of the writing of this book, we would be hard-pressed to find much in that narrative that would illuminate the course of this journey.

Rather we would prefer to put forward this text as embodying a story characterised by discontinuity and dislocation – or, more accurately, (dis)continuity and (dis)location – that mirrors and contributes to the (dis)continuity and (dis)location of the contemporary moment. At which point, we run out of space–time and move on to different meeting places...

Bibliography

Appadurai, A. (1990) 'Disjuncture and difference in the global cultural economy', in M. Featherstone (ed.) *Global Culture: Nationalism, Globalisation and Modernity*, London: Sage.

Appadurai, A. (1996) *Modernity at Large: Cultural Discussions of Globalisation*, Cambridge: Polity Press.

Appadurai, A. (2001) *Globalisation*, Durham: Duke University Press.

Apple, M., Kenway, J. and Singh, M. (eds) (2005) *Globalising Education: Policies, Pedagogies and Politics*, New York: Peter Lang.

Aronowitz, S. and Giroux, H. (1991) *Postmodern Education: Politics, Culture, Social Criticism*, Minneapolis: University of Minnesota Press.

Asad, T. (1986) 'The concept of cultural translation in British social anthropology', in J. Clifford and G. Marcus (eds) *Writing Culture: The Poetics and Politics of Ethnography*, Berkeley: University of California Press.

Ashton, D. and Green, F. (1996) *Education, Training and the Global Economy*, Cheltenham: Edward Elgar.

Ball, S. (1990) *Politics and Policy Making in Education: Explorations in Policy Sociology*, London: Routledge.

Ball, S. (1998) 'Big policies/small world: an introduction to international perspectives in education policy', *Comparative Education* 34(2): 119–30.

Bartlett, L., Evans, T. and Rowan, L. (1997) 'Prologue', in L. Rowan, T. Evans and L. Bartlett (eds) *Shifting Borders: Globalisation, Localisation and Open and Distance Learning*, Geelong: Deakin University Press.

Baudrillard, J. (1983) *Simulations*, New York: Semiotext(e).

Baudrillard, J. (1996) *Selected Writings*, Cambridge: Polity Press.

Bauman, Z. (1998) *Globalisation: The Human Consequences*, Cambridge: Polity Press.

Beck, U. (1992) *Risk Society: Towards a New Modernity*, London: Sage.

Beckett, D. (1998) 'Disembodied learning: how flexible delivery shoots higher education in the foot: well, sort of', *Electronic Journal of Sociology* 3(3): www.sociology.org

Beller, J.L. (1996) 'Desiring the involuntary', in R. Wilson and W. Dissanayake (eds) *Global/Local: Cultural Production and the Transnational Imaginary*, London: Duke University Press.

Benko, G. (1997) 'Introduction: modernity, postmodernity and the social sciences', in G. Benko and U. Strohmayer (eds) *Space and Social Theory: Interpreting Modernity and Postmodernity*, Oxford: Blackwell Publishers.

Bernstein, B. (1996) *Pedagogy, Symbolic Control and Identity: Theory, Research, Critique*, London: Taylor and Francis.

Bhabha, H. (1989) 'Beyond fundamentalism and liberalism', *New Statesman and Society*, 3 March: 34–5.

Bhabha, H. (1990) 'The third space: interview with Homi Bhabha', in J. Rutherford (ed.) *Identity: Community, Culture, Difference*, London: Lawrence and Wishart.

Bhabha, H. (1994) *The Location of Culture*, London: Routledge.

Bigum, C. and Green, B. (1993) 'Technologising literacy: or, interrupting the dream of reason', in A. Luke and P. Gilbert (eds) *Literacy in Contexts: Australian Perspectives and Issues*, St Leonards: Allen and Unwin.

Bigum, C. and Green, B. (1995) *Mapping Machines: Educational Administration and Information Technology*, Geelong: Deakin University Press.

Bigum, C., *et al.* (1997) *Digital Rhetorics: Literacies and Technologies in Education – Current Practices and Future Directions*, Canberra: Department of Employment, Education, Training and Youth Affairs.

Birketts, S. (1994) *The Gutenberg Elegies*, Boston: Faber and Faber.

Bloomer, M. (1997) *Curriculum Making in Post-16 Education: The Social Conditions of Studentship*, London: Routledge.

Blunt, A. and Rose, G. (1994) 'Introduction: women's colonial and postcolonial geographies', in A. Blunt and G. Rose (eds) *Writing Women and Space: Colonial and Postcolonial Geographies*, New York: The Guilford Press.

Borgmann, A. (1992) *Crossing the Postmodern Divide*, Chicago: University of Chicago Press.

Bowker, G. and Star, S. (1999) *Sorting Things Out*, Cambridge, MA: MIT Press.

Brah, A. (1996) *Cartographies of Diaspora: Contesting Identities*, London: Routledge.

Braidotti, R. (1994) *Nomadic Subjects: Embodiment and Sexual Difference in Contemporary Feminist Theory*, New York: Columbia University Press.

Bukatman, S. (1996) *Terminal Identity*, Durham: Duke University Press.

Burbules, N. (1997) 'Rhetorics of the Web: hyper-reading and critical literacy', in I. Snyder (ed.) *Page to Screen: Taking Literacy into the Electronic Era*, Sydney, NSW: Allen and Unwin.

Burbules, N. (2000) 'Does the Internet constitute a global educational community?', in N. Burbules and C. Torres (eds) *Globalisation and Education: Critical Perspectives*, New York: Routledge.

Burbules, N. and Torres, C. (eds) (2000) *Globalisation and Education: Critical Perspectives*, New York: Routledge.

Castells, M. (1999) *The Information Age: Economy, Society, Culture*, vols I, II and III, Oxford: Basil Blackwell.

Chaiklin, S. and Lave, J. (eds) (1996) *Understanding Practice: Perspectives on Activity and Context*, Cambridge: Cambridge University Press.

Chambers, I. (1994) *Migrancy, Culture, Identity*, London: Routledge.

Chappell, C., Rhodes, C., Solomon, N., Tennant, M. and Yates, L. (2003) *Reconstructing the Lifelong Learner: Pedagogy and Identity in Individual, Organisational and Social Change*, London: RoutledgeFalmer.

Clifford, J. (1986) 'Introduction: partial truths', in J. Clifford and G. Marcus (eds) *Writing Culture: The Poetics and Politics of Ethnography*, Berkeley: University of California Press.

Clifford, J. (1992) 'Travelling cultures', in L. Grossberg, C. Nelson and P. Treichler (eds) *Cultural Studies*, New York: Routledge.

Coffin, C., Curry, M.J., Goodman, S., Hewings, A., Lillis, T. and Swann, J. (2003) *Teaching Academic Writing*, London: Routledge.

Cohen, R. (1997) *Global Diasporas: An Introduction*, London: UCL Press.

Cole, D.R. (2005) 'Learning through the virtual', *CTHEORY.net* 3(1). Available at: http://www.ctheory.net/articles.aspx?id=445 (accessed 10 December 2006).

Collinge, C. (2005) 'The difference between society and space: nested scales and the return of spatial fetishism', *Environment and Planning D: Society and Space* 23: 189–206.

Cope, B. and Kalantzis, M. (ed.) (2000) *Multiliteracies*, London: Routledge.

Coulby, D. and Jones, C. (1996) 'Postmodernity, education and European identities', *Comparative Education* 32(2): 171–84.

Crook, S., Pakulski, J. and Waters, M. (1992) *Postmodernisation: Change in Advanced Society*, London: Sage Publications.

Cunningham, S. and Jacka, E. (1996) *Australian Television and International Mediascapes*, Cambridge: Cambridge University Press.

Cunningham, S., Tapsall, S., Ryan, Y., Stedman, L., Bagdon, K. and Flew, T. (1997) *New Media and Borderless Education: A Review of the Convergence between Global Media Networks and Higher Education Provision*, Canberra: Department of Employment, Education, Training and Youth Affairs.

Dale, R. (1999) 'Specifying globalisation effects on national policy: a focus on the mechanisms', *Journal of Education Policy* 14(1): 1–17.

Deleuze, G. (1992) 'Postscript on the *Society of Control*', *October* 59: 3–7.

Deleuze, G. and Guattari, F. (1988) *A Thousand Plateaus: Capitalism and Schizophrenia*, London: Athlone.

Derrida, J. (1981) *Positions*, Chicago: University of Chicago Press.

Derrida, J. (1994) *Specters of Marx*, New York: Routledge.

Derrida, J. (1996) 'Remarks on deconstruction and pragmatism', in C. Mouffe (ed.) *Deconstruction and Pragmatism*, London: Routledge.

Derrida, J. (2002) *Positions*, Chicago: University of Chicago Press.

du Gay, P. (1996) *Consumption and Identity at Work*, London: Sage.

Edwards, R. (1995) 'Different discourses, discourses of difference: globalisation, distance education and open learning', *Distance Education* 16(3): 241–55.

Edwards, R. (1996) 'Troubled times? Personal identity, distance education and open learning', *Open Learning* 11(1): 3–11.

Edwards, R. (1997a) *Changing Places? Flexibility, Lifelong Learning and a Learning Society*, London: Routledge.

Edwards, R. (1997b) '"Plagiarising" the self? Research texts as simulacra', in T. Evans, V. Jakupec and D. Thompson (eds) *Research in Distance Education*, 4, Geelong: Deakin University Press.

Edwards, R. (1998) 'Mapping, locating and translating: a discursive approach to professional development', *Studies in Continuing Education* 20(1): 23–38.

Edwards, R. and Clarke, J. (2002) 'Flexible learning, spatiality and identity', *Studies in Continuing Education* 24(2): 153–65.

Edwards, R. and Nicoll, K. (2004) 'Mobilising workplaces: actors, discipline and governmentality', *Studies in Continuing Education* 26(2): 159–73.

Edwards, R. and Nicoll, K. (2007) 'The ghost in the network: globalization and workplace learning', in L. Farrell and T. Fenwick (eds) *World Yearbook 2007: Educationing the Global Workforce*, London: Routledge.

Edwards, R. and Usher, R. (1997a) 'Globalisation and a pedagogy of (dis)location', in P. Armstrong, N. Miller and M. Zukas (eds) *Crossing Borders and Breaking Boundaries: Research in the Education of Adults*. Proceedings of the 27th Annual Standing

Conference on University Teaching and Research in the Education of Adults, University of Leeds: Standing Conference on University Teaching and Research in the Education of Adults.

Edwards, R. and Usher, R. (1997b) 'Final frontiers? Globalisation, pedagogy and (dis)location', *Curriculum Studies* 5(3): 253–68.

Edwards, R. and Usher, R. (1998a) '"Moving" experiences: globalisation, pedagogy and experiential learning', *Studies in Continuing Education* 20(2): 159–74.

Edwards, R. and Usher, R. (1998b) 'Globalisation, diaspora space and pedagogy', paper presented at the American Educational Research Association Annual Meeting, May 1998, San Diego, USA.

Edwards, R. and Usher, R. (1998c) 'Lost and found: cyberspace and the (dis)location of teaching, learning and research', in R. Benn (ed.) *Research, Teaching, Learning: Making Connections in the Education of Adults*, 28th Annual Standing Conference on University Teaching and Research in the Education of Adults, University of Exeter.

Edwards, R. and Usher, R. (1998d) 'Signing on for a learning society?', paper presented at the European Society for Research in the Education of Adults, European Research Conference, September 1998, University of Louvain, Belgium.

Edwards, R. and Usher, R. (eds) (2003) *Space, Curriculum and Learning*, Greenwich, CT: Information Age Publishing.

Edwards, R., Nicoll, K., Solomon, N. and Usher, R. (2004) *Rhetoric and Educational Discourse*, London: Routledge.

Elam, D. (1994) *Feminism and Deconstruction: Ms en Abyme*, London: Routledge.

Eraut, M. (2004) 'Informal learning in the workplace', *Studies in Continuing Education*, 26(2): 247–74.

Evans, T. (1989) 'Taking place: the social construction of place, time and space in the remaking of distances in distance education', *Distance Education* 10(2): 170–83.

Evans, T. (1995) 'Globalisation, post-Fordism and open and distance education', *Distance Education* 16(2): 256–69.

Evans, T. (1997) '(En)countering globalisation: issues for open and distance education', in L. Rowan, L. Bartlett and T. Evans (eds), *Shifting Borders: Globalisation, Localisation and Open and Distance Education*, Geelong: Deakin University Press.

Evans, T. and Green, B. (1995) 'Dancing at a distance? Postgraduate studies, "supervision", and distance education', paper presented at 25th Annual Conference of the Australian Association for Research in Education, 26–30 November, Hobart, Australia.

Evans, T. and Nation, D. (1992) 'Theorising open and distance learning', *Open Learning* 7(2): 3–13.

Falk, R. (1993) 'The making of global citizenship', in J. Brecher, J. Brown Childs and J. Cutler (eds) *Global Visions: Beyond the New World Order*, Montreal: Black Rose Books.

Falzon, C. (1998) *Foucault and Social Dialogue: Beyond Fragmentation*, London: Routledge.

Farrell, L. (2000) 'Ways of doing, ways of being: language, education and "working" identities', *Language and Education* 14(1): 18–36.

Farrell, L. (2005) 'The problem with "common knowledge" at work', paper presented at the Researching Work and Learning Conference, December, University of Technology, Sydney.

Farrell, L. and Holkner, B. (2004) 'Points of vulnerability and presence: knowing and learning in globally networked communities', *Discourse* 25(2): 133–44.

Featherstone, M. (1991) *Consumer Culture and Postmodernism*, London: Sage.

Featherstone, M. (1995) *Undoing Culture: Globalisation, Postmodernism and Identity*, London: Sage.

Featherstone, M. and Burrows, R. (eds) (1995) *Cyberspace, Cyberbodies, Cyberpunk: Cultures of Technological Embodiment*, London: Sage.

Fenwick, T. (2001) *Experiential Learning: A Theoretical Critique from Five Perspectives*, Columbus: ERIC Clearinghouse on Adult, Career, and Vocational Education, Center on Education and Training for Employment, College of Education, Ohio State University.

Field, J. (1994) 'Open learning and consumer culture', *Open Learning* 9(2): 3–11.

Fitzclarence, L., Green, B. and Bigum, C. (1995) 'Stories in and out of class: knowledge, identity and schooling', in R. Smith and P. Wexler (eds) *After Postmodernism: Education, Politics and Identity*, London: Falmer Press.

Foucault, M. (1979) *Discipline and Punish: The Birth of the Prison*, Harmondsworth: Penguin.

Foucault, M. (1980) *Power/Knowledge: Selected Interviews and Other Writings 1972–77*, Brighton: Harvester.

Foucault, M. (1986) 'Of other spaces', *Diacritics*, Spring: 22–27.

Frith, S. (1996) 'Music and identity', in S. Hall and P. du Gay (eds) *Questions of Cultural Identity*, London: Sage.

Gabilondo, J. (1995) 'Postcolonial cyborgs: subjectivity in the age of cybernetic reproduction', in C.H. Gray (ed.) *The Cyborg Handbook*, London: Routledge.

Game, A. (1991) *Undoing the Social: Towards a Deconstructive Sociology*, Buckingham: Open University Press.

Garrison, D. and Anderson, T. (2003) *E-learning in the 21st Century*, London: RoutledgeFalmer.

George, R. (1997) 'Language and ideology in open and distance teaching and learning', in L. Rowan, L. Bartlett and T. Evans (eds) *Shifting Borders: Globalisation, Localisation and Open and Distance Education*, Geelong: Deakin University Press.

Gibbons, M., Limoges, C., Nowotny, H., Schwartzman, S., Scott, P. and Trow, M. (1994) *The New Production of Knowledge: The Dynamics of Science and Research in Contemporary Societies*, London: Sage.

Gibson, W. (1984) *Neuromancer*, London: HarperCollins.

Giddens, A. (1990) *The Consequences of Modernity*, Cambridge: Polity Press.

Giroux, H. (1992) *Border Crossings: Cultural Workers and the Politics of Education*, New York: Routledge.

Giroux, H. (1993) *Living Dangerously: Multiculturalism and the Politics of Difference*, New York: Peter Lang.

Godin, B. (1998) 'Writing performative history: the new *New Atlantis*', *Social Studies of Science* 28(3): 465–83.

Goodenow, R. (1996) 'The cyberspace challenge: modernity, post-modernity and reflections on international networking policy', *Comparative Education* 32(2): 197–216.

Gough, N. (1998) 'Globalisation and curriculum: theorising a transnational imaginary', paper presented at the Conference of the American Educational Research Association, San Diego, USA.

Green, A. (1997) *Education, Globalisation and the Nation State*, London: Macmillan.

Green, B. (1993) *Curriculum, Technology and Textual Practice*, Geelong: Deakin University Press.

Green, B. (1998) 'All over the world...speculative notes on the global academic', paper presented at the annual conference of the Australian Association for Research in Education, Making Research Count, Adelaide, Australia.

Green, B. and Bigum, C. (1993) 'Aliens in the classroom', *Australian Journal of Education* 17(3): 119–41.

Gregory, D. (1994) 'Social theory and human geography', in D. Gregory, R. Martin and G. Smith (eds) *Human Geography*, Minneapolis: University of Minneapolis Press.

Guile, D. and Young, M. (1998) 'Apprenticeship as a conceptual basis for a social theory of learning', *Journal of Vocational Education and Training* 50(2): 173–92.

Hall, S. (1990) 'Cultural identity and diaspora', in J. Rutherford (ed.) *Identity: Community, Culture, Difference*, London: Lawrence and Wishart.

Hall, S. (1995) 'New cultures for old', in D. Massey and P. Jess (eds) *A Place in the World: Places, Culture and Globalisation*, Oxford: Oxford University Press.

Haraway, D. (1991) *Simians, Cyborgs and Women: The Reinvention of Women*, New York: Routledge.

Hartnell-Young, E. (2003) 'Innovation in practice: from consumption to creation', keynote address, ICTEV Conference, Melbourne, Australia. Available at: www.results.aust.com (accessed 10 December 2006).

Harvey, D. (1989) *The Condition of Postmodernity: An Enquiry into the Origins of Social Change*, Oxford: Basil Blackwell.

Harvey, D. (1993) 'Class relations, social justice and the politics of difference', in J. Squires (ed.) *Principled Positions: Postmodernism and the Rediscovery of Value*, London: Lawrence and Wishart.

Hatano, G. and Greeno, J. (1999) 'Commentary: alternative perspectives on transfer and transfer studies', *International Journal of Educational Research* 31: 645–54.

Hebdige, D. (1990) 'Introduction – subjects in space', *New Formations* 11: vi–vii.

Heelas, P. (1986) 'Emotion talk across cultures', in R. Harre (ed.) *The Social Construction of Emotions*, Oxford: Blackwell.

Heelas, P., Lash, S. and Morris, P. (eds) (1996) *Detraditionalisation*, Oxford: Basil Blackwell.

Held, D. (1993) *Democracy and the New International Order*, London: Institute of Public Policy Research.

Held, D. and McGrew, A. (eds) (2003) *The Global Transformations Reader*, Cambridge: Polity Press.

Henry, M. and Taylor, S. (1997) 'Globalisation and national schooling policy in Australia', in B. Lingard and P. Paige (eds) *A National Approach to Schooling in Australia*, Canberra: Australian College of Education.

Hesse, B. (1999) 'Reviewing the Western spectacle: reflexive globalisation through the black diaspora', in A. Brah, M. Hickman and M. Mac an Ghail (eds) *Global Futures: Migration, Environment and Globalisation*, Basingstoke: Macmillan.

Hirst, P. and Thompson, G. (1996a) *Globalisation in Question*, Cambridge: Polity Press.

Hirst, P. and Thompson, G. (1996b) 'Globalisation: ten frequently asked questions and some surprising answers', *Soundings* 4: 47–66.

Holkner, B. and Farrell, L. (2005) 'The network is down', paper presented at the Researching Work and Learning Conference, December, University of Technology, Sydney.

Jacklin, H. (2004) 'Discourse, interaction and spatial rhythms: locating pedagogic practice in a material world', *Pedagogy, Culture and Society* 12(3): 373–98.

Jameson, F. (1984) 'Postmodernism, or the cultural logic of late capitalism', *New Left Review* 146: 53–93.

Jameson, F. (1991) *Postmodernism or the Cultural Logic of Late Capitalism*, London: Verso Books.

Jarvis, B. (1998) *Postmodern Cartographies: The Geographical Imagination in Contemporary American Culture*, London: Pluto Press.

Jewitt, C. (2006) *Technology, Literacy and Learning: A Multimodal Approach*, London: RoutledgeFalmer.

Jokinen, E. and Veijola, S. (1997) 'The disorientated tourist: the figuration of the tourist in contemporary cultural critique', in C. Rojek and J. Urry (eds) *Touring Cultures: Transformations of Travel and Theory*, London: Routledge.

Jones, G., McLean, C. and Quattrone, P. (2004) 'Spacing and timing', *Organisation* 11(6): 723–41.

Jones, S. (ed.) (1995) *Cybersociety*, London: Sage.

Kaplan, C. (1996) *Questions of Travel*, London: Duke University Press.

Keith, M. and Pile, S. (eds) (1993) *Place and the Politics of Identity*, London: Routledge.

Kellner, D. (1995) *Media Culture: Cultural Studies, Identity and Politics Between the Modern and the Postmodern*, London: Routledge.

Kellner, D. (1998) 'Multiple literacies and critical pedagogy in a multicultural society', *Educational Theory* 48: 103–22.

Kellner, D. (2000) 'Globalisation and new social movements: lessons from critical theory and pedagogy', in N. Burbules and C. Torres (eds) *Globalisation and Education: Critical Perspectives*, New York: Routledge.

Kenway, J. (1996) 'The information superhighway and post-modernity: the social promise and the social price', *Comparative Education* 32(2): 217–32.

Kenway, J., Bigum, C. and Fitzclarence, L. (1993) 'Marketing education in the postmodern age', *Journal of Education Policy* 8(2): 105–22.

Korsgaard, O. (1997) 'The impact of globalisation on adult education', in S. Walters (ed.) *Globalisation, Adult Education and Training: Impacts and Issues*, London: Zed Books.

Kramerae, C. (1995) 'A backstage critique of virtual reality', in S. Jones (ed.) *Cybersociety*, London: Sage.

Kress, G. (1996) 'Internationalisation and globalisation: rethinking a curriculum of communication', *Comparative Education* 32(2): 185–96.

Kress, G. (2003) *Literacy in the New Media Age*, London: Routledge.

Kress, G., Jewitt, C., Ogborn, J. and Tsatsarelis, C. (2001) *Multimodal Teaching and Learning: The Rhetorics of the Science Classroom*, London: Continuum.

Kress, K. (2000) 'Multimodality', in B. Cope and M. Kalantzis (eds) *Multiliteracies*, London: Routledge.

Laclau, E. (1990) *New Reflections on the Revolution of our Time*, London: Verso.

Lakoff, G. and Johnson, M. (1980) *Metaphors We Live By*, Chicago: University of Chicago Press.

Lankshear, C. and Knobel, M. (2003) *New Literacies: Changing Knowledge and Classroom Learning*, Philadelphia: Open University Press.

Lankshear, C., Peters, M. and Knobel, M. (1996) 'Critical pedagogy and cyberspace', in H.A. Giroux, C. Lankshear, P. McLaren and M. Peters (eds) *Counternarratives*, London: Routledge.

Lash, S. (1990) *Sociology of Postmodernism*, London: Routledge.

Lash, S. and Urry, J. (1994) *Economies of Signs and Space*, London: Sage.

Latour, B. (1986) 'The powers of association', in J. Law (ed.) *Power, Action and Belief: A New Sociology of Knowledge*, London: Routledge and Kegan Paul.

Latour, B. (1999) *Pandora's Hope: Essays on the Reality of Science Studies*, Cambridge, MA: Harvard University Press.

Latour, B. (2005) *Reassembling the Social: An Introduction to Actor-network Theory*, Oxford: Oxford University Press.

Lauder, H., Brown, P., Dillabough, J.A. and Halsey, A. (eds) (2006) *Education, Globalisation and Social Change*, Oxford: Oxford University Press.

Lave, J. (1996) 'The practice of learning', in S. Chaiklin and J. Lave (eds) *Understanding Practice: Perspectives on Activity and Context*, Cambridge: Cambridge University Press.

Lave, J. and Wenger, E. (1991) *Situated Learning: Legitimate Peripheral Participation*, Cambridge: Cambridge University Press.

Law, J. (2003) 'Notes on the theory of the actor network: ordering, strategy and heterogeneity', published by the Department of Sociology and Centre for Science Studies, Lancaster University, Lancaster LA1 4YN, UK. Available at: http://www.lancs.ac.uk/fss/sociology/papers/law-notes-on-ant.pdf (accessed 4 March 2006).

Law, J. (2004) *After Method: Mess in Social Science Research*, London: Routledge.

Law, J. and Urry, J. (2003) 'Enacting the social', published by the Department of Sociology and Centre for Science Studies, Lancaster University, Lancaster LA1 4YN, UK.

Lea, M. and Nicoll, K. (eds) (2002) *Distributed Learning*, London: Routledge.

Leitch, V. (1996) *Postmodernism – Local Effects, Global Flows*, New York: State University of New York.

Lemert, C. (1997) *Postmodernism Is Not What You Think*, Oxford: Basil Blackwell.

Levin, B. (1998) 'An epidemic of education policy: (what) can we learn from each other?', *Comparative Education* 34(2): 131–41.

Lingard, B. (2006) 'Pedagogies of indifference: research, policy and practice', keynote address to the British Educational Research Association Annual Conference, University of Warwick.

Lingard, R. and Rizvi, F. (1998) 'Globalisation, the OECD, and Australian Higher Education', in J. Currie and J. Newson (eds) *Universities and Globalisation: Critical Perspectives*, Thousand Oaks, CA: Sage.

Loader, B. (ed.) (1997) *The Governance of Cyberspace*, London: Routledge.

Luke, A. (2006) 'Teaching after the market', in L. Weis, C. McCarthy and G. Dimitriadis (eds) *Ideology, Curriculum and the New Sociology of Education*, New York: Routledge.

Luke, C. (1996) 'Feminist pedagogy theory: reflections on power and authority', *Educational Theory* 46(3): 283–302.

Luke, T.W. (1996) 'The politics of cyberschooling at the virtual university', paper presented at the International Conference of The Virtual University, University of Melbourne, Australia.

Lyotard, J.-F. (1984) *The Postmodern Condition: A Report on Knowledge*, Manchester: Manchester University Press.

Macrae, S. (1997) 'Flesh made world: sex, text and the virtual body', in D. Porter (ed.) *Internet Culture*, London: Routledge.

Maffesoli, M. (1996) *The Time of the Tribes*, London: Sage.

Manicom, L. and Walters, S. (1997) 'Feminist popular education in the light of globalisation', in S. Walters (ed.) *Globalisation, Adult Education and Training: Impacts and Issues*, London: Zed Books.

Marginson, S. (1999) 'After globalisation: emerging politics of education', *Journal of Education Policy* 14(1): 19–31.

Marshall, J. (1997) 'Globalisation from below: the trade union connections', in S. Walters (ed.) *Globalisation, Adult Education and Training: Impacts and Issues*, London: Zed Books.

Mason, R. (1998) *Globalising Education: Trends and Challenges*, London: Routledge.

Massey, D. (1991) 'A global sense of place', *Marxism Today*, June: 24–9.

Massey, D. (1993) 'Politics and space/time', in M. Keith and S. Pile (eds) *Place and the Politics of Identity*, London: Routledge.

Massey, D. (1994) *Space, Place and Gender*, Cambridge: Polity Press.

Massey, D. (1999) 'Imagining globalisation: power-geometries of time–space', in A. Brah, M. Hickman and M. Mac an Ghail (eds) *Global Futures: Migration, Environment and Globalisation*, Basingstoke: Macmillan.

Massey, D. (2005) *For Space*, London: Sage.

Mayor, B. and Swann, J. (2002) 'The English language and "global" teaching', in M. Lea and K. Nicoll (eds) *Distributed Learning: Social and Cultural Approaches to Practice*, London: RoutledgeFalmer.

McChesney, R. (2003) 'The new global media', in D. Held and A. McGrew (eds) *The Global Transformations Reader*, Cambridge: Polity Press.

McGregor, J. (2004) 'Spatiality and the place of the material in schools', *Pedagogy, Culture and Society* 12(3): 347–72.

McWilliam, E. (1996a) 'Touchy subjects: a risky inquiry into pedagogical pleasure', *British Educational Research Journal* 22: 305–17.

McWilliam, E. (1996b) 'Introduction: pedagogies, technologies, bodies', in E. McWilliam and P. Taylor (eds) *Pedagogy, Technology and the Body*, New York: Peter Lang.

McWilliam, E. and Jones, A. (1996) 'Eros and pedagogical bodies: the state of (non)affairs', in E. McWilliam and P. Taylor (eds) *Pedagogy, Technology and the Body*, New York: Peter Lang.

McWilliam, E. and Palmer, P. (1996) 'Pedagogies, tech(no)bodes: re-inventing postgraduate pedagogy', in E. McWilliam and P. Taylor (eds) *Pedagogy, Technology and the Body*, New York: Peter Lang.

Milliron, D. and Miles, C.L. (2000) 'Education in a digital democracy', *EDUCAUSE Review*, November/December, 50–62. Available at: http://www.league.org/mark/digitaldemocracy.pdf (accessed 10 December 2006).

Mohanty, C. (1992) 'Feminist encounters: locating the politics of experience', in M. Barrett and A. Phillips (eds) *Destabilising Theory: Contemporary Feminist Debates*, Cambridge: Polity Press.

Moran, J. (2005) *Reading Everyday Life*, London: Routledge.

Morgan, W. (1997) *Critical Literacy in the Classroom: The Art of the Possible*, London: Routledge.

Morgan, W. (1999) 'Digital rhetorics and beyond: research and practice'. Available at: http://users.wantree.com.au/~peterh/rhetoric/.

Morgan, W. and McWilliam, E. (1995) 'Keeping an untidy house: a disjointed paper about academic space, work and bodies', in R. Smith and P. Wexler (eds) *After Postmodernism*, London: Falmer Press.

Morley, D. and Robins, K. (1995) *Spaces of Identity: Global Media, Electronic Landscapes and Cultural Boundaries*, London: Routledge.

Morrison, M. (1992) 'Part-time: whose time? Women's lives and adult learning', *Centre for Educational Development and Research Papers No. 3*, Coventry: University of Warwick.

Moshenberg, D. (1997) 'Sit down, listen to the women!', in S. Walters (ed.) *Globalisation, Adult Education and Training: Impacts and Issues*, London: Zed Books.

Natter, W. and Jones III, J. (1997) 'Identity, space and other uncertainties', in G. Benko and U. Strohmayer (eds) *Space and Social Theory: Interpreting Modernity and Postmodernity*, Oxford: Blackwell Publishers.

Nespor, J. (1994) *Knowledge in Motion*, London: Falmer.

Nespor, J. (2003) 'Undergraduate curriculum as networks and trajectories', in R. Edwards and R. Usher (eds) *Space, Curriculum and Learning*, Greenwich, Conn.: Information Age Publishing.

New London Group (1995) *A Pedagogy of Multiliteracies: Designing Social Futures*, Sydney: NLLIA Centre for Workplace Communication and Culture, occasional paper no. 1.

Nicoll, K. (2006) *Flexibility and Lifelong Learning: Policy, Discourse, Politics*, London: Routledge.

Nicoll, K. and Edwards, R. (1997) 'Open learning and the demise of discipline', *Open Learning* 12(3): 14–24.

Paechter, C. (2004) 'Metaphors of space in educational theory and practice', *Pedagogy, Culture and Society* 12(3): 449–64.

Pecheux, M. (1982) *Language, Semantics and Ideology: Stating the Obvious*, London: Macmillan.

Perry, N. (1998) *Hyperreality and Global Culture*, London: Routledge.

Peters, M. (1996) *Poststructuralism, Politics and Education*, Westport: Bergin and Garvey.

Pile, S. (1997) 'Introduction: opposition, political identities and the spaces of resistance', in S. Pile and M. Keith (eds) *Geographies of Resistance*, London: Routledge.

Pile, S. and Keith, M. (eds) (1997) *Geographies of Resistance*, London: Routledge.

Pile, S. and Thrift, N. (1995a) 'Introduction', in S. Pile and N. Thrift (eds) *Mapping the Subject: Geographies of Cultural Transformation*, London: Routledge.

Pile, S. and Thrift, N. (1995b) 'Mapping the subject', in S. Pile and N. Thrift (eds) *Mapping the Subject: Geographies of Cultural Transformation*, London: Routledge.

Plant, S. (1995) 'Crash course', *Wired*, April: 44–7.

Poppi, C. (1997) 'Wider horizons with larger details: subjectivity, ethnicity and globalisation', in A. Scott (ed.) *The Limits of Globalisation: Cases and Arguments*, London: Routledge.

Porter, D. (ed.) (1997) *Internet Culture*, London: Routledge.

Poster, M. (1990) *The Mode of Information*, Oxford: Polity Press.

Poster, M. (1995) 'Postmodern virtualities', in M. Featherstone and R. Burrows (eds) *Cyberspace, Cyberbodies, Cyberpunk: Cultures of Technological Embodiment*, London: Sage.

Poster, M. (1997) 'Cyberdemocracy: Internet and the public sphere', in D. Porter (ed.) *Internet Culture*, London: Routledge.

Poster, M. (2001) *What's the Matter with the Internet?*, Minneapolis: University of Minnesota Press.

Power, S. and Whitty, G. (1996) 'Teaching new subjects? The hidden curriculum of marketised educational systems', paper presented at the American Educational Research Association Annual General Meeting, May, Chicago.

Rattansi, A. (1995) 'Just framing: ethnicities and racisms in a postmodern framework', in L. Nicholson and S. Seidman (eds) *Social Postmodernism: Beyond Identity Politics*, Cambridge: Cambridge University Press.

Reich, R. (1993) *The Work of Nations: A Blueprint for the Future*, London: Simon & Schuster.

Rheingold, H. (1993) *The Virtual Community*, Reading, MA: Addison-Wesley.

Rizvi, F. (2000) 'Inernational education and the production of global imagination', in N. Burbules and C. Torres (eds) *Globalisation and Education: Critical Perspectives*, New York: Routledge.

Robertson, R. (1992) *Globalisation: Social Theory and Global Culture*, London: Sage.

Robins, K. (1993) 'Prisoners of the city: whatever could a postmodern city be?', in E. Carter, J. Donald and J. Squires (eds) *Space and Place: Theories of Identity and Location*, London: Lawrence and Wishart.

Robins, K. (2003) 'Encountering globalisation', in D. Held and A. McGrew (eds) *The Global Transformations Reader*, Cambridge: Polity Press.

Rogers, C. (1961) *On Becoming a Person*, London: Constable.

Rojek, C. (1993) *Ways of Escape: Modern Transformations of Leisure and Travel*, Basingstoke: Macmillan.

Rose, N. (1996) 'Identity, genealogy, history', in S. Hall and P. du Gay (eds) *Questions of Cultural Identity*, London: Sage.

Rosen, M. and Baroudi, J. (1992) 'Computer-based technology and the emergence of new forms of managerial control', in A. Sturdy, D. Knights and H. Wilmott (eds) *Skill and Consent: Studies in the Labour Process*, London: Routledge.

Rowan, L. and Bartlett, L. (1997) 'Feminist theorising in open and distance education: local and global perspectives', in L. Rowan, L. Bartlett and T. Evans (eds) *Shifting Borders: Globalisation, Localisation and Open and Distance Education*, Geelong: Deakin University Press.

Rowan, L., Bartlett, L. and Evans, T. (eds) (1997) *Shifting Borders: Globalisation, Localisation and Open and Distance Education*, Geelong: Deakin University Press.

Rustin, M. (1987) 'Place and time in socialist theory', *Radical Philosophy* 47: 30–6.

Rutherford, J. (1990) 'A place called home', in J. Rutherford (ed.) *Identity: Community, Culture, Difference*, London: Lawrence and Wishart.

Said, E. (1989) Representing the colonised: anthropology's interlocutors', *Critical Inquiry* 15(2): 205–25.

Scott, A. (1997) 'Introduction – globalisation: social process or political rhetoric?', in A. Scott (ed.) *The Limits of Globalisation: Cases and Arguments*, London: Routledge.

Scrimshaw, P. (1997) *Preparing for the Information Age: Synoptic Report of the Education Department's Superhighways Initiative*. Available at http://edsi.ngfl.gov.uk/cgi-bin/edsi. cgi?DOC=P2&SECT=&PARA=237

Shah, S. (1994) 'Kaleidoscopic people: locating the "subject" of pedagogic discourse', *Journal of Access Studies* 9: 257–70.

Shields, R. (1997) 'Spatial stress and resistance: social meanings of spatialisation', in G. Benko and U. Strohmayer (eds) *Space and Social Theory: Interpreting Modernity and Postmodernity*, Oxford: Blackwell Publishers.

Singh, M., Kenway, J. and Apple, M. (2005) 'Globalising education: perspectives from above and below', in M. Apple, J. Kenway and M. Singh (eds) *Globalising Education: Policies, Pedagogies and Politics*, New York: Peter Lang.

Smart, B. (1999) *Facing Modernity: Ambivalence, Reflexivity and Morality*, London: Sage.

Snyder, I. (ed.) (2002) *Silicon Literacies: Communication, Innovation and Education in the Electronic Age*, London: Routledge.

Soja, E. (1989) *Postmodern Geographies: The Reassertion of Space in Critical Social Theory*, London: Verso.

Soja, E. and Hooper, B. (1993) 'The spaces that difference makes: some notes on the geographical margins of the new cultural politics', in M. Keith and S. Pile (eds) *Place and the Politics of Identity*, London: Routledge.

Spivak, G. (1993) *Outside in the Teaching Machine*, London: Routledge.

Star, S.L. (1989) 'The structure of ill-structured solutions: boundary objects and heterogeneous distributed problem solving', in L. Gasser and M. Huhns (eds) *Distributed Artificial Intelligence*, Vol. II, London: Pitman.

Strathern, M. (2000) 'The tyranny of transparency', *British Educational Research Journal* 26(3): 309–21.

Stronach, I. and MacLure, M. (1997) *Educational Research Undone: The Postmodern Embrace*, Buckingham: Open University Press.

Study Group on Education and Training (1997) *Accomplishing Europe through Education and Training*, Brussels: European Commission.

Tabbi, J. (1997) 'Reading, writing hypertext: democratic politics in the virtual classroom', in D. Porter (ed.) *Internet Culture*, London: Routledge.

Taylor, S., Rizvi, F., Lingard, B. and Henry, M. (1997) *Educational Policy and the Politics of Change*, London: Routledge.

Thamen, K. (1997) 'Considerations of culture in distance education in the Pacific islands', in L. Rowan, L. Bartlett and T. Evans (eds) *Shifting Borders: Globalisation, Localisation and Open and Distance Education*, Geelong: Deakin University Press.

Thompson, J. (2003) 'The globalisation of communication', in D. Held and A. McGrew (eds) *The Global Transformations Reader*, Cambridge: Polity Press.

Tomlinson, J. (2003) 'Globalisation and cultural identity', in D. Held and A. McGrew (eds) *The Global Transformations Reader*, Cambridge: Polity Press.

Tuomi-Grohn, T. and Engestrom, Y. (eds) (2003) *Between Work and School: New Perspectives on Transfer and Boundary-crossing*, London: Pergamon.

Tuomi-Grohn, T., Engestrom, Y. and Young, M. (2003) 'From transfer to boundary-crossing between school and work as a tool for developing vocational education: an introduction', in T. Tuomi-Grohn and Y. Engestrom (eds) *Between Work and School: New Perspectives on Transfer and Boundary-crossing*, London: Pergamon.

Turkle, S. (1995) *Life on the Screen: Identity in the Age of the Internet*, New York: Simon & Schuster.

Turner, B. (1994) *Orientalism, Postmodernism and Globalism*, London: Routledge.

Urry, J. (1995) *Consuming Places*, London: Routledge.

Urry, J. (2000) *Sociology Beyond Societies: Mobilities for the Twenty-first Century*, London: Routledge.

Urry, J. (2003) *Global Complexity*, Cambridge: Polity Press.

Usher, R. (1993) 'Re-examining the place of disciplines in adult education', *Studies in Continuing Education* 15(1): 15–25.

Usher, R. (1998) 'The story of the self: education, experience and autobiography', in M. Erben (ed.) *Biography and Education: A Reader*, London: Falmer Press.

Usher, R. and Edwards, R. (1994) *Postmodernism and Education: Different Voices, Different Worlds*, London: Routledge.

Usher, R. and Edwards, R. (2007) *Lifelong Learning – Signs, Discourses, Practices*, Dordrecht: Springer.

Usher, R., Bryant, I. and Johnston, R. (1997) *Adult Education and the Postmodern Challenge: Learning Beyond the Limits*, London: Routledge.

Virilio, P. (1986) *Speed and Politics: An Essay on Dromology*, New York: Semiotext(e).

Volet, S. (1999) 'Learning across cultures: appropriateness of knowledge transfer', *International Journal of Educational Research* 31: 625–43.

Wah, R. (1997) 'Distance education in the South Pacific: issues and contradictions', in L. Rowan, L. Bartlett and T. Evans (eds) *Shifting Borders: Globalisation, Localisation and Open and Distance Education*, Geelong: Deakin University Press.

Wark, M. (1997) *The Virtual Republic*, Sydney: Allen and Unwin.

Warschauer, M. (2002) 'Languages.com: the Internet and linguistic pluralism', in I. Snyder (ed.) *Silicon Literacies*, London: Routledge.

Waters, M. (1995) *Globalisation*, London: Routledge.

Webster, F. (1995) *Theories of the Information Society*, London: Routledge.

Wenger, E. (1998) *Communities of Practice*, Cambridge: Cambridge University Press.

Wiseman, J. (1998) *Global Nation? Australia and the Politics of Globalisation*, Cambridge: Cambridge University Press.

Yoshimoto, M. (1996) 'Real virtuality', in R. Wilson and W. Dissanayake (eds) *Global/Local: Cultural Production and the Transnational Imaginary*, Durham: Duke University Press.

Index